CONVERSATIONS
WITH
POWER

To our FUNre
Leader Justn Gold

We are so proud of
you! Go for it...

Love,
Aunt Melanie
Uncle Ken -
Ben

CONVERSATIONS WITH

POWER

WHAT GREAT PRESIDENTS
AND PRIME MINISTERS
CAN TEACH US ABOUT LEADERSHIP

BRIAN MICHAEL TILL

palgrave
macmillan

CONVERSATIONS WITH POWER
Copyright © Brian Michael Till, 2011.
All rights reserved.

First published in 2011 by PALGRAVE MACMILLAN® in the
U.S.—a division of St. Martin's Press LLC, 175 Fifth Avenue,
New York, NY 10010.

Where this book is distributed in the UK, Europe and the rest of
the world, this is by Palgrave Macmillan, a division of
Macmillan Publishers Limited, registered in England, company
number 785998, of Houndmills, Basingstoke, Hampshire
RG21 6XS.

Palgrave Macmillan is the global academic imprint of the above
companies and has companies and representatives throughout
the world.

Palgrave® and Macmillan® are registered trademarks in the
United States, the United Kingdom, Europe and other countries.

ISBN: 978-0-230-11058-8

Library of Congress Cataloging-in-Publication Data
Till, Brian Michael.
    Conversations with power : what great presidents and prime
ministers can teach us about leadership / Brian Michael Till.
        p. cm.
    Includes index.
    ISBN 978-0-230-11058-8 (pbk.)
    1. Heads of state—Biography.   2. Heads of state—
Interviews.   3. Political leadership.   I. Title.
D412.7.T55 2011
321.0092'2—dc22

                                                    2010046921

A catalogue record of the book is available from the British
Library.

Design by Letra Libre, Inc.

First edition: May 2011

10 9 8 7 6 5 4 3 2 1

Printed in the United States of America.

For Dana Swan

CONTENTS

INTRODUCTION

n late October 2004, two weeks before the most important election of his life, Sen. John Edwards was at Haverford College, on Philadelphia's Main Line. Although no one knew it at the time, the Democratic Party's young vice presidential nominee was reaching the crescendo of his career.

It was the first time I had seen a major political figure; the first time I felt the air of an ego-charged hall. It's quite easy to dismiss a politician from behind broadsheets and flat screens. In person, though, is quite often another matter, regardless of one's political bent. Edwards, with his boyish hair and distant gaze, spoke powerfully in our red and black field house that day, his shirtsleeves rolled to his elbows and his voice gravelly from weeks of campaigning. He pilloried George W. Bush for his mismanagement of the war in Iraq and his unwillingness to tackle the broken American health care system.

But, more than anything the enchanting pol said, I was struck by the near ravenous pulse around him. As his speech came to a close, star-struck undergraduates, normally somber and awkward classmates I would have thought immune to Edwards's populist exhortations and polished charm, crushed forward toward the security line. They were only looking for a handshake, a moment of eye contact, an autograph that they'd almost certainly lose. Yet they charged the rope like Midwest linemen. Edwards, too, bounded forward, as insatiably eager to work the line as my classmates and I were to meet him.

"I have noticed that a politician always has a special halo around him," Václav Havel, the slight Czech playwright and president, told me when we met in Prague. "It has nothing to do with whether he is a good politician or a complete fool; the position itself lends that person a special aura."

My classmates and I didn't know then that Edwards was at his peak; that his immaculate comb-over cost the campaign $400 per cut;[1] or that, three and a half years later, he would father a child with a mistress in a torrid and bizarre affair—complete with sex tape and Oprah Winfrey special—as he once again sought the presidency, and while his late wife, Elizabeth, faced down stage IV breast cancer.

These auras that dominate our televisions and newspapers are, in the end, entirely human. Uncomfortably human. They have bad breath and say uninteresting things; they're as prone to temper as much as brilliance; they're as disposed to simple pleasures and laughter as soaring rhetoric. The leaders profiled in this book—though I'm humbled to have met them all—are an entirely human lot, and their power in actuality resides with the crowd. It is a gift that *we* confer upon them. Their celebrity springs from our collective attention as much as any fiber of their own.

And so their failings, too, rest in part with us. When they fail to cut the world anew, or to provide fertile ground for innovation, or to shove against humanity's natural inclination for idleness, we, too, fall short. When they are lambasted in editorials and laughed at in bars, we are really, in the end, only laughing at ourselves.

IN THE MIDST of a heavy hangover and a bout of youthful indignation, I wrote an opinion piece for the *San Francisco Chronicle* in the spring of 2007, titled "Graduating to Starbucks." This book was largely born from that column. It centered on the dim prospects college grads faced amid the global financial collapse; it was inspired by a commencement speech given that year by Barbara Ehrenreich, a talented author and chronicler of the American working class.

"Parents, guidance counselors, and principals alike, they all assuaged us," I wrote, "keep working hard, get into a good college—your future will be bright. They cajoled us, all the while electing leaders that ran up the deficit without hesitation, leaders that refused to listen to the science community about the dangers of global warming, and refused to take steps to adjust our economy while lifting trade barriers."

There's an inertia that leads each era's young to believe that their world is far worse for wear, stripped raw by the previous generations. There's also the jeremiad complex;[2] America, from its outset, has been stocked with doomsayers, those certain that failure is both imminent and irreversible. Each decade has spawned its own brand of fatalism: those who thought race wars would rip the nation in two; those certain that fascism could not be overcome; those who cowered at Sputnik's lunch and the missile gap with the Soviets.

Yet, even recognizing the American propensity for gloom, understanding that we may well be hard-wired to see the worst, the breadth of the challenges we face today remains staggering. For the first time, a generation—these "millennials"—might be justified in its hostility. Around us, the accomplishments of post–Cold War leaders appear ripped at the seams. I was a year old when Mikhail Gorbachev and Ronald Reagan sat together in a square, white house on the desolate Reykjavik coast and imagined a world without nuclear weapons; yet there are still tens of thousands of warheads in bunkers and storehouses, still thousands deployed around the world, and fringe regimes in Tehran and Burma remain bent on joining the nuclear club. I was two when Gro Brundtland, the Norwegian prime minister and physician, wrote the manifesto that gave rise to the Kyoto Protocol and the notion of sustainable development. I was three when the first Palestinian intifada erupted.

Stephen Flynn, a scholar at the Council on Foreign Relations who writes on issues of American infrastructure, noted in the *Atlantic* last summer, "My daughter was 6 when the World Trade Center Towers went down, 8 when lights went off on the East Coast, and 10 when a major US city drowned—I saw things built, she's seen them fall apart."[3]

After centuries of resource wealth, today we face scarcity—of arable land, fresh water, oil—that will be exacerbated by the effects of climate change.[4] There is a serious question whether this planet can sustain the 9 billion inhabitants it'll boast by 2050. And we feel it; we know it, deep in our beings. America and the world look, to many young eyes, like they have been left on autopilot.

But I have found profound inspiration in these conversations. Indeed, far more than I expected. Nearly all these leaders agree that tremendous opportunities were lost at the hinge of the Cold War, yet none—save, perhaps, West Germany's Helmut Schmidt—have given in to fatalism. Despite acknowledging the breadth of these challenges, despite recognizing the stasis between a public that prefers not to hear difficult truths and leaders who choose not to speak them, they remain faithful—wedded to the optimism that drew them into political life.

THERE IS A TENDENCY in this country to feel absolved from the nastiness of politics. The notion of civic responsibility is anachronistic, even laughable, to many in this generation. We've grown up in the era of shareholder responsibility, amid absolute certainty that stability and safety are indelible. But that's changing beneath our feet, and we can feel it. The challenges we find before us are simply too massive for a culture of indifference.

A year and some months after writing my commencement column, I was in Omaha, driving a rented van across the heartland between the Democratic and Republican national conventions of 2008. Frustrated by the chasm between rhetoric and the magnitude of the challenges at hand, it struck me to ask former heads of state what ought to be done. They, having retired from office, are far more likely to speak candidly. And after fighting countless political battles, they understand the levers and pitfalls of the game better than most.

So, as the world affixed its hopes to something new and bold— a young black senator with a funny name and a sharp mind—I set out in the opposite direction, in search of the old guard, hoping to sit down with some of the world's most powerful and influential retirees, intent to capture their reflections and guidance for a generation to follow.

This unlikely journey, which began in a white Washington winter, ends here, blocks from the Kremlin amid a red October. It was made possible by broad strokes of luck and the goodwill of countless friends and strangers; but it was born from frustration, palpable across my generation, and the hope that the ideas within might, somehow, help us to chart a tenable future.

—*Moscow, October 2010*

Chapter One

THE SOCIOLOGIST

FERNANDO HENRIQUE CARDOSO

PRESIDENT OF BRAZIL

1995–2003

November 2009

IN AUGUST OF 1965, the thin and professorial Fernando Henrique Cardoso, then only thirty-four, found himself at his father's funeral, flanked by roughly a hundred fellow mourners, almost all of them clad in military green and brass. One of the more decorated men approached Cardoso's cousin, who, in turn, approached Cardoso. "The general offered condolences on behalf of the military," the cousin told him in a hushed tone. "He also said that you will need to leave Brazil as soon as possible."[1]

The day before, Cardoso had been in Chile, watching from exile as a military junta continued to consolidate power over his native Brazil. He received a telegram that read simply, "Sapo morreu." Cardoso's father, a general, was gone; his exiled son did not even know he was sick, let alone close to death. In Brazil, by custom, the deceased are typically buried within twenty-four hours; Cardoso faced the choice of returning to Brazil despite an outstanding arrest warrant and jail sentence handed down in absentia, or missing his father's funeral.

IN MARCH OF 1963, Cardoso was among the first targeted by the new government. Within hours of the coup, the military apprehended and interrogated a young sociology professor from the University of São Paulo. Bento Prado, a colleague of Cardoso's, managed to convince his captors that he was not Fernando Henrique and earn his release. News of Prado's arrest reached Cardoso who, with the help of a friend's contacts with Air France, found a single airport north of São Paulo where his name did not appear on the no-fly list. He fled, leaving his wife and children behind.

The community of exiled Brazilians that assembled in Chile expected the military to hand power back to civilians within several years. The intervention was well precedented and welcomed by a large portion of the population who charged that democracy had led to stagnation and immense corruption. But the junta held power for the next twenty years. Cardoso's sentence, though, was overturned in 1967, when an amicable military judge, who would later be targeted by the junta himself, offered absolution and an impassioned diatribe against the dictatorship.

During the 1960s, Cardoso drew respect from abroad for his work in exile. He joined the United Nations' Economic Commission for Latin America and the Caribbean, and his affection for Marxism and the left cooled as he watched communist East Germany and North Korea fall drastically behind capitalist counterparts. His book "Dependency and Development in Latin America," co-authored with Enzo Faletto, was one of the most important social science works of the decade. It challenged Latin American thinkers to abandon doctrinal affiliations and elaborate theories and to instead ground their work in the plausible. It rejected the notion that Latin American nations were the victims of foreign imperialism and needed to cut ties with the developed nations, while also acknowledging that their leaders have a limited scope of power, given their dependence on the United States and others. The work gained substantial notoriety and led to prestigious offers for Cardoso to teach abroad. Instead, he returned with his family to the University of São Paulo, where he taught and began a career as a dissident.

The next year, in 1969, the university announced the forced retirement of 70 professors, including Cardoso. Over the next decade, a number of his friends joined the armed resistance. He recalls in his memoir, "Social and political life tended to blend into one. On one occasion, I found myself in a car with a group of friends as we delivered a small shipment of machine guns to someone's house. This was done nonchalantly, as if it were one of several errands to be run that day."[2]

Cardoso remained political in his dissent, however, writing commentary for magazines and running for senate in 1978. He planned the campaign as a protest. His political rights—the privilege to vote and to stand for election—had been stripped along with his position at the university, and he thought there was little chance he would be allowed onto the ballot. But when the military attempted to outlaw his campaign, the Brazilian media ran with the story—the squashed candidacy of a humble professor espousing democracy. The regime was forced to let Cardoso stand for office; he became an alternate senator representing São Paulo.

In the end, it was more likely the failure of the military to keep the economy afloat rather than the work of Cardoso or other dissidents that led to the regime's demise. But, amid the fight, Cardoso made a powerful ally: a small but fiery union leader, the seventh of eight children and the only one to complete primary school. Luiz Inácio Lula da Silva, or Lula, as he is now known around the world, would be first a comrade to Cardoso, then a political rival, then finally a successor as president.

BRAZIL, A NATION OF nearly 200 million people and tremendous natural resources, is the world's fourth largest democracy. It remains alarmingly poor. Cardoso, first as a finance minister and then as president, pulled the fledgling economy into the modern era. He was rewarded in 2001 when Goldman Sachs's chief economist coined the term "BRIC" for the most promising middle powers: Brazil, Russia, India, and China.

The title of Cardoso's autobiography is *The Accidental President*. It is certainly a stretch, but there is some truth to the idea. After the public wrangled power back from the military in 1985, the presidency suffered a number of tragedies. The first president became gravely ill the day of his inauguration and died a month later. Two of the next three presidents would leave office amid impeachment, corruption, and scandal. And, in 1992, when a little-known vice president named Itamar Franco rose to the presidency, he appointed Cardoso as his foreign minister. The hapless Franco faced the same problem that had plagued the Brazilian economy for more than a decade: extraordinary inflation. He burned through three finance ministers in one seven-month period. Though calculations vary, inflation was well over 1,000 percent in 1993, and certainly over 2,000 percent in 1994. Economists generally put healthy inflation between 2 and 5 percent.

In May of 1993, Cardoso stopped in New York on his way home from an official trip to Japan. There, at dinner with the Brazilian ambassador to the UN, he took a phone call from the president, who asked him to consider becoming finance minister. Cardoso had no interest in the job and went to bed thinking he had convinced the president to address the matter upon his return. He awoke to headlines announcing his appointment.

When we sat down, I asked him what chance he thought he had to succeed in those first days. He laughed. "Twenty percent," he said. "The president was psychologically unstable."

I asked if he believed the president was legitimately imbalanced, or if that was hyperbole. Yes, he replied emphatically. "I had the capacity to convince the president and to calm him down, and, to some extent, he gave me power and he transferred responsibilities to me." Cardoso drafted the *Plano Real,* which combined a new, more stable currency fixed closely to the value of the US dollar—which the government took pains to introduce cautiously—with severe reductions to the bloated government budget. The measures, despite many forecasts to the contrary, worked. Cardoso's path to the presidency as Franco's successor was born.

The second major achievement of Cardoso's career came in the realm of public health. Brazil was on course to face one of the world's most severe HIV/AIDS epidemics during his presidency; Cardoso and health minister José Serra launched one of the world's most effective responses to the disease. It coupled coordination with charities and private organizations (often called NGOs—nongovernmental organizations) with awareness campaigns and access to free treatment. To accomplish this, Cardoso took on the manufacturers of antiretroviral drugs, which allow those with the disease to continue living, often for decades, after the virus has progressed substantially. The corporations that had developed the complex pill regimens—like Merck & Co., Pfizer, and the Swiss firm Hoffman–La Roche—were then charging well over $10,000 per year per patient for the treatments. Cardoso encouraged Brazilian drug companies to break international patent laws to produce generic versions. In response, the Clinton administration, on behalf of the American pharmaceutical companies, brought a case against Cardoso at the World Trade Organization. The case was dropped on World Aids Day in 2001 by George W. Bush.

THE MORNING WE WERE slated to meet, I found Cardoso eating breakfast alone. We met on the periphery of the Club de Madrid, an assembly of former heads of state that convenes annually in the Spanish capital. His demeanor juxtaposes simplicity and elegance. He has a deep, even regal voice, thin metal-rimmed glasses, and thick gray hair that he often keeps long in the back. He is overwhelmingly affable, a good deal more humble than most egos that have suffered eight years of motorcades and honor guards. And he lacks the intellectual arrogance befitting a man with a wall of honorary degrees—more than twenty—and consistently ranked among the world's foremost intellectuals. The cover story of the *Economist* the week we met was titled "Brazil Takes Off," and it lauded his work laying the foundation for the modern Brazilian economy. He smiled with cheeks full of breakfast as I handed him a copy, thanked me, and added it to a sizable stack of papers he had already amassed for the flight home.

There's an American tradition to leave a letter in the Oval Office to the next president, sort of advice and things like that. If you were to give two or three pieces of advice to the next generation of leaders, what would they be?

It's difficult to advise a new president, because everyone wants to start the world from the beginning, and you have to understand and accept that. But I would say, first of all, you have to listen more than you think, listen to others. It's not enough to listen to your people, your team; you have to listen to people's anxieties. People's anxieties are not expressed through words. You're asking me about what are the challenges of the time. So we have to be capable to make a kind of compromise between real politics, your people, your team, who says you have to do this and that, and the more ample expectations of the country.

And don't forget that at some point in time, it's better to leave the office for another person. Because even if you are very good, it's important to leave, and not because of corruption—because it's not inevitable that power will corrupt you—but because of the fact that routine is maybe worse for a nation than personal corruption. As more time comes and goes, you believe that you know everything. And that's not true. If you don't understand that it's better for you to leave the office to others, you become an obstacle.

It's interesting that you say you start to think you know things better than others, because other presidents have said that, too. I wonder, how else did you feel yourself changing?

I don't know. My family was involved in power, so I had some indirect experience. Anyhow, I never imagined how difficult it is to exercise power, how cruel it is to do that.

What do you mean?

Cruel, because, you have to fire good people, you have to say "no" to people who are asking you valid, demanding questions. For instance, in some circumstances we had to say no to increasing salaries for people who could use it, because the global situation didn't allow for it. So, it's hard to be a serious political leader. If you are a populist, it's very easy. But if you have a project, and you have to enforce your project, you have to put it into practice, then you have to say, "no, no, no," even when people are asking you for things you'd love to say "yes" to. So it's not easy; it's very hard to do that.

So politics is a matter for strong people. Then you have also to understand that people will criticize you, judge you, and will consider you not in terms of your real ideas or intentions or even behavior, but based on your image. You have to understand that; otherwise, you cannot handle the situation because you have to read in the newspapers stupid things, silly things, aggressive things, that aren't even about you, but about the image they have of you.

I used a tactic to be able to deal with that kind of situation. If a friend of mine or a member of my party said something very critical and in personal terms, I preferred not to read it. Once, one of these old oligarchs in Brazil gave a press interview criticizing me very dramatically in bad terms, and unjustly from my point of view.

Sometime later he wanted or needed to be close to me again, and he came to see me and he brought a copy of the interview in his pocket to justify, to make excuses for the things he had said. When he started speaking, I said, "don't waste your time. I never read your interview." It was true. I preferred not to read; otherwise, how could I ever speak with this man again?

Were you surprised by the lack of knowledge of other leaders? You refer to George W. Bush asking if you had many black people in your country, and Ronald Reagan in Brasilia remarking how happy he was to be in Bolivia.

Yeah, it's shocking to see how it is. Once I had a boss, a Spanish sociologist at the UN. He was a wonderful man, and he used to say, "Fernando, it's better not to know those who command the world." It's a bit like that. You cannot imagine those who are the leaders in the world, that they lack knowledge about specific situations. They have to have other qualities, though.

Let me ask you about another aspect of power. Václav Havel compared being president to being on a submarine, in that you're constantly surrounded by the same people and that it can be difficult to get outside information. Other leaders have spoken about how difficult it is for aides to say "no," or to deliver bad news, because so much of their influence depends on having a good relationship with the president. Did you experience that?

Yes. This is absolutely true, but there are mechanisms to avoid the situation. In my case, I always had some people around me to say whatever they wanted. First, inside of my family—my wife was very clear in taking positions and not necessarily agreeing with me, and she was strong enough to sustain her opinions. Second, you have to read papers, because newspapers normally give the opposition voice, and you have to take into account what they have to say.

Another very hard situation when you are in power is having to deal with those who want to approach you too much, to be around you. And you have to protect yourself from those who'd say "yes, yes and yes." The president requires some formality. I am an informal person, it's easy to talk to me, but being president cannot be like that. You have to have those who are really capable to speak to you more openly, but, in general, some ritual is necessary to keep distance from your friends, because friends can be transformed into chains of bad influence.

But it's very important to listen to ordinary people. I used to swim almost every morning when I was the president, and I had people from a hospital close by come to train me. I used to talk to them, but, even more so, I used to talk to the man who was in charge of the swimming pool, an old man who had been there for a long time, very simple. And I encouraged him to talk about different questions—his life, what people say, so on and so forth.

My father was a military man and he participated in different revolutionary movements, democratic movements, in Brazil, and ended up in prison with his brother several times. They were treated well, but my father said, "all the time I tried to talk to my guard. At the end, my guard was transmitting my news to my brother in another part of the prison." Even in prison you have to talk to your guard, he taught me. You have to talk, have to listen; this is the way we can avoid being inside the submarine. It is feasible.

Speaking about these qualities required of a leader, Ronald Reagan used to say, I can't imagine anyone being a head of state without having been an actor or having some theatrical experience. Does that ring true to you?

I think that what Reagan said is correct nowadays. Leadership now requires a capacity for mass communication, requires one to have some actor's qualities to perform. And this is both good and bad. It's bad because actors are not necessarily intellectual leaders or inspirational leaders. Look, for instance, what has happened in Latin America—Hugo Chávez in Venezuela. Chávez is a good actor. Our presidencies overlapped for a few years, and normally at summits, when we have a family photo with all the presidents, he is normally the last one to come, to attract attention. And sometime he comes with a football or some kind of ball in his hands, or a hat. He's an actor.

TV is the main instrument to communicate now; it's almost impossible to succeed if you can't work in that medium. Look what has happened now in China. It's very interesting, because Chinese leaders have always exercised their leadership in secrecy, not publicly. Part of the game was to not be present. Now they are changing. President Hu [Jintao] may be the first one that the Chinese can follow by watching TV. And now when there is a disaster in China, the ministers and the president go there. That's quite new in China, and it's because they know there's been an important shift.

Take the case of climate change. I think a man like Obama, who is a good performer, has to put that capacity to use. Since we have to behave symbolically, it's not possible anymore just by using words to convince people because we have to convince the masses—not intellectuals, not students—it's a masses thing.

The main virtue of Lula, my president, as a leader, is that he uses symbolism to communicate. I think Obama has the same possibility, and I don't want to compare them, but look at Gordon Brown. It's difficult to see Gordon Brown convincing the masses; very difficult. That's why in the climate change debate what Al Gore did was very, very important.

I accept invitations to go to dinner with football players because football players are reverential to people. And it's important that these new actors and symbols become more aware of their role and what is necessary to be done in the world. We cannot change without these people.

It's interesting because they're not just football players anymore—they used to be faces, dots on the television, but now they're voices as well.

Yes, they can symbolize something, why not use them? The United Nations is trying to use celebrities for instance in the fight against poverty or for education—

Angelina Jolie, all of these people—

That's right. And also Formula One racecar drivers, and people like that. I think they are necessary. In other terms, what is politics today? It's no longer congresses of old parties; that's the past. So how to convince people about climate change, how? We have to use mass media and these personalities to inform them. But this requires not just journalists; it requires political leaders and inspirational leaders from society.

We have, right now, a lack of inspirational leaders in the world. I'm not referring to people who are just capable—lots of people are capable to lead. It's more than that to be able to inspire you facing these big issues.

Utopians.

Utopians. What are the big issues? Well, climate change, the nuclear threat, poverty, diseases, and maybe in the future others as well—because what's happening is demography itself is changing.

The two things I'm most eager to ask you about are climate change and AIDS. Your government led the world in its response to the

HIV/AIDS epidemic. One of the ways you did that was by tackling drug companies, negotiating with them for lower prices on antiretroviral drugs. Do you recall any of the conversations you had with Bill Clinton on that issue?

What I really recall were discussions with Clinton when the Kyoto Protocol negotiations were underway on the issue of climate change. It was extremely difficult for him because of the American position. At that time, we negotiated only on the phone, and I had him on the phone several times because it was necessary to allow for some concessions from both sides to finally have an agreement. After that, America decided not to implement the treaty; it couldn't get through the Senate. It's a pity. Clinton, I remember, called me desperately once, because he said, "I have no room to maneuver. The pressure on me is enormous, but I think that it's important to reduce emissions."

So that was Clinton. It was always very easy, very simple to talk to him. It was not necessary to convince him about issues. He was always enthusiastic about what we did with AIDS; he has always been very favorable to that, even if quietly.

I want to stick with this, because it's an important moment, the decision on antiretrovirals. It's really the first time, in a period of worshipping the free market, that we decide that human interest and needs must supersede the market. And we're at a moment now when there's another huge challenge in climate change, and there's a hesitancy to move as aggressively as you did on HIV/AIDS. The numbers are astounding. There was a recent poll in the Times *of London that stated only 41 percent of Brits believe climate change even exists;[3] 36 percent of Americans believe that it's human driven. The percentage of people that believe the globe's warming, regardless of whether it's human driven or not, has dropped 20 percent in the last three years in the US.[4] So I wonder, do you agree—*

It's terrifying.

So at this moment do you agree that governments need to intercede where we, the public, don't yet fully understand the severity of what we're up against?

I think so. Look, going back to your question about AIDS, in that case Brazil has been very active. Largely because of my health minister, José Serra, who is the governor of São Paulo now—he's an economist, got his PhD at Cornell. It was enough to look at the data coming in and see that the Brazilian situation would be a disaster.

You were on par with South Africa in terms of how bad it could get, where, in some places, a third of the population has the disease.

Yes. It was very bad. We had to do something. First, we approved a bill in Congress offering free medicine to everyone, rich or poor. Secondly, we decided to organize a specific group inside the Ministry of Health to deal with just this issue. Third, we asked for organizations working with people infected with HIV to help us in monitoring programs and to build trust in the government's capacity. Fourth, we decided to show to the public through awareness campaigns that there is a disaster coming, but that we have the instruments to cope with it. Brazil is a Catholic country and the church is against the use of condoms. But we decided to show on TV—and very crudely at that—how to use condoms. Very crudely—to shock people. So we gained the public's support.

At the end, well, there remained the enormous cost of treatment. The Brazilian law has an item that says that in the case of dramatic necessity, an emergency, the Brazilian authorities have the power to break the patent and to try to do reverse engineering and produce products in Brazil. So I decided, let's go that way. Since we have technological capacity and since we have the political will, we have the two factors that are very important in threatening the multinationals. So, largely at least, they decided to accept our proposition of reduced prices.

So, I think that Brazil is now losing an opportunity to again lead the world regarding the CO2 question. We have been in the past on Kyoto. We have been in the lead on HIV, why not now? Why this vague discussion about what we'll do to preserve our growth? We have an enormous growth potential using our comparative advantages in the case of climate change.

Because you would agree there's really not a leader. There's nobody pushing other nations—

Yes, I agree there's a vacuum. But I don't know why Brazilians are not pushing more strongly, because this is our opportunity. In this case—and it's a strategic decision—Brazil has become a global player. But we have yet to seek more profoundly, what do we want to do as a global player? Do you want to repeat the path of other countries in the past, or do we innovate?

We have the possibility to innovate in my opinion. We cannot compete with the USA or even Russia in terms of armaments. This is ridiculous. But we can play a very important part of the game if we insist on climate change, clean energy, fight against poverty. These are the areas in which Brazil has a comparative advantage. We have, as you know, tremendous ethanol capacity. What sense does it make to destroy, to burn and damage forests? It's senseless. You know the burning of the forest—not just damage to the forest in general—is responsible for close to 75 percent of Brazilian CO_2 emissions?

So why should we repeat this mistake? We have to grow but not at any price. So I think it's a lack of leadership that we suffer.

If you look back on your career, what was your greatest mistake? If you could do one thing over, what would it be?

My worst mistakes? [a scoff of a laugh] Several things. First of all, I was probably too ambitious in proposing too many reforms simultaneously. Societies are not ready to change, much less in several ways at once. So I would be less ambitious and more efficient in concentrating my efforts, more focused.

At the beginning of my government, we still had to get inflation under control to regain fiscal stability, because states within the country had these tremendous obligations in the area of social security. Like you are trying to do now in the United States, we also had to reorganize the health system. We also had tremendous problems regarding the political system—the number of parties, the system of votes. I decided *not* to start by proposing political reforms, because if I had started with political reforms, probably the nation would have exploded, and the other reforms wouldn't have had a chance. But maybe it would have been possible at the beginning to be more insistent on some political reforms, because this remains a problem. So this, I think, could be a mistake.

It was not that I didn't act because I didn't recognize that changes were needed, but we decided it was necessary to start by moving with the basic forces. Let's break some monopolies, let's reorganize the state pension apparatus.

Another thing was crime and security. This is a tremendous problem in Brazil. Really a tremendous problem. The problem is that citizens' security is in the hands of the states, not the federal government. But, I think Brazil requires federal leadership on this issue. So, I think it was a mistake to not be more serious in dealing with that.

Let me ask you about the post–Cold War years. My generation looks at nuclear proliferation that continues, climate change that we don't have an answer to yet, millennium development goals unmet, this global economy that's wildly and precariously imbalanced—there are saver nations such as China and Germany and the Middle East, and huge debtors like the UK and US. These were the challenges for the post–Cold War generation and they've fallen short largely. Do you think history will judge it and the leaders of the powers during this period harshly?

If you compare the current leaders with the leaders at the end of the Second World War, then yes. But I am still highly impressed by what I read about those men. There is a fantastic book of the correspondence between Roosevelt and Stalin. Roosevelt had a clear, idealistic idea about what to do after the end of the war. And Roosevelt had it set in his mind that it would be necessary to include the Soviet Union, not Russia, but the Soviet Union, in that game. So he was very indulgent vis-à-vis Stalin's demands. And Stalin was much worse if we compare him to Putin in terms of psychology, because Putin is not warm, but he's not—how can I put it—tricky. Stalin was tricky, and he was playing with Roosevelt, and Roosevelt stuck with the position that we needed the Soviet Union after the war.

They organized the world. The United Nations that they built prevented the big international clashes. Not specific wars, not all wars, but there have been no more big clashes. So they are responsible for that, even Churchill. Churchill was a man of the past, of the British Empire. Roosevelt was a man of the future, and Stalin of the present. So, Roosevelt was making mistakes sometimes tactically, because of his foresight, and Stalin made strategic mistakes because of his tactics. But now, who can be compared with these big men? Who really has big ideas about these new issues and these really grand visions?

So how do we need to reorganize the world for this century?

Well, it's not an easy question. You asked about your generation, the point is the world has changed enormously. Corporations today are being reorganized in a different way—much more open, much more democratic, much less vertical, much more horizontal—and using new technologies. And now more and more people want to be participants in the deliberations, and can be, because of the Internet. The world is running through networks that can jump borderlines and even language—because there's only one language now, it's Internet language. Which is not English, it's a mix, it's code. But, it will be necessary to understand—I will use a strong word—the sense of the humanity. This has never been taken into account, humanity as such.

We have national interests, class interests, the workers, the entrepreneurs, Brazil, United States. Now it is a little different, because climate change refers to humanity; the nuclear threat affects not one nation, but humanity. So I think it's necessary to have a kind of leadership able to arrange national interests, class interests, even personal interests, with the interests of broader humanity. It is easy to express this of course, but difficult to implement. I belong to a small group of people led by the former prime minister of France, Michel Rocard, that proposed the United Nations accept the principle of interdependency.

What's the difference, right? Well, the United Nations has been composed by nation-states, governments. Now we are ready for it to slowly open to NGOs. But what is important is to change the mindset. We are interdependent now.

Interdependence could imply disguising domination by a group of nations. It has to be different than that. We have, within the UN family, an international penal court. This is important because there is no more national sovereignty inside that court. An American could be judged there—the United States has rejected that, but the structure exists, if the US would allow it. In the case of genocide, for instance, we see it function as a court for humanity, not a national system or national idea of justice.

So, I think to be in accordance with the spirit of the new era, it requires leaders who have the capacity to take into account a new approach.

What is the risk of being too much of an idealist? I guess it's the same that Roosevelt incurred, and he was blamed in several places. But if you don't have utopians, you cannot move. Utopians cannot be fulfilled by definition. In Greek, utopian means one with no place, someone who cannot exist—

But they pull everybody else forward.

Yes.

So there are successes we look at—European Union, the euro. Then there are perhaps failures—the United States is not subscribing to the International Criminal Court. There's this tension between where need we go and the current state system. Is it malleable enough? Can we bend it to where we need it to be?

Up to now, it hasn't been. Imagine Obama. He knows what we're speaking about right now; he understands and feels this. But he's the president of the United States of America. Even the ritual process of the inauguration in the United States is a Roman spectacle. He assumed the American past altogether, the Founding Fathers, slavery. It was symbolic. So he has to play a role. He's not just his ideas, he's the president of the United States of America, and America means all of that.

So how does he reconcile the vision that all of that is not enough for these challenges with the reality that it is the base for his power? It's extremely difficult. It will take time to conciliate the national egoism with humanitarian necessities; it will take time.

Cardoso offers a sense of rather extraordinary ambition. In our conversation, he recalled a question posed to him by Bill Clinton: What is your nation's greatest fear, and what is its greatest hope? In his memoir, Cardoso writes, "Our hope is to become a prosperous and just world power, worthy of our continental size." He continues, "As

I told Clinton, the reality in Brazil has been much closer to our national fear: that we will never realize our destiny, that we will remain imprisoned by the memorable line from Stefan Zweig: 'Brazil is the land of the future, and it always will be.'"[5]

The distance between Brazil's reality and its massive ambition has narrowed since Cardoso's rise. His two monumental accomplishments—in successful battles with HIV/AIDs and hyperinflation—show that government at its best can deliver astounding triumphs in the face of crisis. Alongside the British Petroleum disaster in the Gulf of Mexico in July 2010 and the financial collapse of 2008, two great failures so early in a century, it is quite easy to succumb to the government loathing preferred by the Reagan disciples—the view that government is inherently inept and failing.

But Cardoso's capacity to speak candidly to those challenges; to move his public to action; to instill faith in the government's plan and to then deliver on that vision, should offer hope well beyond Brazil for what government can achieve in the modern era.

There is also the imperative of personal action. This book, in many ways, is a roster of those compelled to extraordinary roles by the circumstances around them. Among those that Cardoso met while biding time in Chile was Ricardo Lagos, the future Chilean president. His mother-in-law, coincidentally, lived across the street from the Cardosos in Santiago. In 1973, Lagos was slated to become the Chilean ambassador to Moscow, but soon had his career interrupted by a violent coup. Chile, the Latin American nation with the richest tradition of democracy, the one nation Cardoso had thought immune to communist hysterics, fell to the tidal wave of fear gripping the Cold War world.

That year, as the country became less politically stable, Cardoso sent his wife and children back to São Paulo. In August, Cardoso joined Lagos for a dinner celebrating Lagos's imminent departure for Moscow. Clodomiro Almeyda, the Chilean foreign minister, joined them; he asked Cardoso how much longer he planned to remain in Chile. Perhaps a month, Cardoso responded.

"Well, you may get to see the page of history turn," the minister told him.[6]

Chapter Two

THE MATADOR

RICARDO FROILÁN LAGOS ESCOBAR

PRESIDENT OF CHILE

2000–2006

ON THE MORNING OF September 11, 1973, Chilean president Salvador Allende, wearing a tweed jacket and a gray knit turtleneck, found himself barricaded inside his presidential palace, clutching an AK-47. He and sixty-seven other men—most all of them government officials—were locked in battle with the Chilean military outside. By 11 A.M. General Augusto Pinochet, the coup-maker laying siege to the palace, was irate that Allende and his aides had yet to surrender. He ordered an air assault on the compound. Two Hawker Hunters, squat fifties-era British fighter jets, arrived an hour later. They made four passes and dropped eighteen bombs. National heirlooms, antique furniture, and paintings by some of Latin America's most noted artists went up in flames. Around 1:15 P.M., Allende received word from his chief of police that the military effectively controlled the entire country. Realizing imminent defeat, he announced a surrender. He shook hands with each of those that had fought alongside him, then retreated upstairs. As troops stormed the palace, he yelled, *"Allende no se rinde!"* He took his AK-47, a gift from Fidel Castro, clutched it between his thighs, and fired two shots into his head.

The timorous-looking Pinochet, with pale blue eyes and a small, wide face, took control of the government and held it tightly for seventeen years. Of the numerous dictators who rose in Latin America during the last half century, Pinochet stands among the most iconic and enduring. He also remains perhaps the most controversial. Upon his death in 2006, Chileans offered a schizophrenic response. Hundreds gathered with candles and banners outside the hospital where he lay; others popped champagne and threw confetti on Santiago's streets.

THE 1973 COUP TYPIFIES American interference in Latin America during the 1960s and 1970s, a policy steeped in Cold War hysterics and amplified by Cuban bellicosity, most poignantly with Fidel Castro's training of rebels from throughout the region. Allende, though a Marxist, had been democratically elected and showed little interest in becoming the emperor of a distant Soviet satellite. Nonetheless, in 1970 President Richard Nixon told the CIA to "make the economy scream" and ordered "everything short of a Dominican Republic–type action"—that is, a military occupation—be done to stop Allende's election.[1] Throughout the hemisphere, what the US termed a Cold War proved quite hot for millions of others. In Guatemala as many as 45,000 people were "disappeared"; in Argentina the military junta killed perhaps 30,000; in the Dominican Republic, El Salvador, and Panama U.S.-backed authoritarians stomped out the left along with countless others of no political ideology whatsoever. Hundreds of thousands of innocents were killed, and hundreds of thousands more tortured within inches of their lives.

AT 2:15 A.M. ON the morning of September 8, 1986, almost thirteen years to the day after Pinochet's coup, policemen brandishing submachine guns stormed the bedroom of Ricardo Lagos. The day before, militant Marxists had attacked Pinochet's motorcade, killing five of his guards and wounding eleven others. The general's car was hit by a shoulder-fired rocket at such close range that the ordnance didn't have time to arm; it ricocheted off with an impotent "clank." Pinochet, unharmed, was sped back to his country estate in a gray, bullet-pocked Mercedes.[2]

At the time, Lagos was a prominent member of the opposition, though decidedly democratic and nonviolent. He served as president of the Democratic Alliance, an umbrella group of parties that opposed Pinochet. It included democratic-socialists, Christian democrats, even members of the extreme right—that is, those too conservative to support Pinochet. He spent the bulk of his time keeping that coalition aligned, and, with the floundering economy as a catalyst, trying to bring unions and other broad swaths of society back into the political fold.

Nonetheless, he was arrested and taken to the Carabineros prison on San Martin Street in Santiago. He would learn later that a former student of his, a law graduate from the University of Santiago, had recognized his name in the stack of arrest warrants issued that night and immediately dispatched his own detectives to arrest Lagos.

"Don't worry, Mr. Ricardo, we are from the Investigaciones," one of the officers told Lagos during the dark raid. The irate professor had no idea what the words meant. Others rounded up by the military that night, including José Carrasco, the president of the national association of journalists, were summarily executed. The detectives who apprehended Lagos tried to pick up Carrasco as well but were too late.[3]

An international campaign for Lagos's release began immediately, led by friends in Santiago and former American colleagues at Duke University, where he had studied for a PhD. Jimmy Carter wrote a letter urging the regime to free him, and when Spanish foreign minister Francisco Fernández-Odoñez refused to meet with his Chilean counterpart at the UN, Lagos was released. The young inspector had given him his life back in exchange for a three-week prison term.

THE DECISIVE MOMENT in the demise of General Pinochet came on April 25, 1988. On that night, the streets of Santiago were eerily empty. For the first time since Pinochet's coup, a political program, *De Cara el Pais,* Face the Nation, aired on television. Lagos and a fellow representative from his recently formed political party, the Party for Democracy, sat at a round table debating three hostile journalists. Lagos, dressed in a blue suit and a mosaic tie, swiveled in his chair to look directly into the camera. "To me," he said, "it is incomprehensible that a Chilean would be so power hungry as to hold on to it for twenty-five years." He raised his right index finger and assailed Pinochet for recanting on a promise to relinquish power. "And now you promise the country eight more years, with torture, assassinations and violations of human rights," he told the camera.[4] Marco Antonio de le Parra, a Chilean playwright, would later write, "His finger is the finger of Chile."[5]

Pinochet wanted to send soldiers into the streets in response. Those around him cautioned against such a caustic reaction. Instead, lawyers at the Interior Ministry were tasked with finding grounds for prosecution; they found none.

Heraldo Muñoz, who would later serve as Lagos's deputy foreign minister, recalled taking the train to a rally in Santiago with

Lagos several days later. "We did not grasp the impact of the broadcast," he wrote. "[P]eople tried to touch him and hug him . . . [we] did our best as his improvised bodyguards, but by the time we got to the stage our shirts had been pulled out of our pants, buttons were missing, and we were soaked in sweat."[6]

Lagos would become the regime's main enemy. On June 9, the general, who never referred to Lagos by name, said on live television: "I say to those bad Chileans who insult us on television because they know we are in a democracy and we are not going to do anything to them: be careful, because patience has a limit."

When the national referendum was held that October, 400 international observers, including US senators Ted Kennedy and Richard Lugar and former presidents Gerald Ford and Jimmy Carter, as well as Bianca Jagger—ostensibly in the country as tourists because of Pinochet's objections—watched as the Chilean people voted "no" to another eight-year term for the general by a majority of 55 percent.

ALTHOUGH OUT OF POWER, Pinochet, with legal immunity and the title "senator for life," continued to wield influence through the 1990s. Civilian presidents regularly sought his approval before controversial decisions, particularly on issues involving the military. And an investigation of his regime's human rights abuses released a year after he stepped down proved embarrassingly sympathetic; it failed to name any of the crimes' perpetrators and ruled out prosecution based on its research.

In October 1998, while Pinochet was in London for medical treatments, Spanish judge Baltasar Garzón, who had previously brought charges against members of the Argentine junta, issued an arrest warrant for the aging dictator. Scotland Yard, acting on a warrant filed via Interpol, arrested him at the London Bridge hospital. The British Parliament was bitterly divided over whether Pinochet should be privileged to diplomatic immunity. He remained under house arrest in Britain for seventeen months. After public calls for his release from both Margaret Thatcher and George H. W. Bush, Jack Straw, the British foreign secretary, arranged for a return to Chile in March 2000.

What should have been a quiet arrival turned into a boisterous affair. When Pinochet's military transport plane arrived at the Santiago airport, the allegedly ill general stood from his wheelchair and strutted across the tarmac as a military band played his favorite songs. Lagos, then the president-elect, was furious but could only watch. While in office, Lagos decided to stay removed from the judicial drama that played out, as the courts stripped Pinochet of his immunity—before reversing the decision and then, ultimately, reconfirming it—then debated whether he was mentally strong enough for trial. Lagos also reopened investigations into atrocities committed by the regime.

AS PRESIDENT, LAGOS TOOK the existing economic principles of the country—implemented by the Chicago Boys, Chilean free-marketeers trained at the University of Chicago and installed by Pinochet—and coupled them with significant social investments. Many of the Pinochet-era reforms, referred to as neoliberal principles, are the bedrock of contemporary economic consensus: they hold that the state has little role in industry; that governments should not run large deficits and should limit regulation, subsidies, and price controls; that currency values should be determined by the markets; that protectionist tariffs on imported goods should be lifted, even if cheaper, imported goods will undercut domestic production; and that nations should seek to export as much as possible. The philosophy, later espoused by Ronald Reagan and Margaret Thatcher—who sent an aide to Santiago for a six-month study of Pinochet's reforms before attempting her own—is now commonplace.[7] At the time, however, it remained largely untested. The Chilean economy stuttered, then gained ground before losing steam in the 1980s; it only took flight once civilian rule was reinstated.

The principles became collectively known as the Washington Consensus; it became doctrine in the 1990s and was espoused by the US government and the world's major lending institutions—the World Bank and International Monetary Fund. Their implementation became the standard metric used by corporations and banks considering investments in foreign countries, as well as their currencies and debt.

The critique of this approach, offered by Lagos and many others on the political left, centered on the stratification it created, concentrating wealth in the hands of the elite while having little effect on the poor. Lagos ran on a platform of making the surging economy benefit all Chileans; a full 30 percent of the nation was unemployed in 1983 under Pinochet's regime. When Lagos left office in 2006, unemployment stood at 8.1 percent.[8] First as minister of education, then as minister of public works, and finally as president, Lagos melded a reverence for the free market—signing free trade pacts with the United States and European Union—with ideas from the left: comprehensive health care reform that maintained a dual track of both private and public systems; campaign finance reform to publicly fund political parties; and labor reforms to include unemployment insurance and expand workers' rights. He levied private funds to build public roads, an idea emulated around the world, leading to a $2 billion investment in otherwise remote areas. He left office with an approval rating above 70 percent, and showed the world how free markets and socialism could coexist in Latin America. Yet despite the success of Brazil and Chile, other countries in the region—notably Venezuela under Hugo Chávez and Bolivia under Evo Morales—have empowered populists rather than market-friendly social democrats, as the political pendulum has swung back to the left.

I want to go back to that famous night in 1988 when you stared down Pinochet. Had you planned to speak that candidly? Had you practiced, or were you moved by the moment that night?

We were in the middle of a campaign for a plebiscite. We were facing a question of whether people would register to vote or not, because, according to Pinochet, you had to register in order to vote. Secondly, how could we make sure that votes would be counted; to be involved in the count, you needed to have somebody from a political party recognized by the dictatorship, so we had to register a party. To register a party meant that we needed to have 35,000 signatures, so it was all very difficult.

I knew that I had to go on TV in order to explain to people that if they registered to vote, and then if they dared to register to have a party, then it would be a different thing. But, in fact, we started to see people registering for the party right away, and because of that, they had to invite me to debate on TV because I was an official political party's candidate. So I went on TV first to thank those that dared to put their names on that list to say they were for a party against Pinochet, and, secondly, I went on to ask others to register to vote to defeat Pinochet.

Now, what happened is that during the campaign, whenever I addressed Pinochet straight, rhetorically, well, people were very moved by that kind of thing. I did the same thing that night that I had done all over the countryside. The only difference is that when you are now talking to an audience of millions of people, well, of course, the result was very amazing.

And were you worried that night? Did you think there was a chance they would come after you? What did your wife say to you? Did she say, "Ricardo you've gone too far?"

I had been in prison two years before, so they thought that it was likely I'd be taken back. My youngest daughter at that time was thirteen years old, and she heard Pinochet's minister of the interior say that they would take actions against me, and she was very upset and afraid.

Jump forward, as you're waiting to assume office ten years later, your predecessor as president had organized a return for Pinochet from prison in Spain. It was supposed to be a quiet affair, and it turned into this spectacle. Were you worried that this would either destabilize the country or just wildly distract it enough to undermine you? And was waiting so long before you ran for president a strategic decision? You had an incredible platform to run for president right away, but you ran for the Senate instead.

[In 1990] I told the Chilean people that I was not the best candidate. I didn't say it this way, but people understood when I said, "Look, I'm not going to stand because I was so antagonistic to Pinochet." It was like a matador, you know, fighting with a bull. I mean, if you run for president you have to have very clear ideas why you think this is better for the country if you are elected. And I thought that in 1990, right after we defeated Pinochet in the plebiscite, I was not the best candidate, even though I had backing.

Back to 2000 while you're waiting to assume office and Pinochet returns and there's this unrest, you weren't worried that it would—

No, not at all, not at all. I knew that I was going to be in office ten years after we defeated Pinochet. I knew that once I was in office I was going to be in command.

And while you were president, there was this drama that played out over whether he was fit to stand trial. At one point, in 2004, the Court of Appeals said he's fine—his dementia is not that bad. As someone that knows many people who were killed by the regime, as someone arrested by the regime, is it frustrating to look back? He died with 300 indictments, but no conviction. Is that sufficient for justice or is that bothersome to you?

"I think that what you have achieved as a country in the area of human rights has not been done by any country in the world." How about that statement? Do you know who told me this? Bill Clinton. I explained to him, "Look, we had an official commission with regard to those that disappeared and with regard to those that had been executed. When the [1991] report came out, many people said, 'I don't believe that.'" Then, years later, I conducted another investigation. It's the only one as far as I know that exists in the world with regard to the issue of those that have been imprisoned and have been tortured. Thirty-five thousand Chileans declared themselves to this presidential commission. Twenty-nine thousand were recognized as people who were imprisoned because of political reasons and had been tortured.

For me, it was essential that the tribunals in Chile be able to judge Pinochet, and they did. They had to be able to strip his immunity as a former chief of state, which they did, and, as with all litigation of that kind, it took a long time. Pinochet died, but at least the number of indictments that he has against him is quite large. The fact is that, now, the chief of his police is in prison; the number of people now in prison or the number of people now being indicted for crimes against human rights is extremely big. So I think that we have fulfilled our job in that sense.

You've spoken about the need for democracy to deliver. Today in the Americas, we've seen a shift left politically, effectively and peaceably in Chile and Brazil, certainly less effectively and more radically in Venezuela and Bolivia. I wonder if it was a mistake of the Washington Consensus to not allow developing nations to deliver more to the poor, to not allow them to spend more on health and education over the past two or three decades?

Well, I always say that Chile is not a bad student with regard to the Washington Consensus. We did all the things of the Washington Consensus, but we went beyond that, because the Washington Consensus—

But beyond it in a way many countries were advised not to . . .

Well, that's the point. You had to. I mean the Washington Consensus is common sense economics, that's all. But common sense economics also will have to teach you that you cannot build a society like a market. If you use the market to build a society, you will reproduce the inequalities that exist in the market. Therefore, society has to be built not around consumers' wishes; society has to be built according to citizens' wishes, and as citizens, all of us are equal. That's a big difference.

When citizens say, "I want to make sure when there is growth that a percentage of that growth will go to education, that a percentage of that growth will go to health, to social housing, to infrastructure, or to buy armaments"—that's a decision for the citizens. And what is important is that in a society having growth, how do you make sure then that the growth will produce a society that is more just, more calibrated? In other words, how do you build social cohesion? A society in which everybody feels that he is receiving part of what he has given for the country?

And given that many places haven't succeeded in building that condition, and given the current financial collapse, as well as the fact that climate change will disproportionately affect poorer nations, do you think this coming decade will see a good deal of unrest and a turn away from democracy?

It's difficult to say, because, as you said, we are in the middle of a huge economic crisis, but at the same time, we were able to react with stimulus packages. At this particular moment in time, all of us are Keynesians again. And it seems to me that this is the real issue, because today we know how to defeat poverty. There is no excuse, other than the political will, and therefore I think that in the future, countries have to take care of themselves. I don't believe that it's possible to have a democracy that doesn't deliver, because, in the end, that democracy will fail. And to deliver means to listen to the citizens, not to the consumer. The market is very important, but the market has never been the way to build a society.

If there is one thing you understood at the end of your presidency that you wished you had grasped in the beginning, what would it be?

What I would say is that you have to believe in what you say. This sounds very simple, but you have to be convinced in what you transmit to the people in order for people to vote for you. When you are unable to deliver because of particular circumstances, then you have to be able to explain that to the people. That's essential.

One of the things underway during your presidency was the information revolution, which has drastically changed the way leaders must interact with their publics. Information about what a president's doing, information that may or may not be true about the dangers of potential legislation, all of this is readily accessible now, and feedback to officials, via email and YouTube and such, is also much easier. The shift really happened in the years you were president, between 2000 and 2006. What advice do you have for leaders about this new information age and how do you have to lead differently as a result?

With regard to the new information age, I think that in developing countries particularly you have to avoid having the information age mean that there's going to be a digital divide in our societies—between those that have access and those that don't. How are you going to have job training to teach the skills that are necessary for today?

We did something very interesting in Chile; we had a joint venture with the Bill and Melinda Gates Foundation that established

Internet connections, digital access to all the books all over the world in every public library all over the country. Once we had that, then we started making on-the-job training for the people. Can you imagine, some fisherman in the remote area of Chile, far away on a small island in the extreme south of the world, knowing through the Internet whether they should sell fish to the Madrid market or in the Barcelona market depending on the prices that day? I went there once and I couldn't believe what the change means for those fishermen, once lost on this small island but who are now connected. That's the kind of new world that we are creating.

You mentioned before this shift in technology that a leader has to take four to six challenges that he knows the public can understand and has to prove himself on those issues. Does that still ring true to you in the information age?

I think so. That's very important. My priority was health reform. A leader now has to be in everyday contact with the people. During my six-year term, every day I had a public activity that would have to be on the evening news in every house.

This is fascinating because we look at Obama now and people say he's overexposed. Is there such a thing now? That's really the question.

No. I don't think so. They told me, "Look, you are not going to be able to keep the exposure that you have now after six months, people will get tired of you." I kept the exposure during my six years. That's the only way you're going to pass legislation. On health reforms, you better explain very clearly what are you planning to do, and then again when you have problems in Congress or when you have a problem with corporations. Physicians, in my case, were not very happy.

The college of physicians in Chile was run by somebody from my own party, but he was very much against best-practice protocols we wanted to put in place. They decided to go on strike, and I went to the public and said, "Okay, I accept their challenge." I challenged the physicians in my country to go on strike, but to strike not only in the morning when they work for the public sector, but also to strike in the afternoon when they work for the private sector. Oh, my goodness, it was awful.

Because they were just planning to strike in the morning?

Of course, of course. In the private sector they would have lost a lot of money. I said to them, "You are socialists in the morning and you are capitalists in the evening." [a scoff]

In the last 20 years, what's the most important way your thinking about the world has changed?

Well, because of the Internet and the revolution of the digital age, we are still unable to see, because we are in the middle of the wave. The wave is still building. You have to think about the fact that after Gutenberg created the printing press it took 200 years to publish a newspaper. In the early eighteenth century, when you published the first paper, it was almost another 100 years before you had a revolution in France. And it was only after the revolution that human beings thought that it was possible to go back to a system of government that the Greeks used to call democracy.

In other words, don't you think that democracy is the byproduct of the fact that you have a paper? Is it possible to think that the democratic government can exist without the citizens being informed? Are we going to be able to go back to the Agora of the Greeks? When they all met in the square to discuss the public problems, the public policies of the government, that was the Agora. That was democracy. All of the citizens were "informed citizens." The important issue is the extent to which democracy is going to be transformed from the way that we know it, given the immediate access that you have in today's world.

What are the changes that *you* would have, your generation? To have a plebiscite almost every day is going to be possible—there's a question and everyone just presses a button and that's it? [astonished laugh]

Members of my generation look at how far we have to go to get a climate change protocol in place. We look at nuclear proliferation that continues; a global economy that's imbalanced and moves in cycles of boom and bust. These are the challenges that the post–Cold War generation should have addressed. Do you think history will judge it harshly?

Yes. This is the first generation that is facing a global problem that has to be tackled in a global way. This is the first case and, in the future, quite a number of problems are going to be global. If you move from nationalist states to a global problem that has to be tackled globally, that means, to some extent, you will have to resign your own sovereignty in your own country.

You have to tell the United States that you want to monitor, to receive reports, and to verify that their own report is true with regard to emissions. And you have to say the same to the Chinese, the Indians, and the Brazilians. Oh, my goodness, so you are going to have an authority *above* the authorities of those countries, because they don't trust the others, or simply because you want to be transparent vis-à-vis the international community? That's the kind of thing that we are talking about now, and this represents a tremendous change. It's very much like in the end of the Middle Ages, when the duke, the count, the feudal lord—they all had to give up sovereignty for the benefit of the national state, to the king. Now we are in a similar process.

On the challenge of climate change, you've posed an intriguing idea—that the current tariff system in international trade should morph into a system in which the penalties levied in global trade would be based on their C02 emissions. The more a country emits, the more penalties that are levied. But, with only a fraction of the world even recognizing the dangers inherent in this, do we have any chance of putting that kind of framework, or really any framework, in place before the worst comes to bear?

It seems to me that the scientific reports are extremely clear. What is worse, the scientific reports lately are all tending to what we thought was the worst-case scenario before. And, therefore, what we used to have—the kind of negotiations to reduce emissions to no more than 450 parts per million—now the scientific community is saying that it's not going to be enough, and emissions must be reduced to 350 parts per million if mankind is going to survive. So the question of scientific evidence is very clear.

Now the time has come, what about the political will? What about politicians saying, "Just do it?" I know it's difficult.

In a democracy, normally, politicians are used to thinking about the next election. The next election is in three years', four years' time at most. Nevertheless, to be a leader, one has to think about the next generation, not the next election. That's the big difference. You have to be able to explain to your people how important it is to prepare the world for the next generation, and that means that you have to win the next election if you're playing in the right way. And this is the only way to exercise political leadership.

It seems to me that the question of climate change is one of those areas where we face a global problem. Not a single country, no matter how important the country is, can solve it alone. And no matter where you are, you are going to emit, and your emissions will affect me, no matter where I live. And my emissions will affect you. This is the real issue, and, therefore, the question is: Is the US willing to take leadership in this area? And, what about the rest of the world?

But there seems to be a deadlock between the US and China since the failed summit in Copenhagen in December 2009. Do you sense the rest of the world is going to become incredulous that these two powers just can't manage to work together?

I think that is true to some extent. I wouldn't like to say that there is something like a G-2, but now the major emitters also realize the fact that the US and China have 40 percent of total emissions. Well, an agreement between those two countries is going to be very important.

At least at Copenhagen they agreed that the issue of deforestation is as important as any of the other issues with regard to the question of emissions. Why do I say that? Because deforestation is responsible for 18 to 20 percent of total emissions. Now, after Copenhagen, you are willing to pay not to cut trees, and that is an important step forward.

I think the biggest failure was in regard to what is going to be the baseline on emissions. The Chinese, on a voluntary basis, are saying that they would like to have a reduction in emissions, and, more importantly, say that they are going to increase their renewable sources of energy. The US is going to finish in second or third place.

I'm okay with finishing second or third in the race for new technologies so long as we can get an agreement in place to actually start employing them.

Well, reality today means that more and more people would like to know how much is emitted when they go to buy something. In Sweden's supermarkets they put the emissions on products that people are going to buy. The other day I bought a ticket to go to Europe, and, the ticket, Air France, says what you are going to emit with so many miles.

Now, why do I say this? Look, the Europeans are saying they are going to decrease their emissions by 20 percent and increase their energy efficiency by 20 percent by 2020. Now, this is an official agreement of the EU, and they are going to impose a penalty for those products that come from countries where they emit more. And we are now talking about 20 percent of the world's market.

But stop there. We are heading from an era of plentiful resources to an era of scarcity, whether it's oil, arable land, water. How do we, as a younger generation, start to shift our values to mirror the challenge we have to face?

It seems to me that the new generation already has much clearer values regarding this issue. In the second half of the twentieth century, countries used to be measured by their per capita income. Well, let me tell you, in the first half of the twenty-first century, countries are going to be measured not only by their income but by their emissions per capita, because all of us know that if there will be 9 billion people in 2050, mankind cannot emit more than 2 tons of carbon per person each year. If the US now emits 22 tons per person, and the EU between 10 and 12, Latin America up to 12, well how are we going to be ranked?

We've got a new yardstick. What is the per capita emission in your country? I'm quite sure that this new generation will also have this second measurement in the back of their brain.

The US Department of Defense, a body rarely assailed for liberal leanings and even more rarely endorsed by environmentalists, concluded in the 2010 Quadrennial review: "climate changes are already being observed in every region around the world, including the United States and its coastal waters. . . . Assessments conducted by the intelligence community indicate that climate change could have significant geopolitical impacts around the world. . . . [It] will contribute to food and water scarcity, will increase the spread of disease, and may spur or exacerbate mass migration. . . . It may act as an accelerator of instability or conflict."[9]

In 2008, for the first time in tens of thousands years, perhaps since humans appeared on earth, both the northwest and northeast shipping channels of the Arctic, north of Siberia and Canada, respectively, were navigable due to the melting arctic icecap. Humanity is like a frog in a slowly boiling pot, Nobel Prize–winning economist and *New York Times* columnist Paul Krugman noted, blissfully unaware of the looming danger. But the same dynamism that created this problem, if harnessed, through more efficient means of energy and the kind of conscientious consumerism that Lagos notes, might save us, too.

Eventually, we will have to kick fossil fuels; it is not a question of choice. And humanity, even if warming has momentarily slowed, is now exceedingly vulnerable to small shifts in climate. A rise in average global temperatures of 7.2 degrees Fahrenheit, which the Met, Britain's national meteorological service, predicts will occur within the next fifty years, will be the tipping point for global instability. Rainfall, they predict, will drop off by 20 percent in western and southern Africa, where populations are most vulnerable to food scarcity. Rain will increase by 20 percent in the subcontinent, in India and Pakistan, where major population centers are situated in flood plains. The science behind climate change is beyond reproach. The question is how long we, as a nation, will choose to look the other way.

Lagos's intuitions about the changing landscape of media, and its implications for leaders of the twenty-first century, mark an important lesson: overexposure no longer exists. Political genius requires—and publics demand—leaders who communicate without reprieve. The German philosopher Max Weber, in his celebrated 1917 lecture "Politics as a Vocation," suggested, "Modern demagoguery"—a term that, in his use, does necessitate evil—"makes use of oratory, even to a tremendous extent, if one considers the election speeches a modern candidate has to deliver. But use of the printed word is more enduring. The political publicist, and above all the journalist, is nowadays the most important representative of the demagogic species."[10]

Weber's era has come to a close. Today's politician, more than at any point since the Greeks, can reach an audience without filter. Leaders now have direct channels to their publics, and video-recording assures the spoken word endures as well as its written counterpart. Web pages—aggregating speeches, video clips, sched-ules, and press releases—coupled with a general distrust of the media, bode well for an era in which publics will be more inclined to get information directly from candidates, rather than traditional news outlets.

A very simple idea, affirmed in a number of other interviews, also emerges: To run for president and to serve well in that capac-ity requires an exceedingly lucid vision. In 1864, Abraham Lincoln noted in a letter, "I claim not to have *controlled* events, but confess plainly that events have *controlled* me."[11] Though the American Civil War dwarfs many of the challenges confounding heads of state today, nearly all recognize the validity of the statement. Napoleon, too, noted the phenomenon: "I never was truly my own master; but was always controlled by circumstances," he told biographer Emmanuel-Augustin-Dieudonné-Joseph, comte de Las Cases, while on his island-prison, St. Helena, in 1816.[12]

When the winds of politics and global anarchy kick up, the hori-zon is easily lost. Great leaders, in those times, have the capacity to remain on an even keel, to not lose sight of the vision or doctrine for which they were elected. Those elected by happenstance, without a broad vision they intend to implement, are certain to fall short.

There also comes a reiteration of something Cardoso suggests: the importance of listening. Defeats are surprisingly common: Tony Blair, Bill Clinton, John F. Kennedy, Ronald Reagan, Franklin Roo-sevelt, George H. W. Bush, Barack Obama, and countless others suf-fered tremendous defeats in their political careers. When I asked Lagos what he had taken from his two failed bids for office, he noted, "You have to learn to listen."

Lagos and Fernando Henrique Cardoso should be coupled in history. Both started their careers from positions on the political left; both were exiles and ardent opponents of right-wing dictatorships; and both, upon reaching power, stood for a third way. They sought to couple the power of the free market with a vision for government that extended beyond the limits Chicago economists envisaged.

Today, Lagos finds himself linked to another global figure, a woman nearly 8,000 miles away, in Oslo, Norway. Gro Brundtland, the former Norwegian prime minister and former director-general of the World Health Organization, is, alongside Lagos, a UN Special Envoy for Climate Change.

Chapter Three

THE VIKING WARRIOR

GRO HARLEM
BRUNDTLAND

PRIME MINISTER
OF NORWAY

1986–1989, 1990–1996

ON A BRIGHT NOVEMBER afternoon in Nice, I took a taxi up a winding route that dead-ends atop one of four narrow hills just west of the city proper. Each crest stretches toward the sea from the inland, like a set of fingers working their way south in search of the Mediterranean. I navigated a pair of security gates and intercoms wielding scrawled notes and fumbled, high school French. "You're here to see *who?*" a watchman's accented, bodiless voice spurned back through a metal box.

Brundtland's husband, Olav, still recovering from a severe stroke, greeted me once I reached the door. Their marriage is a political oddity—Gro, the mother of four, a socialist prime minister, and a physician; Olav, a conservative intellectual, professor, and columnist, but a father above all. "If the dusting gets done," their daughter Kaja told a reporter in 1987, "it's by my father."[1]

"Now before we begin, I have to ask you," Brundtland said, as she served tea on her back porch. "It's just that we get a number of requests and respond to very few of them. How did you get here?" She asked flatly. "Why you?"

To call Brundtland a tough woman would be a considerable understatement. With Nordic blue eyes, short hair, and a wide—if hesitant—smile, she is a presence that fills the room. In the film of her life, the lead could only be played by Judi Dench. She served as the Norwegian prime minister for nine years, led the World Health Organization for the subsequent five years, and is now a United Nations Special Envoy for Climate Change. In 1994, the British *Independent* wrote of her, "Mrs. Brundtland has never been one to tone down an argument for the sake of cosiness. She is a Viking warrior incarnate."[2] She is also the daughter of physician-turned-politician Gudmund Harlem, who held two cabinet posts and was active in the Nazi resistance.

Norway, a relatively small nation with tremendous oil reserves, found itself on the doorstep of the Soviet empire during her years as prime minister; neighbor Finland found itself pressed against the door itself. When Brundtland met Mikhail Gorbachev in 1986, it was the first time in twelve years that a Norwegian prime minister had been granted an audience with a Soviet premier.

GRO—THE NAME MOST Norwegians refer to her by, and which she prefers—brings an interesting dimension to the discourse as one of the world's relatively few female former heads of state. In recent years, as women have taken on far greater leadership roles in society, and outpaced men at universities in nearly all developed nations, it has become clear that the future will be decidedly more female, and justifiably less male. The recent financial collapse accelerated the shift: in the United States more than 80 percent of job losses were suffered by men.[3] And a Pew study of wages in the United States concluded that the median income for married women age 30 to 44 had outpaced that of their male counterparts in 2007.[4]

Political leadership in many nations, though, lags behind. The US Senate, for instance, has only 17 women today; in the British House of Commons, 143 women were elected to the 650-seat parliament in the 2010 elections. Female membership in the Norwegian assembly, the Storting, has hovered around 37 percent; elsewhere in Western Europe figures remain comparable. Margaret Thatcher, while prime minister of Great Britain, appointed a single woman to her cabinet; Gro's was nearly perfectly gender balanced.

International development, too, is undergoing a slow, gender-driven renaissance. Muhammad Yunus, the winner of the 2006 Nobel Prize in Economics, revolutionized aid with microloans in Bangladesh, given almost exclusively to women too poor for conventional lending. Yunus found that nearly all repaid his bank as model debtors. Noted *New York Times* columnist Nicholas Kristof's book *Half the Sky*, cowritten with his wife, Sheryl Wu Dunn, is a celebration of "the girl effect," the idea that aid, if concentrated on women, is far more effective, and may have a chance of righting the gender imbalance of the developing world and its resulting—and rampant—domestic and sexual violence.

Gro recognized these dynamics earlier than most. Her 1986 report for the UN, titled "Our Common Future," offered a prescient understanding of how gender disparity would likely slow development. The report also resulted in the 1992 Rio Earth Summit, which established the framework that matured into the Kyoto Protocol, a treaty setting "binding targets for 37 industrialized countries and the European community for reducing greenhouse gas emissions."[5] The treaty was ratified by all major emitters except the United States; it led to emissions trading structures in the European Union and Japan, by which governments issue permits for the release of greenhouse gases, which businesses buy and sell to mirror their needs. To date, caps on emissions have been placed too high to seriously limit emissions, and, following the breakdown of talks in Copenhagen for a successor treaty to Kyoto—which expires in 2012—the future of carbon trading is uncertain.

IN THE MID- 1980S, when the price of oil collapsed, Brundtland's Norway found itself in a devastating position financially. As prime minister, she convinced the nation to accept a two-year wage freeze across income brackets in 1988 and 1989. Nominal raises of less than 5 percent were allowed, to stave off inflation. It was an act of political brinksmanship, and a plan that required selling a complex and unpalatable vision to her public.

Gro, while prime minister, also suffered immense personal tragedy. Her youngest son, Jergen, who had battled depression since age seventeen, took his own life in 1992. He was twenty-five. Brundtland, then the soul of her Labour Party, resigned leadership of the party but remained as prime minister. Four years later, when she thought a successor had built up reasonable stature, she abruptly submitted her resignation to the Norwegian king. Her husband, Olav, waited for her outside the prime minister's office in Oslo, the car already packed full with "clothes, tools, and a case of light beer." They retreated to their winter cottage on Lake Mylla. The photographers and journalists that had assembled shouted questions; "they got only a smile."[6]

One of the most terrifying things about climate change is how far we still have to go to convince not only publics but also societal lead-

*ers about the danger. President Václav Klaus in the Czech Republic,
José María Aznar of Spain, basically half of the US Senate . . .*

You know, last year I was in Virginia at Thomas Jefferson's
house, and I was given something called the Thomas Jefferson Award.

I couldn't believe what happened. There were three awardees;
one was Senator [John W.] Warner from Virginia, and also your
Supreme Court Justice Antonin Scalia. I knew a little about Scalia,
but not everything, and I certainly didn't know the things he could
say about climate change. But it showed me that even as late as the
middle of 2008, a Supreme Court Justice could stand up in a dinner
speech after me and push aside what I had said.

My reflection, as I was there in Thomas Jefferson's house, was
that Jefferson with his scientific mind—you know, with his real in-
tellect; he read what was available at his time—had no chance of
knowing what we know today. I just made a brief dinner reflection.
I said, "Because of human activities now, the sum of them lead to
changes that are destroying and affecting our planet." So Scalia stood
up and said, "There is no link between climate change and human activity." That was his main point in his speech. But you know—
Jefferson was crying.

Everyone in the room, I can tell you, was shocked.

*I was with Fernando Cardoso of Brazil, and he said: "We've learned
now that the US can't lead the world on its own, that it takes everybody together. But the world can't do it without the United States."
Given that we really only have a couple of years to get ahead of the
worst effects of climate change, do you think we'll get there? Do
you think our minds will sort of bend enough, and we'll be able to
adapt?*

I cannot *not* believe it. I mean I am basically a combination of
an optimist and a realist. This is how I have worked, solved, ana-
lyzed, given priority to what I put my effort into since I was a girl.
And it still has not left me. So even if only thirty-something percent
of the United States understands that Scalia is wrong, the leadership
of the US now knows it.

Bush knew it! He said it, and he didn't believe it in his first
term. By the middle of his second term, he had enough insight,

enough reports coming to his desk that he started to stop saying these kinds of things. He said, I think it was January of 2008 in his State of the Union Address, that we have to realize there is a link between human activity and the risk of climate change. He understood that he had been on the wrong track. So certainly, the present administration fully knows. Now, how would it then be possible *not* to start moving much more clearly in the right direction within the next year or two?

But Clinton knew as well and we didn't move forward—the Senate didn't ratify Kyoto.

But meanwhile the number of political leaders around the world who are aware is much higher than it was in Clinton's time, I think.

Since we're talking about this current moment, I want to ask about backlash within broader populations. The BBC released a poll recently, done really around the world. It found that only 11 percent of people thought the free market system was working well; 23 percent thought that the system was fatally flawed.[7] To what extent do you worry that we could see a backlash from this crisis against capitalism, against democracy?

There is a risk, but frankly I think that a balanced approach will appear.

Yes, absolutely, it's a pessimistic picture. But how do we share with what I will call the "broad public" the kinds of things that you and I are talking about now? It is rather complex. And it's so easy to put out a statement saying that if you do this or that every problem will be solved. This is every election, every campaign that I see. People are not really given the right messages about the complexity of decisions and the priorities that we have to make.

You know, the Norwegian people learned a lot over my years, and it helped. When that economic crisis hit Norway in 1986–1987, it was a combination of both a global economic crisis and Norway having lost its competitive advantage, having fallen down with regard to its productivity. Our wages were too high, our cost levels were too high, and we were losing competitiveness. Then, like now in your country, people had been borrowing too much because the banks were running after you to give you money, and the conservative government at that time let the banks do this. There was very little regulatory effort.

When I had to take over in 1986, there was a global economic crisis, and, in addition to all these weaknesses in the Norwegian economy, oil prices fell from $30 to $10. This was a catastrophe. The United States can live with deficits for many years, even decades now, as we have seen. Norway can't.

So, what we had to do was work with the labor unions, which, in Norway, have a much stronger place in society, because they are serious, moderate unions that are realistic. We were able to say to the Norwegian people: "There will be no wage increases for the next two years because we are in a crisis; this is what we have to do in order to avoid unemployment and really a much worse situation for everybody." And for years I had to travel around explaining to Labour union leadership and the Norwegian people, "I'm sorry. We are seeing to it that you are able to stay in your house, that you are able to keep your jobs, to generally keep unemployment down, but we are not going to have a chance to give you increased standards of living until we have worked ourselves out of this situation."

I'm telling you this because it was possible to explain to the Norwegian people that this was necessary, and we generated enough support to make it work over several years, until we came through the crisis. But, after, the Norwegian economy has since been sound. We have had increased oil income. We have a pension fund that we started that now has 300 billion Norwegian crowns, which is not used, except for 4 percent every year in the budget. People have gotten used to an increasing standard of living, and now, in the debate between political parties for the last election, they suggested that basically everything under the sun can be done.

I love that you're speaking to this because there's an adage in American politics that "Nobody gets elected by saying they're going to raise taxes." In moments of crisis, you can sometimes speak honestly about these problems, and we almost see the same thing in America today: People are just living so far beyond their means, but we've yet to see politicians speak really candidly to the truth. I mean, part of it is a public that doesn't understand, but part of it is that the public is in denial.

Yes. It's a combination. It's a combination.

And I wonder if this isn't the biggest challenge for modern democracy as a whole? The dangers that an uninformed public—or a public that is choosing to simply look the other way—are posing everywhere?

Yes—you know the more ambitious we become about solving complex and interrelated global problems, the more this is our dilemma. More knowledge has to be shared to keep democracy working. And, as I sometimes say to people who are frustrated, when I speak with really good-natured environmentalists or students, who say, Why can't this be done? I say, "If there was an alternative to have a global dictatorship, and we could decide that now, we would have to do that because of what we now know scientifically about climate change. But we don't have one, and we are not going to have one—not a government at the global level and certainly not today." And it *would* have had to be a dictator at the global level, because there is no way to get a democratically elected government above and beyond every other country. And this is the troublesome thing.

Now, you mentioned taxes. I had a learning experience quite early. I was prime minister in 1981, after the elected prime minister left because of an illness and I took over for the last nine months of the term. We were planning the budget for the coming year, which is presented in October, two or three weeks after the elections. The conservatives and the other non-social-democratic parties won that election. It was a bad economic situation—interest rates were up to 13 percent.

But, as we discussed what the budget should look like, we had a discussion in the cabinet about the exact taxation level, whether we should increase the taxation to raise half a billion Norwegian crowns, which was a considerable sum at that time.

Now, I'm telling you this because, after the election was lost and we came into opposition, I saw how the new government and the parties of the center right were using that budget. It was very easy for those parties to give people the impression that we were for high taxes for everyone, not only for the ones with the highest incomes. It is always very simple to scare people. And when we came to the next election, we did not, in our program, repeat increasing the taxes.

We changed the taxation system to get more revenues, but in different ways to avoid the dilemma of getting the conservatives all over us, hammering down on us, and scaring the public about the taxes.

So then, when I was back in government and everything went wrong, as I told you, in 1986–1989, when oil collapsed, I told the people that we would not increase their taxes, but rather would not increase their income. It's really the same thing, but it worked. They accepted not increasing incomes, because they understood that if the pay per hour or per month for workers would be increasing, we would get inflation. We would not be able to pay our debts, et cetera. People understood it. But it amounts to the same thing, doesn't it?

And also, the other thing which we managed to do, we made a law just to prohibit income increases for anyone. And that passed in Parliament with the center of Norwegian politics behind it.

I want to jump back to what you were talking about before, about a leader as an educator. Do you think that, paradoxically because of the information revolution, governing democratically has become harder? People are now closer to their representatives and president than ever before. It's so easy to find out what she is doing, where he stands on specific things, but it remains very difficult to understand issues fully. So ironically, is it possible that it's made things harder, that technology has made governing more difficult? It's very easy to scare people, and it's very easy now, in turn, for vocal minorities to make their views sound quite loud.

You know, frankly, I think yes, it has. Because if I go back in our history, people trusted the leaders of the Labour Party who rebuilt Norway after the Second World War. It was probably more like Roosevelt, if you go back to your 1930s, after the crisis. We had had a war. Norway was built back up. They had trust in the leaders, and the leaders deserved it. They did the right things, and they spoke well in their speeches when they traveled the country, explaining issues to people. So yes, you are right, but I don't see an alternative. I mean I'm not suggesting dreaming backward; it's not possible. We just have to move on to try to explain and to try to get more information through, and to get even more participatory approaches.

Now, in the United States you have too few people voting, and that's a tragedy in itself. It means that, in fact, the democracy is not working, because so many people are not there, even every four years for the presidency. In my country now, it used to be—if you go twenty years back—80 percent were voting, at least in the national elections. Now, we are down to around 72, 73 percent. But still, three-fourths of the people have voted for the parties for Parliament and therefore for the kind of government we have.

What was the most important advice, political advice, that anyone gave you?

Well, I think it must have been my father's first advice. My father was a minister in the government for ten years. The advice he gave me was quite important in my first months and weeks, and that's a very decisive part of any new challenge.

He said, "Remember that anything that is on your desk that you haven't given a response to means part of your ministry is not working as effectively as it can. For the efficiency of your ministry and for the staff of several hundreds that you have, make sure that you are not a block in the system." This was very important.

The second thing my father told me was, "If you are in Parliament, never say anything that you are not sure of. Never take any chances when you are uncertain or you don't know enough to answer a question. Say, I'm not sure, this I will have to check; I will come back later and give you a full response." In a parliamentary system, if a minister takes chances and if a minister says anything wrong, you can be finished in a moment.

So these two things were important, but the prime minister also gave me one big and important piece of advice. I asked, "What do I do with all the officials in the ministry who may have other political views than the Labour Party? How do I deal with that?"

He said, "Gro, forget about it. Deal with everybody as if they are your party colleagues." It is a fundamental wisdom.

On a personal level, picking up this concept of information technology and citizens knowing everything that you do—in your book you mentioned, for example, going shopping at Christmas and basically becoming trapped—how did that change affect you?

I think this is a big problem. When I started, when I said yes to the prime minister in 1974 to become his environment minister, I had no clue about the things we are talking about now. How it would affect my family was not part of my consideration. My consideration was: Can I say no? Am I good enough to say yes? Can I do it? And can my husband and I find ways to deal with the caretaking of the children and so on? The perspective that you were going to be under attack every day, every hour even, was not on my mind because it wasn't that way in 1974.

And then, the years have passed and it's become worse and worse and worse. And now, I would not advise any of my children to become a politician, to go into what I did. I wouldn't. And it's terrible to say so because it's against all I believe in. But if I think about the person, and the challenges that the person can face in the future and the dilemmas, I would say, "No, don't, unless you really are so burning for it that you choose to do it, even knowing that it may become difficult for your children, for your wife, for your husband."

I had no idea how it could and would affect my children. And they kept it from me until they were grown up, because they tried to protect me. And only when they were twenty-five, thirty, and this was all history, did they explain some of the things that they encountered that were hurtful and difficult for them, yes.

And so when you write about that—you write about every item in your grocery cart being scrutinized, and people eavesdropping on all your conversations—was there ever a moment where you thought about leaving public life simply because it had become so invasive?

No, because this all happened gradually. So I let my husband do more of the shopping than before, and I stopped taking my two terrible boys. That Christmas the youngest ones understood how afraid I was with all these people watching, so they were using it to manipulate me. We were shopping and people were watching, and they were pointing, "Mom, I want this, and this!" My goodness. Oh, it was a drama, yes. The two of them were doing it laughing. So I said, no more Christmas shopping.

I started understanding that I have to protect my family, myself, my husband by not letting the journalists into my house. You see, while these years passed, my feeling of responsibility toward my party, toward my country, grew every year until the end of the story. So I could never make my personal considerations in front of my responsibility.

But, I mean, if a young person asks me now, "Should I do it?" it's a different story because you can tell them, "Your life will be very different from all your colleagues and everybody else if you do it." But I couldn't make that assessment, except after our son died.

My children were not elected—this is the point. This is what I realized gradually when things happened to my children that were linked to my work. I had to say to a journalist, "Don't you think? How can you expose a sixteen-year-old boy because he is my son?" And he said, "Well, this is the right of the public to know." And I said, "No. This boy has not been elected. He never sought office. He has a right to privacy and he is not even a grown-up. He's a child of sixteen." But people have to think about it. They didn't even reflect until I started explaining it, I think. And then some of them started nodding, realizing what it meant. You have to explain it.

That was when I realized that I could not continue being both the prime minister and the other. It was kind of a crossroads; this terrible event forced me to make some assessments. And people were begging me, "You mustn't leave." So I decided I will leave from the party leadership, because then a new leader can build up the future and I can do the governing of Norway for the next few years.

I want to ask you about being a woman and a leader. During the campaign, Hillary joked with Barack that he had an unfair advantage because she had to wake up an hour earlier to get her hair done...

[*knowing laugh*] But you know, there is some truth to this—and she was overdoing it there in a way, but, I mean, that's part of joking. Because you *are* required more than a man would be to look good, to look rested, to have nice hair, not to have forgotten to put on your makeup. There are a lot of things that relate to women that don't to men. You sometimes change the color of your shirt and the color of your tie, but basically, otherwise, nothing.

But there is a difference, and nobody, of course, would have asked a man at that time, "What about your children?" and all of these things. They still don't. They don't ask a man about how can he deal with being this or that because he has three or four children. Nobody would say it today. Even today in Europe, even in Norway today, there is a difference in how people react, respond, reflect. Although there has been a lot of change, we still have different expectations of female and male leaders.

Watching Hillary's campaign, you also saw this tension between feminine and tough.

It's very difficult.

What advice do you have for women who are trying to ascend to these top political rungs all around the world?

It's a difficult challenge. It is. But I'll tell you one thing that I have repeated when young women have asked me similar questions. One thing I'm sure about is that if you have a high-pitched voice, like many women have, that becomes thin and not easy to hear. You have to speak up. So I usually tell women, "You must train your voice and you must use it by being heard." Because you are not going to be respected fully if people don't sense that you speak with a certain authority, with determination. Using your voice in such a way that it carries in the room is an important thing, because men—and even many women—when they hear male voices they listen, and when they hear a female voice they often relax because it's a thinner, secondary voice. In every meeting, you will hear this. But some women have the ability to speak out, to speak with a certain amount of authority, and to really use their voice.

On this theme of women and leadership, you talked about women in Norway eclipsing men in the universities. We've seen the same thing in nearly every developed nation. And if we look at development in recent years, so much has been written about how aid, if focused on women, through microloans and other means, is much more successful. Do you think the world would be in a better place today if there had been more female leaders?

I think so. It's just that it would have been a better balance. And it would have meant that in more countries there would have been more people, also females, who have been given the opportunities, who have been given the chance to talk, who have been educated and can be a part of society at the leadership level. Mostly, societies in which you get women as leaders have gone through certain stages of improvement, of achieving participatory approaches across male and female, which means that those societies would be more democratic. And more women leaders would mean that you have come to a better stage of using all your resources in a better way.

So that would be one important thing. But I also do think that if you, in a collegium or a forum of leaders, have too much imbalance, the kinds of experiences that women tend to notice, that women tend to pursue and then tend to understand will be underrepresented in the debate, which is not a good thing.

Do you recall experiences in which you were slighted by male leaders or, maybe more subtly, when your gender was deftly used against you?

I had a conservative leader who was my main opponent for many years. Those years when he was prime minister and I was leader of the opposition, he often said, "Mrs. Brundtland this and that," and the way he used "Mrs." instead of saying "Gro," or saying "my honored opponent," or using other ways to address the parliamentary leader of the Labour Party—it framed whatever he would say. I sensed that it was condescension. But you have to be cautious about saying something, because people can think you are making an issue of something which isn't. But gradually, people started reacting to it, and you had people writing and saying, "Why does Mr. Willoch talk this way to Mrs. Brundtland?"

When I was a young prime minister of forty-six, most of the people I worked with in bilateral meetings were older than me, and, except for Margaret Thatcher, they were all men. And I connected with them by being very direct, speaking my mind, using my knowledge, experience, sometimes using examples from my own life. Instead of somebody conveying some kind of brief from the bureaucracy, you become a person. It has to be very direct, personal, open, and frank, because you have a limited amount of time. You have to make a personal impression on that counterpart.

This is what I did with Gorbachev. I recall explaining to him my concern about narcotics and drugs in the Soviet Union. I said, "So how are you planning to deal with this? Because you have now told your country that alcohol is a problem that has to be dealt with. But, you know, we also have narcotics, and in Norway, and we have been struggling to deal with both of these issues. So how are you proposing to deal with this in Russia?" And he started explaining that, "No, we really don't have too much," then he broke himself off.

He started saying, "We don't have a narco—." I said, "Well, it's really impossible, because in Norway, we've been working so hard and we still haven't gotten very far." He said, "My daughter is a medical doctor and she knows about these issues." And then I realized that I was reaching his mind with what I was saying. He understood that since Norway had a problem in narcotics, we obviously have a problem here, too. He didn't say it expressly, but he told me that he was going to look into it without saying so. Three weeks later, maybe four, there was a big announcement from Moscow about the challenge of narcotics and drug use in Russia. So he had gone to his people and said, "I'm not accepting that you say that we don't have a problem."

But, of course, when you are talking with a Soviet leader and you are from small Norway, a neighboring country, you are very attentive to every detail. You have two hours at the most and it could be a year till you see him next.

I met Ceauşescu in Romania in 1983. At the time, he was the most progressive with regard to nuclear weapons and other foreign policy issues. But he was so streamlined in everything he had to say. It was nice, polite, just glossing over everything. It was not possible to reach into him. He was prepared in a kind of Teflon way, very different than with Gorbachev when he looked into my eye and said, "I have a daughter who is a medical—." It was fascinating to see his mind moving.

To come back to the question of the early 1990s, at this historical hinge, do you agree that there was a lost moment with Gorbachev, not only on nuclear disarmament, but on thinking about defense in general?

On everything.

That Bush and Clinton could have gone to Russia and even China and said, "We are wasting tremendous resources on defense."

I think more could have been done in the 1990s. Frankly, it could because the momentum was there. You had Gorbachev. Now, twenty years later, we have seen on the television the celebrations after the Berlin Wall fell. You can see the degree of enthusiasm that had built up before those moments, and there was more to be gained from it. Things were lost.

Now, you can say who lost them? It's not a simple answer, because in Russia, as Gorbachev was toppled, you ended up with Yeltsin, who was quite some person. And, of course, behind these people, in the wings everywhere around the world, you had the KGB and others with power to really make it difficult for the leaders. So obviously, despite the enthusiasm for a kind of a new society in the former Soviet, well, it was a little more difficult. And, of course, the analysts in the United States and other places, they could not tell such a good story so long as Gorbachev was still in power.

But, I mean, he told me that they were after him, when he was supposed to come to Oslo in December [of 1990] when he had won the Nobel Peace Prize. And it was quite a shocking moment in my life, I must say, to see the leader of the Soviet Union, of the *Soviet Union,* sitting beside me explaining his difficulties leaving his country. How he was not allowed to go to Oslo—

By the apparatchiks? What did you sense? How did you react?

It was surely a shocking experience. It was so emotional, it was so personal. The man was holding my hand and speaking to me as an old friend. And, of course, we had met before. He felt confident that I was his friend and I could feel it. I could sense it. There was only an interpreter standing behind us. We were sitting there. But, I was not aware of how bad the situation was until that moment, what kinds of barriers he was up against and the counterforce against his radical changes. And then, of course, he was toppled later.

As Brundtland showed me out, I raised the issue of Yeltsin's alcohol abuse. A few weeks before we met, it emerged that the first democratically elected Russian president, while visiting Bill Clinton in Washington, had been found on Pennsylvania Avenue by the Secret

Service, drunkenly searching for pizza, dressed only in his underwear. The next night, when he tried to get out again, a brief standoff took place when he was mistaken for a "drunken intruder."[8]

"Yes, he was quite some person," she repeated. She recalled ordering that he not be served alcohol at state functions in Norway, but found that he arrived already inebriated. I recalled a picture of Yeltsin in her memoir, at what appears to be a state function, borishly holding Gro under one arm and the Queen of Norway under the other. "Raspberries and cream," he had told the assembled photographers, referencing Gro's white pantsuit and the queen's red dress. I asked if he had been drunk at the time, "Quite," she replied.

For all the comedy that such anecdotes now evoke, there should be an equal part horror. In 1995, an American rocket ferrying a Norwegian weather satellite set off the old Soviet warning system. The trajectory of the flight resembled a US strike from a submarine somewhere in the arctic. The nuclear football, the black case that authorizes a nuclear launch and accompanies the president at all times, was put in front of Yeltsin. "For several tense minutes, while Yeltsin spoke with his defense minister by telephone, confusion reigned," wrote David Hoffman of the *Washington Post*.[9] With less than eight minutes to decide whether to launch a retaliatory strike, Yeltsin balked, confident that a mistake had been made and that Clinton had no intention of making war.

He, of course, was right. The Norwegian government had notified the Russian command of the launch, but the notice had failed to climb through the dysfunctional bureaucracy. How many vodkas, one must wonder, had Boris had that day? What if he had started the day a bit earlier, or a bit more hungover?

From Brundtland, I draw two lessons. The first centers on crisis: In extraordinary and perilous moments, the public wants to know the extent of the damage or threat, and expects decisive action. If a public is confident in its leader, his or her diagnosis of the problem, and the solution prescribed, their willingness to follow can be stunning. Brundtland's ability to weather the economic wilt of the 1980s by devaluing the currency, clamping down on credit, and, most astoundingly, freezing wages for two years, is a testament to what can be achieved amid crisis, and what the public, when forced to listen, can comprehend and accept.

The public, she notes, is more willing to accept shared, palpable sacrifice than uncertainty, or measures that evoke a visceral reaction—like raising taxes.

The second lesson from Brundtland is that "knowledge has to be shared to keep democracy working." Today, despite the dawning of the information age, accurate information feels as out of reach as ever. A plethora of political commentary and opinion, rather than fact, has been the result. Many citizens decline serious political thought because of the maze of maddening deceit and misinformation that seems to surround politics. Our major American news agencies, themselves once the bulwark between spin and fact, have become exceedingly politicized.

The first steps to tackling the challenge may already exist. The Congressional Research Service, a professional, apolitical think tank within the US Congress, uses taxpayer dollars to fund short, simple papers on nearly every issue imaginable—the Iranian nuclear threat, the state of the war on drugs, potential ramifications of new legislation and analysis of passed legislation. Making the material accessible to the public—an idea that has been raised many times on Capitol Hill, but never seems to muster the momentum to come to fruition— could be an important first step toward realizing the potential for shared information.

If Brundtland found herself on the steps of the Soviet fortress peering in, battling to convey information across, Václav Havel, the poet-prince of Czechoslovakia, was on the other side of the garrison, pounding relentlessly at its gates and trying to tell his story to the world. He is the author of a twentieth-century fairytale, and one of the most iconic dissidents of the Cold War.

Chapter Four

THE PLAYWRIGHT

VÁCLAV HAVEL

PRESIDENT OF
CZECHOSLOVAKIA
1989–1992

AND THE CZECH REPUBLIC
1993–2003

IN NOVEMBER 1989, CROWDS swelled in Prague's Wenceslas Square for eleven consecutive nights, chanting toward the castle high on the hill above the city and its communist occupiers: "*Havel, na Hrad!,*" "Havel to the Castle." At the foot of the square's statue to the patron saint of Bohemia, they lit candles and laid flowers alongside pictures of young dissidents killed by Nazi occupiers during the Second World War and by Soviet troops during the annihilation of the Prague Spring, in 1968. They held their keys aloft, jingling them as if to sound a final bell. It was the Velvet Revolution, and among its authors was the slight but reconciled Václav Havel. His is one of the twentieth century's most unique curriculum vitae: playwright and brewer; soldier, welder, dissident and philosopher; prisoner, then president.

At seventy-four, Havel is a frail man. Almost five years in prison and a lifetime of smoking have brought an already feeble frame close to death several times, and, as we spoke, his words were interrupted by a churning cough. He developed severe pneumonia while in prison. He was saved by an international campaign led by his wife, Olga, to free him. The discovery of a cancer, misdiagnosed first as another pneumonia, led to the removal of half his right lung, in 1996.

Havel was born into a wealthy Prague family in 1936. Their privilege was inverted when communist forces came to power twelve years later. The most prominent families were exiled from the capital, their properties confiscated and replaced with tiny villas near the German border. Havel's father, a well-connected developer and restaurateur, managed to keep hold of two rooms in the family's Prague apartment. For the meek and pudgy Václav—Vasek, as he was known as a boy—the loss of fortune was oddly liberating. He had been alienated by his wealth amid so much poverty. In his words, he would have "gone on to study philosophy at the university," and, after graduation, "ridden around in an imported sports car without having done the least thing to deserve it," if the communists had not come to power.[1]

Instead, he was banned from the universities and had to contrive his way into night classes meant for middle managers of the communist bureaucracy. After compulsory military service, during which he wrote several outlandish plays that were staged by unit mates, he advanced cautiously into literary circles. He lingered on the periphery of conferences and publications sanctioned by the regime, where he found that deference toward state propaganda and writing was expected. He quickly found a voice critiquing his contemporaries who were co-opted into the "gray" malaise of communist writing and life.

In 1956, at a writers' conference hosted by the party journal *Květen,* Havel, then barely twenty and, allegedly, shaking at the podium, first assaulted the establishment. Surrounded by Czech and Slovak literary luminaries, he assailed their work for its unwillingness to deal with darker shades of humanity, for its exclusion of great writers who had lived before the rise of communism, for the lack of outlets and a general unwillingness to push the bounds of the medium. Around that time, he began expecting the regime to arrest him. He took to carrying an emergency packet with him wherever he went. It held soap, toothbrush and toothpaste, cigarettes, and a change of underwear.[2]

HAVEL SLID EASILY INTO the counterculture of sixties-era Prague, with its late nights and liquor, love affairs and rock 'n' roll. He married Olga Šplíchalová, a Bohemian girl that his doting mother wildly disapproved of, and fell in love with a small theater on the Balustrade. Olga worked there as an usher and Václav spent nearly every waking minute immersed in production—writing, taking tickets, designing sets, cleaning up after audiences.

In 1968 Havel watched as the Prague Spring was crushed by Soviet troops. Alexander Dubček, the first secretary of the Communist Party of Czechoslovakia who had allowed for the thaw of culture and thought, was ousted from his position and replaced by two decades of strict totalitarianism. Havel, who was in the northern town of Liberec at the time of the invasion, saw tanks roll over barricades, burying Czechs in the rubble, and troops open fire on crowds.

Havel took over the airwaves from an underground radio station to organize the town's resistance. A local band of hooligans, known as the Tramps, joined the police in trying to thwart the Soviets. Over the radio, Havel provided news updates and ideas for resistance; the Tramps, with their long hair and vagabond attire, bedeviled the foreign troops by changing street signs. "And thus arose a strange collaboration," Havel later recalled, "for two days members of the Pastor's Gang wore armbands of the auxiliary guard, and three-man patrols walked through the town: a uniformed policeman in the middle with two long-haired Tramps on either side."[3]

A week later, Dubček capitulated to the Soviet invaders; the resistance in Liberec and Prague broke. Havel's personal resistance, though, continued on. His essays and plays began circulating widely, despite being banned by the hardened regime. Several of his earliest works—*The Garden Party, The Memorandum,* and *The Increased Difficulty of Concentration*—slipped through the Iron Curtain and found their way to stages in Europe and the United States. They lifted Havel to international prestige. In 1976, when he was invited to Vienna for the opening of one of his plays, his passport was revoked. His relationship with the communists became a game of cat and mouse, the regime tracking and jailing him, and Havel, all the while, growing more reckless and more renowned, and thus harder to suppress or eliminate. He later explained how his first and longest prison term, from October 1979 to February 1983—time he spent welding steel mesh and "wringing out sperm-stained sheets"—emboldened him, despite nearly killing him.[4] He no longer faced an abstract fear of what the regime might do to him, but instead possessed a very concrete sense of the likely punishment and his own capacity to endure.[5]

The game ended in November 1989, when Mikhail Gorbachev made clear that Moscow would no longer prop up fledgling satellite regimes with military interventions. The Berlin Wall was beset by chisels and ladders, and, days later, Czechs and Slovaks took to Wenceslas Square. On December 29, the Federal Assembly voted unanimously to make Havel the acting president.

In the following weeks, Havel rode a scooter through the castle's corridors and welcomed his countrymen into the former communist fortress; he threw a "festival of democracy" with mimes and jugglers and hosted a string of celebrities. It quickly became clear, though, that Havel—and the troupe of actors, poets, and dissidents that he brought with him—hadn't the first clue how to govern. Similarly, the nation that had chosen him to lead hadn't the slightest instinct how to behave as a democracy. The Civic Forum, the broad collection of dissidents that he had led and that had morphed into his political party, proved a far better opposition movement than political base.

He would fumble through his first term and half-heartedly run for a second. He has recalled feeling like a fraud while president, like his triumph had been a dream that might evaporate at any moment. Nonetheless, he felt a mandate to gain admission to the European Union and NATO, to ensure that the Iron Curtain would never be drawn back across Eastern Europe. He secured reelection by one vote in the Czech parliament in 1998, and gained acceptance into NATO in 1999. In 2004, one year after he left the castle at the end of his second term, the Czech Republic joined the EU. He left with a nearly 55 percent approval rating and now, the better part of a decade later, is spoken about affectionately by the overwhelming majority of Czechs.

A FEW BLOCKS FROM the Slavia Café—where as a teenager he convened a rogue literary society, called "the 36ers" for those born in 1936—Havel keeps an office in a pastel-green-colored building. Across from a graffiti-covered wall, the sixth nameplate reads, "VÁCLAV HAVEL, KANCLÉŘ." A small, gently faded heart hangs off the final leg of the "R," where the graffitist turned his or her pen to the placard.

The office has the feel of a theater storage closet. In the courtyard outside, an alien statue, befitting a man of absurdist theater, stands guard. It's tall and white, adorned with angel's wings, and stands atop three discarded pistols, its hands outstretched in search of alms or communion. Havel's assistant, Sabina, who has been with him since before the revolution—when she responded to a nondescript ad for a secretarial position—told me that it is on loan from the church in charge of Havel's archives. A low, vaulted ceiling gives the office a cavernous feeling, and we sat in red velvet chairs of a subtly regal shape.

The day that we met Havel's jacket was velvet, too, a darker shade of red nearing black; his trademark mustache remains a resilient gray. On the wall opposite our velvet chairs was a red Tibetan tapestry that, he told me proudly, had been a gift from the Dalai Lama. "There are thousands like it, and each has a different mythical power—but this is the highest," he said, smiling up at the piece. "There are only seven in the world." He pointed to a large gold and silver tray at the center of the table, etched with the preamble to the US Constitution. "From your new president, Obama," he said, looking at me with a sly grin. He nervously thumbed at his glasses case as we spoke, and has a tendency to look toward his lapels or his feet as he speaks. When I posed questions, he sometimes looked to the translator for assistance, but, more often, he launched into a reply, a subtle smile occasionally stealing across his face.

I wonder if you were surprised by how quickly the walls closed in after you became president. At one point, you wrote about wanting someone outside your group to look at a speech, someone who didn't live "on the submarine."[6] *Were you surprised by how quickly relationships changed?*

Well, it was different with different people. I have noticed that a politician—and this is a general phenomenon—always has a special halo around him, due to the simple fact that he holds a particular office. It has nothing to do with whether he is a good politician or a complete fool; the position itself lends that person a special aura. I realized that myself when I persuaded a friend of mine to become minister of foreign affairs. The moment I appointed him, I started to respect him more and was politer to him, despite the fact that we were old friends and had even been in prison together. But this is just a peripheral observation.

Otherwise, reactions varied. Some people were mad at me and accused me of cutting myself off from them. The simple explanation for that was that I didn't have time anymore, which they didn't understand. Others would support me in every possible way; some even worked together with me. Some thought I had become a stranger; others claimed I had deliberately sought out political power, that I wanted to become president and loved being president. Some found me a strange kind of president who thought of the presidency as a sacrifice rather than an honor. So responses were very different.

And the greater their hopes that I would sort everything out, that I would quickly make the world a better place, the more disappointed they became, because in the end, of course, the world did not change for the better and they blamed me for it—and some even became my enemies. The greater the hopes they invested in me, the greater their disappointment. And this is what I told President Obama when he was here in April: The whole world had pinned their hopes on him, believing he would change the world for the better, and when it turned out to be impossible, some people would start hating him. And he said it had already started to happen.

Your mother urged you to create an illegal literary society, the 36ers, as a teen, which would have likely landed you in jail if you had been a few years older. As you grew older and more reckless, where were your parents in the picture? Did they push you forward or pull you back?

I think my parents sympathized with everything I did, but, at the same time, they were very worried. They didn't want their child to be hurt unnecessarily. My father and my mother, of course, like all parents, perhaps, wanted me to achieve something in life, to become someone important, which is why I'm sorry they didn't live to see my presidency, because then they would have seen me rise to an important position. At the same time, however, they were worried, my mother especially, that I was doing risky things, that I was risking persecution or prison. Because they had gone through difficult times themselves as targets of the "class struggle," naturally they were concerned about me.

It was different when I was writing for the theater, and it was different again after the Soviet occupation, because the whole atmosphere in society changed, and with it, my position in society changed as well.

What moved you to tears as president?

In the first place, I'm not someone who cries often. Anytime I'm aware that there are tears in my eyes, it's always a situation in which I'm absolutely ashamed of myself. I'm capable of shedding tears over a mindless television show, for instance.

But I do not remember ever crying in situations of great historical moment. I was probably too busy to have the time or the energy to get emotional.

You were out of the city when the revolution began; I wonder how you knew the moment was right, and what your strongest memories are from those eleven days?

The time was so full of hectic activity that I wasn't able to absorb all the events and remember everything that happened. By the way, we taped everything. I think it was the only revolution that was captured fully on tape—including all the closed-door meetings—and today these tapes are coming out as books, books about the revolution. I read them with great interest and suspense because I've forgotten half or two-thirds of what happened.

But if a specific moment stuck in my memory, it would probably be a moment before a huge demonstration on Letná [Park] where there were about 750,000 people present. The communists, who were still in power, were flirting with the idea that some sort of mass hysteria might take place that would radicalize the crowd and people would start fighting among themselves, or something along those lines. And there were provocateurs in the crowd whose job it was to trigger this mass hysteria, so we knew that the demonstration had to be brief and conclude quickly, which meant that we couldn't let everyone speak who wanted to because it would have gone on forever. It was very upsetting to have to deny the microphone to our friends. And, this was also immediately after the sanctification of St. Agnes, so it was sort of a breakthrough moment. Jaroslav Hutka, the singer, sang a song to settle the crowd, and then Bishop Václav Maly recited the Lord's Prayer—he was also a fellow prisoner of mine. I felt that this was kind of a turning point, if the demonstration was successful, if nothing unfortunate happened during it, we would win, and moreover, that there was a kind of higher power watching over us, keeping us from harm.

The responsibility was enormous because, to a certain extent, it was up to us, and to me, whether things would really unfold in a peaceful, "velvet" way, as they say, or whether there would be bloodshed. As we learned later, there had been plans, for instance, to have two fighter jets fly very low over the crowd, and though they wouldn't fire on it or do anything, they could well have induced a kind of mass hysteria and rioting in the crowd. Another day, there was an order for tanks to move on the city, and [a communist paramilitary force called] the People's Militia was called up all across the country. So it wasn't entirely clear that it would all happen peacefully. We had a huge responsibility to remain in the driver's seat, because none of us wanted to be responsible, or have the feeling that we were responsible, for bloodshed or the death of innocent people.

Was there a point or a moment where you felt destined or almost compelled by something large? Not necessarily toward the presidency or even to lead this revolution, but that something was guiding you almost?

I can't say I had the feeling that my acts were driven by any sense of historical destiny, or by any uniqueness on my part. Nevertheless, I'm not stupid and I knew that for some people I had become a symbol, an icon. In some ways, the farther away from Prague you were, the greater of a symbol I was for some. I was a kind of mythological figure. Someone trying to break down a wall with his head and everybody makes fun of him, saying it's not worth it, but the wall finally does break down and the person who beat his head against it becomes king and rules over the land for ever and ever. It's the sort of happy ending that Americans like. But I also know some people who could have done my job better than I did; it's just that history determined it would be this way, and not otherwise.

And the people who at various times thought of me as a quasi-mythological figure or, as I saw it, attributed a disproportionate authority to me—I treated them with respect too. I didn't ridicule their deference; I completely understood it. People need hope, and they need someone to personify that hope.

In addition to being an incredible symbol to many people, in addition to all the duties of the president, you took on writing the traditions, the political customs, the awards, the ceremonies for the entire country. You took to arranging the cutlery at state functions yourself. And I wonder if, with all of those jobs at once, if you ever felt like it was just going to crush you?

What can I say? It annoyed me sometimes that I had to receive several visitors a day, some of them only because protocol demanded it. I had to have a conversation with these visitors not really knowing what to talk about and, what's worse, if they were not very talkative, I had to do all the talking. And there was also the danger of mistaking someone for somebody else. All that was in some ways painful, but the most difficult was probably speechwriting, because it was out of the question that someone else would write my speeches for me. Since I was originally a writer by profession, I wanted my speeches to have my own personal stamp, my own handwriting, my own voice. But I had very little time for writing all those speeches. I couldn't wait for the ideas to come, I had to write one, sometimes two, speeches over a weekend, and it was terribly painful.

When I was in prison, where I spent almost five years, I experienced the collective life. There is never a minute to be on your own—you're not even alone in the bathroom—and in this way, being a president is similar to being in prison, because I was always with people, from morning till night, and so those occasional escapes into solitude were quite important for me. There were more occasions to escape as president than there were in prison.

Along with the castle, the president also has the chateau at Lány, not far from Prague, at his disposal, and there I found a relatively quiet place where I could sequester myself and write or read or just loll about and think things over. It was an occasion for me to be on my own. I needed to be on my own sometimes.

After the revolution, you said that the former satellite countries entered a period you called "mafia capitalism,"[7] and that the revolution was not complete. I wonder if, today, if you think that revolution has been completed? And if not, what will the final version look like?

I think it's far from over, that phase of having to deal with mafia capitalism. It's the product of the previous era, when absolutely everything, even the smallest barbershop, was state-owned. So what followed, the massive, historically unprecedented transfer of property—privatization—naturally presented a major temptation for some people, especially in a society that had been so deeply demoralized.

Thus, the so-called post-communism phase came along, when a lot of bad things happened and former communists became the most entrenched of capitalists, and the new legal system wasn't far enough along yet to regulate the various [market] mechanisms, and so forth. It's probably impossible to say exactly when this phase will be over, or when we will reach the point at which we can call ourselves a stable democracy. Our basic experience, however, is that it has taken longer than we thought it would, and that it will continue for some time. The process is at different stages in each of the [former Soviet bloc] countries and it's a very complicated process, but it will certainly be some time before we achieve a parity with the so-called old-line democracies. Maybe it will take a new generation of people to get us there. It has turned out that the complete subjugation of society by communism or, shortly before that, by Nazism, can take decades to recover from.

On the other hand, I would add that we have an opportunity to do more than merely become a democracy as stable as the Netherlands or Spain or England. We have gone through an experience that they have not. Our history came to a standstill, and I often encounter Western politicians who say they envy us because we started again from scratch and were able to avoid some of the mistakes that for them are irreversible. So there was a hope, when they provided assistance to us, that we would be able to pay them back by demonstrating something interesting, something new, ways of dealing with the various dangers inherent in modern civilization, things like that. Unfortunately we haven't been able to show them very much.

It seems—and here I'm talking about my own country—that standardization has become the ideal. The desire to be average, to be like all the others, not to search too hard for new approaches or not to make any special effort. So the ideal is something that lacks any inventiveness or invention.

And on that idea of the revolution still unfolding, do you see progress or do you feel like you've stalled?

It happens in parallel: Some things have stalled or been blocked, some things have proceeded in the right direction. Now, twenty years on, some things have come a long way. For instance, we may now observe how rich and complex our civil society has become. Civil society was practically wiped out by the totalitarian regime. For the communists, it was even more important to liquidate civil society than to nationalize private property. So the restoration of civil society represents a very successful self-structuring from below.

And another success story would be all the small businesses that have popped up, small shops, services of various kinds. There are thousands and thousands of small business people who offer different services. Life is more colorful now compared to life under the communists, where everything was gray and uniform. So there has been a gradual movement forward, but at the same time, parallel to that, political life remains subject to the model of standardization that I mentioned earlier, meaning it's better not to come up with new things, and if anyone does come up with new ideas, kick him in the shins.

People often note that you came to office without formal political training, without perhaps political skills. But leading the Civic Forum of dissidents took tremendous political maneuvering, in terms of keeping these wide-ranging opinions under one umbrella. Did that translate to your presidency? Did the lessons that you learned leading that movement transfer, or was it an entirely different skill set?

I am someone who likes harmony, agreement, ease, and I have a tendency to reconcile people's differences, to bring them together, to put them at ease. This was an ability that, without any special effort on my part, always carried me to the forefront at the various stages of my life. And naturally, I deployed this ability during my presidency. How successfully is another question. But if we remember, for instance, those endless meetings I organized about the issue of dividing Czechoslovakia or about the future shape of the federation, meetings in which I brought Czech and Slovak politicians together, I always tried in every possible way to create an atmosphere of spontaneous mutual trust and harmony. That's one example of how I tried to use this ability of mine as president as well.

Beyond that, I'm someone who loves order. If people have a meeting for whatever purpose, I'm happiest when they come to an agreement and it's written up in proper Czech. I like concrete outcomes, I don't like endless, empty generalizing.

I have a favorite analogy: I like things to be in their proper place, and I'm glad when I meet somebody who had a bald patch thirty years ago and still has a bald patch today—that is, I like it when things have their own identity and continuity. That's why I wrote somewhere recently that the world today is such an enigma, so full of unsolved mysteries, that you have to feel grateful for everything you actually understand, grateful that some things have maintained their identity and their continuity.

There are young people in the world today who are in the situation you and your peers were, in which they have to make a choice—people in Cuba, in North Korea. They have to decide whether to seek something else, whether to fight against the system, or take an easier path and live their life as the system exists. What would you say to those young people?

Well, I wouldn't be so presumptuous as to give them much advice. But I might say in passing that when someone makes the effort to become a dissident and joins the opposition and runs the risk of being persecuted, that fateful step has two positive aspects to it.

The first is that they feel good about being in harmony with their conscience and their beliefs. When you lie a little or make compromises you shouldn't, you can have the ugly feeling of being soiled. If you decide to do something good, regardless of whether that advances your cause or not, you at least have the positive feeling of being on the side of truth. And the second aspect—and the experience of my country and of the other post-communist countries bears this out—is that these seemingly pointless, quixotic efforts may rather quickly turn into something important and may eventually bear fruit. They just may be successful.

There is an American tradition in the last hour of the presidency for the president to leave a letter to the future president; if you had to write such a letter to my generation, what would you write?

I think the greatest challenge for politicians in the future, in general terms, will be to take seriously all the threats inherent in today's global civilization. Even if their opinions are minority opinions, they must achieve a level of credibility and get the support of those who do not share their opinions. Today, politicians seem more in thrall with public opinion, to what the polls or the press or the media tell them, and this is not always a good thing. We need people who can think for themselves. It is riskier, but it would also be more effective in blazing new trails.

Lastly, I am going see President Gorbachev; it has just been revealed that Maggie Thatcher, the British prime minister, several months before the Berlin Wall collapsed, asked him to keep the wall in place because of the ramifications she feared its removal would have on Western Europe. Does that surprise you?

Well, it [Thatcher's request] was a huge mistake, of course, a very short-sighted and pragmatic approach, I think. When the Iron Curtain fell, it opened up enormous opportunities for everyone, and we can also say that tens, if not hundreds of billions were saved because we stopped manufacturing arms, and so on. Of course, it would have been much easier to carry on in the old Cold War way, but I think it's much better that the Iron Curtain came down, both for citizens who lived behind the Curtain, but, to the same degree, for those on the other side.

The lesson from Havel concerns endurance. He is fond of the myth of Sisyphus, the story of a Greek king condemned to roll a boulder up a mountain for eternity. Speaking about the frustrations of the presidency, Havel told a German audience: "At the very deepest core of this feeling there was, ultimately, a sensation of the absurd: what Sisyphus might have felt if one fine day his boulder stopped, rested on the hilltop, and failed to roll back down."[8] Havel, quite simply, had succeeded, but now had no idea what to do. He found that successful democracy, too, requires an unrelenting siege; the swift and momentous change he helped write in 1989 was followed by another incremental struggle, but one that he felt less disposed to tackle. It is a battle in which citizens of all democracies must take part. "Our main enemy today is our own bad traits, indifference to the common good, vanity, personal ambition, selfishness," he said in December 1989. The most dangerous legacy of communism, he suggested, was the "contaminated moral environment" left in its wake.[9]

British professors of psychology Nick Hopkins and Stephen Reicher, in their study of nationalism, argue that great leaders are "entrepreneurs of identity."[10] Havel crafted a new identity for his nation, peaceful and democratic in character, and in 1989, 95 percent of the public in Czechoslovakia voted in the nation's first election. Barack Obama, too, managed to hollow out space for a new identity, inclusive and post-partisan in nature, with nuanced perceptions of conflict and race. It spoke to those who had lost faith in politics, and others who had never been involved. But both presidents have seen their cultures wither. The Czech Republic has found itself slipping back beneath Russian dominance; Moscow deftly exploited Czech corruption and quietly came to dominate its energy industry. Havel's conservative successor rekindled ties with the Soviet capital and refused to fly the EU flag over his office when Prague held the rotating EU presidency, as is customary.[11] In the Czech Republic's May 2010 elections, turnout was down by a third from 1989, to 62.5 percent. That still betters American involvement, which, in presidential cycles, hovers in the low 50 percent range.

The Australian system, I was intrigued to learn, makes voting compulsory; seventeen-year-olds are assaulted with mailings, warning of fines if they fail to vote. Election day marks a national holiday, with barbeques and turnout well above 90 percent. The US system is fully embarrassing for a twenty-first-century democracy. Several former leaders found the fact that voters must register weeks or months in advance and the complexity of ballots in many states simply laughable. We must, as a generation, become entrepreneurs of an identity that demands a better system, better participation, calm and civil discussion, and, above all, selflessness.

As Václav Havel threw stones at the Prague Castle, Mikhail Gorbachev, a compact and bald Soviet of outsized charisma, was in

Moscow, maneuvering through the party ranks. Like Havel, Gorbachev managed to speak to the West in a way few from the region have been able to, before or since. He would bring the rusted Soviet machine to its knees, and negotiate the peaceful surrender to a war the Soviets had lost decades before.

Chapter Five

TWO GORBACHEVS

MIKHAIL SERGEYEVICH GORBACHEV

GENERAL SECRETARY
OF THE USSR
1985—1991

MIKHAIL GORBACHEV SHOULD HAVE never become the Soviet premier. When he was six years old, his grandfather was taken in the middle of the night, a victim of one of Stalin's purges. And he grew up in the Stavropol region of the Soviet East, which was occupied by the Nazis during World War II, when Gorbachev was eleven. Both facts should have stunted his climb through the Soviet ladder, but he clawed his way into the ruling Politburo nonetheless. He was born in a two-room house with a dirt floor in 1931, and, as a boy, spent summers working on a collective farm. After the harvest of 1949, during which he worked twenty hours a day, he and compatriots at the local machine-tractor station were awarded the Order of the Red Banner for outstanding labor. It was an incredibly rare honor, particularly for someone so young, and helped him gain admission to the law studies program at Moscow State University, the premiere Soviet college.

"Russians speak of 'two Gorbachevs,'" Robert Kaiser, the former Moscow bureau chief for the *Washington Post,* wrote in his 1991 biography "the apparatchik and the reformer."[1] The duality seems to remain. He maintains a penchant for long, winding speeches, honed in the Soviet days. The first time I heard him speak, he concluded by noting that his beloved daughter, Irena, who almost always travels with him, had put her hands together, a signal that he should conclude his remarks. I was certain it was a joke; I was assured it was not. His high school girlfriend, Yulia Karagodina, recalled the duplicity of Gorbachev even as a teen. "Once at a Komsomol meeting, in front of everyone at the local movie house," she told the *Post*'s David Remnick, speaking about the local branch of the omnipresent communist youth that Gorbachev led, "he reprimanded me in front of everyone, saying that I'd failed, that I was late. He was shouting a bit, disciplining me. Then afterward, it was as if nothing happened. He said, 'Let's go to the movies.'"[2]

IN THE 1930s, NEARLY five million Soviets died of starvation while Joseph Stalin continued to sell grain abroad to finance his rapid industrialization.[3] Gorbachev recalled in a memoir that, in 1933, "nearly half the population of my native town, Privolnoye, starved, including two sisters and one brother of my father."[4]

Gorbachev's first indication of the chasm between Soviet rhetoric and reality came when he traveled to Moscow to attend university. He found a striking disparity in wealth between his home and the capital city. And the idyllic portrait of collective farms peddled in Moscow was a great distance from the reality Gorbachev knew well. Still, he remained committed to the Soviet ideology. Joseph Stalin died in 1953, after more than thirty years as the Soviet general secretary. "All night long we were part of the crowd going to see his coffin," Gorbachev recalled in a book of conversations with college roommate Zdenek Mlynar, who would become a prominent Czech intellectual and leader of the Prague Spring.[5]

After graduation, Gorbachev returned to Stavropol with his young wife, Raisa, who had been his philosophy instructor at Moscow State. He began his career as an administrator for the Komsomol and rose quickly through the party hierarchy, advancing to agriculture secretary. He benefited greatly from the patronage of several prominent Soviets who vacationed at the Crimean beach resorts and spas in Gorbachev's province. Yuri Andropov, who led the KGB, was perhaps the most important.

Despite several failed harvests in his region, Gorbachev ascended to the fourteen-member ruling Politburo in Moscow at age forty-seven. It was a clique of geriatrics; Gorbachev was nearly a decade younger than the next youngest member, and twenty-one years younger than the group's average age.[6] Andropov became premier in November 1982, but died fourteen months later. The energetic and charismatic Gorbachev was passed over for succession; the feeble Konstantin Chernenko, though, would have an even shorter tenure than Andropov.

Gorbachev would not miss a second opportunity to seize power. He returned home to his dacha at 4 A.M. on March 11, 1985, and found Raisa waiting up for him. Wary of KGB listening devices in their house, they went for a walk as the sun rose. "We can't go on living like this," he told her.[7]

In Washington, Reagan was woken and told of Chernenko's death. "How am I supposed to get anyplace with these Russians," he asked his wife, Nancy, "if they keep dying on me?"[8]

GORBACHEV KNEW BETTER THAN anyone how far the Soviets lagged behind. As a young party official, he had traveled to Italy, the Netherlands, Belgium, and West Germany. He had taken three trips to France and spent several weeks driving around the country in a rented Renault with his wife and two other couples in 1966. In Alberta, Canada, in 1983, he met a wealthy farmer whose dairy cows yielded an average of 4,700 kilograms of milk each year; the Soviets drew less than half of that, 2,258 kilograms per cow.[9] Gorbachev was confounded.

He recognized that political changes would have to precede economic renovations. Gorbachev the reformer dashed forward, calling for glasnost—an openness of critical thought, conversation, and dissent, notions the Russian people had never known. He brought quiet discussions that had happened for years in Soviet kitchens squarely into public. As he pressed forward, Gorbachev was keenly aware of the ill-fated reform efforts of Nikita Khrushchev during the early 1960s. Khrushchev, who had succeeded Stalin, was deposed in 1964 by party stalwart Leonid Brezhnev, whose chest, a popular joke held, required surgical enlargement to fit all of the medals he awarded himself.

Gorbachev the apparatchik, though, was quite cautious with economic reforms. In the summer of 1986, during his second year as the Soviet premier, he launched a crackdown on private farming and other "unearned income." It became known as the tomato war. Amid the near-perpetual Soviet food shortages, greenhouses were smashed and backyard gardens were uprooted; confiscated tomatoes were run over with trucks. The *Lituraturnaya Gazeta*, a weekly journal of political news, published a long story titled "The Criminal Tomato."[10]

Gorbachev was, in effect, crushing one of the few entrepreneurial instincts in the stagnant nation. "The Achilles heel of socialism," he said years later, "was the inability to link the socialist goal with the provision of incentives for efficient labor and the encouragement of initiative on the part of individuals."[11]

A plan to introduce capitalism in five hundred days was drawn up, but then discarded.[12] How, Gorbachev reportedly asked, would the vast middle level—the administrative bureaucracy in the ministries and enterprises that had always blocked reforms in the past—be persuaded to go along with really significant changes?[13]

BRITISH PRIME MINISTER John Major arranged for Gorbachev to attend the G7 in London in July 1990. He came not as the representative of a dominant power, but, rather, with hat in hand, searching for financial support to ease the economic transition. The meeting, Gorbachev's translator Pavel Palazchenko recalls, "seemed like an interrogation." Japanese prime minister Toshiki Kaifu suggested that Gorbachev's plan to free 70 percent of the prices controlled by the state by the end of the year "was not enough."[14] Gorbachev left with nothing. "Only [Margaret] Thatcher," he would recall decades later, who had been deposed by her party six months earlier, "said: 'listen, you've got to support him.'"[15]

A little more than a year later, in August 1991, hardliners launched a putsch against Gorbachev. There had been rumblings of such an assault for months, and George H. W. Bush sent a secret message to Gorbachev through the mayor of Moscow, Gavriil Popov, warning that a coup attempt was likely. Gorbachev was vacationing with his family in Crimea at the time; they were put under house arrest. Tanks rolled through Moscow's streets and took positions in front of the parliament.

The hardliners made two critical mistakes. First, they failed to control the media, and their forced broadcast of the ballet *Swan Lake* was occasionally interrupted by news updates about the coup produced by intrepid journalists. Second, they let Boris Yeltsin out of his dacha. Yeltsin had been elected Russian president in June, two months before, a position still beneath the Soviet Union command. But his political star was rising just as Gorbachev's fell; the pair vehemently disliked one another. Gorbachev, locked in his dacha in Crimea, told an advisor: "This may not end well. But you know, in this case I have faith in Yeltsin. He will not give in to them."[16]

Yeltsin, wearing a bulletproof vest beneath his suit jacket, climbed atop a tank outside the parliament, a nineteen-story behemoth known as the White House. "The use of force is absolutely unacceptable," he declared. "We are absolutely sure that our compatriots will not permit the tyranny and lawlessness of the putschists."[17] His words were broadcast to the nation.

In a city of more than nine million residents, the demonstrations were surprisingly meager, despite six years of glasnost. Most estimates place the crowd between 20,000 and 30,000. Other more generous guesses rarely exceed 100,000. Either figure is paltry compared to the millions who occupied the Eastern bloc capitals two years before, in November 1989, as the Berlin Wall collapsed.

The coup failed two days later, and Gorbachev returned to Moscow. His wife, Raisa, had suffered a mild stroke, and his daughter, Irena, had a nervous breakdown as they traveled home. He quickly found that his power had evaporated. In the week following the coup, Ukraine, Belarus, Kazakhstan, Uzbekistan, and several other republics left the union. A month later, in December, Gorbachev reluctantly relinquished the nuclear football to Yeltsin.

Within three months of the coup, Yeltsin freed prices, property, and trade—all of which had been controlled by the Soviet bureaucracy, rather than supply and demand—nearly all at the stroke of a pen. The moves Gorbachev had been too timid to authorize for six years were executed overnight, and termed "shock therapy." But Yeltsin failed to build the requisite laws and institutions to accommodate such steps, and the economy was ravaged by a handful of oligarchs. They built massive empires of corruption and crime, and now, two decades later, Russia still grapples with the mafia capitalism that took hold. The Russian people had transitioned from the worst of totalitarianism to the worst of capitalism in a span of weeks.

Do you recall the 22nd Congress of the Communist party, in 1961, when Khrushchev announced his plan to build the true, communist ideal in twenty years? It was just a few months after Yuri Gagarin returned from the first space flight. It was really the Soviet peak, and this massively humanist ideal must have felt within reach. It must have felt that you were truly on the right side of history. Do your recall that convention, the feel of those days?

I recall that moment with a conflicted feeling. On the one hand, we believed then that the planned economy and the socialist system, cleansed of Stalinist repression, was going to provide an answer to our needs, and, indeed, the needs of mankind—an abundance of products but also social justice. During those days in the late 1950s and early 1960s the system seemed to be working. But when we went back home, we saw the problems, and questions and doubts arose. Still, it is undeniable that the achievements of that period in science, education, health care, and improved living standards were real. This was the time when reforms should have started. Instead, we allowed the old system of total control to stall the country's development for years and even decades.

You have said that reforms of the Soviet system that you initiated really should have taken twenty or thirty years, but that "passions took hold." If you were to live once more having the hindsight of history, would you have focused on the economic side, choosing a path closer to Deng Xiaoping? Would you make more room for small businesses and the entrepreneurial ideas and instincts that had been denounced for so long?

It is said that one of the great historical mysteries of the twentieth century is why Soviet reformers did not consider pursuing a more pragmatic path, similar to the one followed by the Chinese. This would have meant dismantling the economic structure of state socialism while keeping the political system as it had always been. But, in order to reform our country "the Chinese way," we would have had to have a different country—probably populated by the Chinese.

In China economic reforms faced no resistance from the party bureaucracy. In the Soviet Union the *nomenklatura*—the party and economic bureaucracy—was extremely strong; they had stopped previous attempts at reform, such as the one tried by Prime Minister Alexei Kosygin in the 1960s, and would have killed this reform, too. So, we needed political change. And, of course, we had to consider the will of the people. Our people needed to breathe. They were suffocating without freedom. They needed to be part of a discussion about how they wanted to live.

So, glasnost—this freedom of speech and openness of government—was indispensable. At first we had the illusion that a change within the system could give the country a second wind. But, fairly soon, I and my close associates concluded that we needed to replace the system whose main elements, such as monopoly of power in the hands of one party, lack of private property, and ideological rigidity, had not changed since Stalin's time. Of course, we could talk all day about the errors and mistakes we made; whether I should have moved sooner, or faster, or perhaps gone slower on some things. The most critical decision was to begin the process of change. And, you must understand that there is no country more difficult to reform than Russia. We were able to take the process far enough to the point of no return, so that no one could turn back the clock. Perestroika did result in a change from a totalitarian state toward a democratic one. For the first time in Russia's thousand-year history, we had a real, contested election. Freedoms of speech, of assembly, of association, of travel, freedom of religion took root in the country, as well as private property and entrepreneurship. A systemic transformation was achieved in just a few years and practically without bloodshed. I think we can be proud of that.

In your conversations with Zdenek Mlynar, one of your roommates at university, who later became a leader of the Prague Spring, you noted that until Khrushchev made his revelations about Stalin in 1956, you had no idea of the state of affairs, and that, until you became general secretary in 1985, there was still a lot you didn't know. What do you recall learning upon your ascent that was most shocking? Anything that truly sent a shiver down your spine?

You know, when I was in the tenth grade I chose as the theme of my graduation essay a line from a poem about Stalin: "Stalin Is Our Battle Glory, Stalin Is the Flight of Our Youth." I believed in Stalin and I believed in communism. We knew about the injustices and the repression during Stalin's time but, most people, including my grandfathers, one of whom barely escaped death in 1937, tended to absolve Stalin and put all the blame on his henchmen. I had to live through a lot of things and rethink my positions constantly. It was a complicated road. Khrushchev's speech was a milestone, but even he didn't reveal all the truth. When I became general secretary, I saw papers signed by Stalin that left no doubt that he was personally responsible for massive, arbitrary repression—for example, the killing of thousands of Polish officers at Katyn. Eventually, I came to the conclusion that Stalinism was an ideological basis of an unjust totalitarian system that could not be justified.

I knew well the conditions under which we lived. I can still remember the 800-mile train ride I took north to Moscow from my village of Privolnoye when I was going to begin college at Moscow State University in the fall of 1950. On that train trip, I passed through cities like Stalingrad, Rostov, and Voronoezh that were still in ruins from the war.

As a university student, I lived in the Stromynka student hostel that housed up to 10,000 students, with eight or more to a room. The place had a kitchen and a toilet on each floor but no proper bathing facilities. My friends and I had to use a public bathhouse in order to get clean, which we did only several times a month. We did not even have a closet in which to store our clothes; we had to store them in suitcases under our beds.

I left Moscow in 1955, with my wife Raisa, whom I met and married while still at the university, and returned to Stavropol, to work at the territorial prosecutor's office. I did that for just seven days and then was sent by the Territorial Party Committee to work in the youth organization, the Komsomol. It was a period of great optimism, an exciting, freer time in which a newer atmosphere existed, particularly after Khrushchev denounced Stalin at the 20th Communist Party Congress—the conditions of scarcity were going to end soon. That is what we thought.

I would have had to have been blind not to see that everything was not perfect in my country. Working in one of Russia's regions, I saw that many of the problems could not be solved at the regional level, but I hoped that if I had a chance to work in the central government, solutions could be found. It was only later that I and others began to question important aspects of the system—lack of freedom, its stifling of initiative, its inability to adapt to change. Also, Raisa and I traveled a lot, including abroad. So there was some basis of comparison between East and West. Before I became party secretary I probably had traveled more than any other Soviet leader.

During a trip to Canada in 1983, as chairman of a Soviet agricultural delegation, I spent ten days asking lots of questions while touring farms, cattle ranches, and even supermarkets. I remember at one cattle farm I asked to meet some of the workers. The head rancher told me that he ran this large ranch of several hundred acres by himself, with the help of only a few day workers. I could not believe this. How could such a ranch be run so efficiently? It was at the end of this trip that I had serious discussions with our ambassador to Canada, Alexander Yakovlev. It was at the home of Eugene Whelan, who was Canada's agriculture minister. The discussion took place before dinner, because Whelan was stuck at the office. So Alexander and I took a long walk among the cornfields. Somehow, we clicked. We talked as much about democratic ideas as we did about the economy. It was then that some of the ideas for radical changes that became known as perestroika came up. I ended up bringing Yakovlev back to the Soviet Union. First he worked in a think tank—the Institute of the World Economy and International Relations—and later he became a member of the party Politburo. He was one of those who shared my belief that we needed real change.

But to suggest that there was any special, magical moment when it was revealed to me what we needed to do, the answer is no. It was more of an evolution. There were moments and events that made one think that something was badly wrong. For example, the winter of 1984 was quite bad, extremely cold, in which so many of our electric plants were on the verge of breaking down. It was at that time that I was working on a speech to the party conference in December on ideology, in which I talked about restructuring.

In retrospect, your family suffered enormously given what they had to endure at the hands of your political opponents—

My family paid an exceptionally high price for the changes initiated by me and my associates. If anyone had any idea how much they suffered, particularly when the political struggles intensified, all the sleepless nights and countless dangers and the worries. And then, of course, all of the nasty things that my political opponents said about Raisa. The trauma of the three-day coup attempt in August of 1991 resulted in Raisa suffering a severe attack of hypertension, later diagnosed as a stroke. She was extraordinarily concerned about my safety and what might happen to our family. When we returned to our residence in Moscow after the coup, the first thing she did was burn all of the correspondence that we had shared between ourselves out of fear that someone might get their hands on it. Raisa's suffering is the thing that I regret the most.

Almost everyone I've interviewed agrees that, in the long lens of history, the first post–Cold War leaders will be judged harshly for not seizing that moment from 1989 to 1991 to reimagine the world, for not better handling the twilight of the USSR. Given that the fall of the USSR was not the first, and will certainly not be the last, decline of a superpower, what lessons should my generation pull from this?

Western leaders could have moved more quickly and recognized the changes we were implementing and provided the Soviet Union with serious financial assistance that would have made it easier for us to make structural reforms in the economy. But that did not happen. There was a critical year during the Bush administration between 1989 and 1990 when substantial aid from the United States could have made a difference. At the time, we were not asking for subsidies or handouts. I am sure that we would have been able to avoid economic collapse and repay any loans. But Western leaders stood on the sidelines, remaining forever skeptical. Doubtlessly, the reason was lingering suspicions from the Cold War.

And when Yeltsin adopted the "shock therapy" approach in the early 1990s and Russia's economy collapsed, with the country's most precious assets plundered, the West seemed to enjoy that. They offered us a lot of economic advice, much of which was, frankly, useless because it was not adapted to our unique circumstances. I remember when Bill Clinton first came to Moscow as president of the United States. He asked me what kind of advice I had for him. After everything that I had experienced during the previous few years, my answer was simple: Treat Russia with respect because Russians do not appreciate it when someone pats them on the back in a condescending way.

We, as a planet, find ourselves heading toward an iceberg ecologically. Arable land, fresh water, oil, climate change—these are all imminent problems, but our governments are, frankly, stymied. Is liberal democracy compatible with the challenges of this century?

Let me begin with a simple statement. History is not predetermined. There is always an alternative to everything. Of course, history is all about the making of decisions, and it is the history of people and of society that is most important. The philosopher Goethe once said, a person can be considered to have accomplished something if he can catch the flying history by its coattails.

Having said that, I understand, perhaps better than anyone else, the enormous changes that must take place if our planet is going to survive. But, I don't believe that a new world order can be primarily constructed by only leaders, diplomats, or negotiators. If we have any chance of making the necessary changes that we have to, particularly in regard to the environment, it is going to be up to common citizens to become more involved in these issues. We must rely upon the human being—what I call the human factor—to act as the driver of change. For starters, we need to get rid of all the suspicions that exist between different nations. We need to build trust. If we join forces, we can change things for the better.

Do you realize that the first United Nations conference on the environment took place in Stockholm in 1972? And where are we? It's clear that politicians are lagging behind the pace of change, and that no one country, even the most advanced democracies, has all the answers. If you think you do and that everything has been decided correctly here, you could not be more wrong. All democracies have to be forever nurtured further and further. And in the end, it will be up to the people of each country to really force their leaders to come to terms with the great crises that our planet faces.

I have said that the United States, too, needs it own perestroika. When I first said so, to an audience of thousands in a big midwestern city, they gave me a standing ovation. It's because so many Americans feel there is something wrong about a system based on over-consumption and hyperprofits at any cost without regard to social or environmental needs.

There's a tradition of leaving a letter to your successor in the Oval Office. If you were to craft a letter to my generation about the most important lessons on leadership you've learned over the course of your career, what might it say?

If I were to give advice to your generation, I would say that one must believe that morality and politics can be compatible, but it is not a game for the faint-hearted. I was in politics for more than fifty years. In order to reach the Politburo, I had to struggle. I knew the system from within. I knew the power of the *nomenklatura* and how the bureaucratic machine could break and corrupt even good people. As a young man I deeply resented the arrogance and lack of accountability of our bureaucrats. Most of them just followed the rules and went through the motions with total indifference.

I even thought of quitting politics on three separate occasions, but I didn't. I had a hot temper, too, and I had to struggle to not let it spill over into my public persona. But, you know, luck often has a lot to do with one's success. The Stavropol town of Kislovodsk, which was under my jurisdiction, is where many high-ranking Soviet officials would go to relax and enjoy the mineral spas. That is where, in August of 1978, I happened to meet Yuri Andropov. He had been in charge of the KGB since 1967, and he became one of my mentors and, then later, general secretary. He was not a faceless apparatchik; he was thinking about the country's future and wanted to initiate change, but he died before he could start.

You also need the ability to learn. Just imagine—when I was starting my political career, live TV was unknown. When I served as first secretary of the Territorial Party Committee, I was afraid of the television cameras. But all of that changed. Later, television interviews became my strong point. Tom Brokaw told me that someone preparing to interview me asked him how he should go about it, what kind of questions he should ask. He replied: "Based on my experience, you may ask him anything at all: He will still say what he wants to say."

"There is nothing more difficult to take in hand, more perilous to conduct, or more uncertain in its success than to take the lead in the introduction of a new order of things," wrote Niccolò Machiavelli, the Italian student of political philosophy.[18]

Gorbachev had the courage to recognize a historic tide, and to move with it rather than against it. But those who lead in tremendous moments of change must stay ahead of the wave, and Mikhail Sergeyevich failed to move his economy in tandem with the political opening of glasnost that he authored. He was, though, among the most pivotal leaders of the century, and among its most inspiring and visionary. During a 1991 arms control summit in Moscow, he asked George H. W. Bush whether the United States had decided what kind of Soviet Union it hoped would emerge—a weak, broken state, or a prosperous incarnation? "I hope very much that the answer to the question I put to you," Gorbachev said, "will be the United States wants to see a more dynamic, progressive, and secure Soviet Union. So far as we are concerned, we want to see a United States that is prosperous, and strong, and secure, and that is our close partner." He added, "We want this no less than you do. We want our two countries to be more dependent on each other."[19] Gorbachev, despite having grown up in a closed society, had come to understand the value of interdependence and dynamism better than his American colleagues.

As Gorbachev's Soviets turned inward, grinding conflicts around the developing world began drawing to a close. Over the previous four decades, anticolonial wars of independence had often morphed into struggles to determine the future of the state—either communist or democratic—which Americans and Soviets were more than happy to support. But after the Berlin Wall collapsed, the mercenary and patron relationship shifted dramatically. Without sponsors to fuel the carnage, armed movements around the world found themselves orphaned and usually too impoverished to continue on their own.

Andrew Mack, a professor of international relations and former aide to UN Secretary-General Kofi Annan, directed a study of polit-

ical violence in the decade following the Cold War. He found that
the demise of the Soviet Union had staggering ramifications. The
number of major conflicts around the world, those in which a thousand or more people died, fell by 80 percent. The total number of
wars being fought at a given time dropped by 40 percent. The average number of deaths per conflict fell to 600 in 2002, from its height
of 37,000 in 1950. The Mujahideen and Mohammad Najibullah's
Afghan communists, UNITAS, RENAMO, FNLA, and the ANC—all
militant, ideological, and formidable—were all abandoned. The Cold
War, in Mack's analysis, had driven a third of all conflicts during the
second half of the twentieth century.[20]

In Pretoria, South Africa, the Berlin Wall's sudden collapse
changed the political landscape for F. W. de Klerk, the last white president of the nation and, at fifty-three, the youngest leader in the country's history. For his regime—thoroughly sanctioned for its vehement,
racist apartheid laws—the Soviet decline allayed fears that the black
majority's struggle for equality was a Soviet-backed plot, a Trojan
horse sent from Moscow.

Less than three months after the wall came down, de Klerk
shocked the world by lifting the ban on the African National Congress (ANC), the communist party, and other black political federa-
tions. Apartheid was stumbling through its final paces. The
segregation of schools and neighborhoods, prohibitions on marriage
and sex between races—the entire structure stood poised to implode.

The leadership of the ANC, including the iconic Nelson Mandela, had spent the previous three decades in exile or prison, most of
them in Lusaka, Zambia, or on Robben Island, a windswept Alca-
traz-like jail six miles off Cape Town's shore. They were suddenly
free to wrest power from de Klerk and his Afrikaner brethren, either
peaceably, through negotiations, or violently, through the brutal civil
war that many thought inevitable.

Chapter Six

THE LAST AFRIKANER KING

FREDERIK WILLEM DE KLERK

PRESIDENT OF
SOUTH AFRICA
1989–1994

ON FEBRUARY 2, 1990, at the height of summer in Cape Town, an extraordinary energy reverberated through the coastal city. Young white Afrikaners mixed with blacks and coloureds[1] as they marched down the city's Grand Parade and through its Greenmarket Square, carrying the black and gold banners of the still-banned African National Congress (ANC) and signs demanding the release of the party's leader, Nelson Mandela. In front of the Parliament, camera crews from every corner of the globe waded into lines of marchers.

Alistair Sparks was one of the two hundred reporters gathered for the president's opening address to Parliament that day. Roughly half an hour before de Klerk began, the journalists were locked in an anteroom and given advance copies of the speech. The partymen waiting inside the halls of the National Assembly hadn't seen it; not even de Klerk's conservative wife, Marike, had read the speech, finished just before midnight. The newsmen expected something significant from the young president, at least an overture toward ending apartheid, perhaps the release of Nelson Mandela later in the day. Instead, they witnessed what Sparks termed "a quantum leap"; it was followed by several more.

"My God, he's done it all," Sparks murmured to David Ottaway of the *Washington Post* as he flipped through the text.[2]

The speech felt much longer than it should have; reprinted in a book by de Klerk's brother, Wimpie, it totals just twelve pages, and it took de Klerk little more than half an hour to deliver. But with the deliberate tone, and de Klerk's usual stoic oratory, the minutes felt decidedly longer. With a chest full of medals, he stood before the assembly. "The steps that have been decided, are the following," de Klerk read. "The prohibition of the African National Congress, the Pan Africanist Congress, the South African Communist Party and a number of subsidiary organizations is being rescinded." Hisses and cheers rose from the chamber. He went on to lift restrictions on emergency law, announced that political prisoners would be freed, and limited detentions without prosecution to six months.

"I repeat my invitation with greater conviction than ever: Walk through the open door, take your place at the negotiating table together with the government," he said. "Henceforth, everybody's political points of view will be tested against their realism, their workability and their fairness. The time for negotiation has arrived."

"The eyes of responsible governments across the world are focused on us. The hopes of millions of South Africans are centered around us. The future of Southern Africa depends on us. We dare not falter or fail," de Klerk finished, his eyes finally lifting from the page.

Nine days later, Nelson Mandela—who had actually requested additional time to prepare for his release—was finally freed, after twenty-seven years in prison. De Klerk had made one of the boldest and most unexpected moves in political history.

NOTHING ABOUT DE KLERK'S background portended the changes he would introduce. He was elected to Parliament at thirty-six, reached the cabinet by forty-two, and, in the years after, did almost nothing to distinguish himself from the *verkrampte,* or unenlightened, wing of the party. The term was coined by his older brother, Wimpie, a respected newspaper editor and intellectual who never shied from critiquing or complimenting his brother. F. W. is widely believed to have opposed the 1985 repeal of the Immorality Act, a law banning sex between races, and, in 1987, as minister of education, he plainly supported segregated schools and passed measures to cut funding for universities that failed to curb unrest and students who participated in protests.[3]

De Klerk was a party man in every sense. His father, known to the white Afrikaner nation as Oom Jan (uncle Jan), was an accomplished member of the dominant National Party, serving in several cabinet posts and rising to president of the Senate. His uncle served as prime minister, and his grandfather had been a close friend and political ally of Paul Kruger, the patriarch of the South African state. To further complicate the familial drama, a year after de Klerk's quantum leap, his twenty-four-year-old adopted son, Willem, became engaged to the beautiful daughter of a coloured political leader, after dating in secret for two years. The de Klerks allegedly learned of the relationship when a jeweler called their home regarding the engagement ring. The marriage was called off just over a year later, under immense pressure from Willem's mother, Marike, according to the fiancée's account.[4]

In 1990, the exiled leadership of the ANC, including future presidents Thabo Mbeki and Jacob Zuma, invited F. W.'s brother, Wimpie, to join a delegation of intellectuals visiting them in England. Wimpie told them not to be deluded into thinking his brother was any kind of messiah. The message corroborated what Wimpie had written in March 1989, a month after his brother's quantum leap: "he is too strongly convinced that racial grouping is the only truth, way and life."[5]

THE THREE MILLION SPEAKERS of Afrikaans—a harsh mix of Dutch, Portuguese, Khosa, and Bantu—made up less than 7 percent of the nation during de Klerk's years, and roughly 60 percent of the white population. Descendants of the Boers—the Dutch, German, and French Huguenot settlers of the seventeenth, eighteenth, and nineteenth centuries—the Afrikaners consider themselves a distinct ethnic group. The rest of the contemporary white population consists mostly of the descendants of settlers from Great Britain, whose colony South Africa became at the end of the Napoleonic wars in 1806. During the 1970s and 1980s, the Afrikaners, having lived on the foot of Africa for three and a half centuries, came to see the struggle to maintain apartheid as a matter of life and death—a fight to protect a culture with no other homeland. Not to endorse the system made one a traitor to the race. The Afrikaner character and its apartheid structure was, in their opinion, born from a rugged, survivalist gene, not colonial arrogance or misguided xenophobia. But by 1990, the weight of history was leveled against de Klerk and his people.

In previous decades, his National Party had found shelter beneath the umbrella of the Cold War's broad, ideological fracture. The government in Pretoria had cemented a rapport with the United States at the close of the Truman years, when the regime backed the Americans in the Korean War. Gold and mineral rich, Pretoria also

signed an agreement to sell coveted uranium ore, enriched for nuclear warheads, to both the United Kingdom and the United States.

Two decades later, in 1975, the fall of Saigon jarred the world.
It showed the limits of the American public's willingness to fight in
remote corners of the globe, and, in its wake, Secretary of State
Henry Kissinger quietly made southern Africa the new fault line between the Soviet bloc and the West. The recently relinquished Portuguese colonies of Angola and Mozambique, on South Africa's
coastal flanks, became the newest pitch for Cold War adversaries.

South Africa was thus drafted into the game of giants, playing
for allies in several of Africa's national liberation movements. To its
east, Pretoria found itself funding Renamo, the Mozambique resistance movement, in a fifteen-year civil war that cost nearly a million
lives. To the west, the Cubans, backed by the Soviets, had been exporting Castro's revolution to Angola since the 1960s. The conflict
escalated substantially in 1975, once the colonial overlords were toppled; the conflict spun into one of the most intricate of the Cold War,
with more than 50,000 Cuban troops on the ground. Various war-
lords and militiamen of maddeningly shifting alliances vied for control, and South Africa, goaded by the United States, pressed north
into the territory late in August of 1975. It would become known as
the Border War.

All of this brought South Africa in line with the capitalist West;
its brutal segregationist structure was a secondary concern alongside
the great game with Moscow. There were limits to the compact,
though. For one, South Africa had been forced to withdraw from the
British Commonwealth in 1961, under pressure from the Canadian
prime minister, John Diefenbaker.

In the late 1980s, Martti Ahtisaari, the great Finnish architect of
peace, set to work on the mess in southern Africa at the behest of
the United Nations. He charted an agreement for South Africa to
withdraw to its present-day borders, to remove Cuban troops from
Angola, and to grant independence to the state of Namibia in 1989.
The agreement held, and the thick, dour Finn went on to cast similar magic in Aceh, Indonesia, as well as in Kosovo. He won the Nobel
Peace Prize in 2008 for his life's work. The successful resolution of

the Namibian equation, in addition to Gorbachev's reforms, is among the factors de Klerk cites for instilling the confidence to dismantle apartheid.

FOUR AND HALF MONTHS before his quantum leap, at his inauguration, the new president had been beset by tears. The short and bald de Klerk is an intensely religious man, a member of the most strictly Calvinist church in South Africa, and the tone of the day was decidedly fated. "In tears, he told us we should pray for him—that he knew he was going to be rejected by his own people, but that he had to walk this road and that we must all help him," his brother later said. It takes a leap to imagine the reserved de Klerk saying this, but there is little disputing the historic power of the moment, or the fact that his brand of faith provides for such a prophetic tone. His favorite pastor, Pieter Bingle, gave the inaugural sermon that day, basing his sermon on Jeremiah 23. He said that de Klerk was "standing in the council chamber of God," that he must respect the Afrikaner traditions yet also have the courage to forge ahead. In a 1990 interview, de Klerk referred to the presidency not as a job, but as a *roeping,* or calling, which men occasionally receive from god.[6]

Upon becoming president, de Klerk found that his predecessor, the irascible P. W. Botha, known as "the old Crocodile," had authorized secret negotiations with Mandela's ANC. The discussions had been taking place over the previous three years, and Mandela, de Klerk learned, was living in Cape Town. With attentive jailors alongside, he was slowly acclimating to life off of Robben Island. There were drives into the countryside and walks near Sea Point beach. "Once, we stopped at a petrol station to fill up, down near the foreshore in Cape Town," Mandela later recalled, "and I got out of the car and spoke to one of the pump attendants. I made a mistake by greeting in the African way and it caused quite a commotion. They seemed to realize that I was somebody."[7]

De Klerk and Mandela met only once prior to de Klerk's speech in February 1990. Some contend that the meeting came only at Wimpie's urging. There were few photographs of Mandela available to the president—his pictures, writings, and any discussion of him whatsoever were outlawed—and de Klerk recalls each sizing the other up for a long moment. "So this is Nelson Mandela," he thought in the silence.

Together they shepherded the nation from tumultuous, vehemently racist white domination to resilient, majority-rule, free-market democracy. They shared the 1993 Nobel Peace Prize amid the struggle, which culminated with Mandela's election in 1994, and de Klerk's acceptance of a vice presidency. The legacy of apartheid remains strong, though. The white population of South Africa, roughly 11 percent of the country, remains disproportionately wealthy; a 2010 United Nations study concluded that South Africa's cities were the most unequal in the world.[8] Roughly half the nation lives below the poverty line, and HIV infection rates in black communities remain astoundingly high, nearing 40 percent in some places, and at 33 percent nationally for women between the ages of twenty and thirty-four.[9]

During the transition, de Klerk, Mandela, and other members of the Convention for a Democratic South Africa (CODESA) worked tirelessly to agree upon a new constitution. De Klerk's central aim was to protect the political and property rights of disempowered minorities—which he and his Afrikaners were destined to soon become—and to siphon off power for such groups both in the parliament and the new president's cabinet. De Klerk's demands were well beyond what the dominant ANC thought justifiable; Mandela called the blueprint a "loser-takes-all" equation.[10] De Klerk was also determined to steer the nation clear of left-leaning groups intertwined with the ANC.

While negotiations for a new constitution dragged on, de Klerk, in his March 1993 address to Parliament, officially acknowledged South Africa's ascent into the echelon of nuclear states, as well as its decision to retreat from the exclusive club. The nation had already dismantled its six nuclear weapons. It remains the first and only instance of a nation developing then relinquishing a full program.

IN PREPARING FOR MY meeting with de Klerk, I read and watched a number of interviews he had given in recent years. Often reporters, many of them well schooled in the history of South Africa, spent their minutes trying to pierce the iron shield, insisting that de Klerk had known about—if not ordered—mass murders and assassinations. Each was bent on being the one to prove that de Klerk had been complicit.

Those I've spoken with who know de Klerk disagree with the proposition that he's a racist, as do several of the reporters who covered the nation's transition. Others argue that he couldn't possibly have climbed through his party's ranks without espousing open bigotry. In either case, I saw little reason to repeat the course that had failed so many others.

De Klerk stepped from the elevator with a tight brow, wearing a white shirt with an open collar and a gold-buttoned blazer. He's of average height and bald, save for a muff of white above a thick, rugby man's neck. He has bulky hands and smallish fingers that have a tendency to reach for the table as his voice peaks, one pad tapping for each point he delivers.

If you look back over the course of your political career, what's your greatest regret?

It relates to the security situation during the transition between my time and Mandela's. When we returned to the negotiations, the one concession that I made which grated on me was to accept that, irrespective of the seriousness of crimes, people who committed crimes with a political motive would be released or entitled to amnesty.

I advocated the Norgard principles that were applied in Namibia, which drew a distinction between simple political crimes and those that were committed with aggravating circumstances. The Norgard principles said that such violent political criminals should not be entitled to amnesty and to pardon. My security ministers and advisors put a lot of pressure on me to say, "No, accede to this request," because, also from their side, there were people who would then qualify for amnesty.

And the ANC was adamant that they wanted, for their people, blanket amnesty irrespective of the seriousness of what had been done, irrespective of the fact that cold-blooded assassinations took place, irrespective of the fact that bombs were put in sports stadiums which killed innocent civilians. I then made that concession.

On the ANC side, I had to release somebody who, in cold blood, took a bomb and threw it into a bar in Durban and killed a number of innocent civilians. It was a murderous, callous act. Applying the same principle, I had to release a white mass murderer who took an automatic weapon, got onto a bus, and shot either twelve or twenty black people in cold blood. It went against my grain, and if I think back, it is the one decision where I should not have followed the advice of my advisors. I should have kicked in my heels on that.

Your predecessor, P. W. Botha, really laid the foundation for your sweeping changes. He held discussions with the ANC leadership for three years, but failed to take the decisive steps. I wonder why you think that Botha had the courage to begin these secret negotiations, but lacked the tenacity to cross the Rubicon, even though it had become clear that there was less of a divide than expected between what Mandela envisioned and what the National Party could tolerate?

P. W. Botha did, indeed, lay the foundations for our reform process. It is, however, not quite true that he conducted secret negotiations with Nelson Mandela for three years. As far as I can recall he met Mr. Mandela only once. However, he did give Minister Kobie Coetsee the green light to hold exploratory talks with Mr. Mandela. These talks did not constitute "negotiations" because Mr. Mandela had originally embarked upon them without the knowledge or approval of the ANC leadership in Lusaka. It was about the possibility of future negotiations and not about substance. At that time, there was still a substantial political divide between the South African government and the ANC. In the final analysis, P. W. Botha was a reformer and not a transformer. He thought that apartheid could be reformed in such a manner that white South Africans would be able to retain sovereignty in substantial parts of the country. He was not prepared to cross the Rubicon to a society in which all South Africans would share political power on an equal and constitutional basis.

With the hindsight of history, how credible was the threat that communism posed to Pretoria? The Border War, even after the United States withdrew its support, remained in Angola and the future state of Namibia, and your intelligence services and police proved adroit in dealing with uprisings in the townships. Was it a mistake to think that communism ever posed an existential threat to the state?

Absolutely not. This was not a question of "reds under beds." The communist threat was very real. Part of the contest between the free world and the Soviet bloc was taking place through third world liberation struggles. One of the main battlegrounds was southern Africa where South African forces had, until as late as the end of 1987, been involved in large-scale battles with Cuban and Soviet-led forces in Angola.

We were also deeply concerned about communist influence in the ANC. We knew that virtually all the members of the ANC's National Executive Committee were also members of the South African Communist Party (SACP). We knew that Communist Party cadres controlled key functions within the ANC alliance, most notably its armed wing, Umkhonto we Sizwe.

We also knew that the SACP proposed a two-phase revolution—a national liberation phase that would include all forces opposed to apartheid during which the ANC would be the vanguard party, and a second "democratic" liberation phase that would culminate, under the leadership of the SACP, in the achievement of the democratic revolution and the establishment of a "people's democracy."

Things moved rather quickly once you made the decision that the ANC would be allowed, that the Communist Party would be legalized once more, and that Mandela would be freed. I wonder when you told friends and colleagues, what were their reactions like?

The decision to make the far-reaching announcements, which I made on February 2, 1990, did not fall out of the air. It was not a sudden sort of instinctive decision. It was the result of very careful planning. Even before I became president, under my predecessor, we regularly held what we called "bush conferences," where the members of the cabinet, under chairmanship of the leader of the party and the president, would talk very, very openly about the issues that faced us.

I intensified this process after I became leader of the party. I started working very hard on keeping my team of fellow leaders and the other leading figures in the party together. One of the results of the preceding work before I became president was that already we had defined a new vision for our party. And that vision said, we will abandon the concept of separate development which was originally called apartheid, and we will embrace a new vision of one united South Africa. No longer divided into so many nation states, but one united South Africa, more or less, on a federal basis, in which there will be no discrimination on the basis of race or color, in which all statutes would be cleared of provisions authorizing or allowing discrimination.

So, did you lose any friends?

The people who opposed the necessity for change were already no longer my political friends. The friendships that I have lost, I lost in the early '80s when there was a big split in the National Party and when a right-wing group broke away and established what they called the Conservative Party, and amongst them were a few very intimate friends of mine who entered politics with me, whose children were best friends with my children. And our friendship suffered as a result of our political divergence.

One of my main tasks after the split, as the leader of the National Party in the Transvaal, which was the strongest place for this new right-wing party, was to fight them. I was right at the front of the National Party's fight against the attack from the political right, which exacerbated the distancing which took place between me and some of my former friends.

After we started with negotiations, the National Party, under my leadership, began losing support amongst the white electorate. We had won an election in September 1989, but by early 1992, in by-elections, which are held whenever a member of parliament died or was appointed an ambassador or something and a vacancy occurred, we started losing constituencies which we had won handsomely in September 1989. Suddenly we were losing to this party to the right.

So they were claiming I no longer had a mandate for what I was doing, and it was the one time when I, fairly unilaterally, without broadly consulting my party, decided this cannot go on. And that I had to confront the white electorate with a simple question, "Do I continue with what I was doing, negotiating this new South Africa, or do I give in to the pressure from the right, and accept that I do not have a mandate." I was being pressured by the party from the right to call a new general election.

One morning I called the party leadership of the National Party together and said, "Look, I have decided we need to have a referendum to pose a simple question to the white electorate to say, 'You now have a very clear picture of where we are going. You must now give me a "yes" or a "no." If the "no"s win, I will call a general election for the white electorate. If it is "yes," then my mandate is settled.'"

If I were to have put that decision to a vote in the executive committee of my party, I think I would have lost. I just made the announcement that we would rather ask the people. The leadership accepted it, and when confronted with that question, 69.9 percent of the whites, voted "yes," we must continue.

And if you ask me today, then I would say that, more or less, the one third who voted "no" still hate my guts. They accuse me of selling out. They accuse me of having given away everything which had been built up. But, more or less, the majority of the 69.9 percent realize that we averted a catastrophe, that, notwithstanding the problems we still have today in South Africa, we basically took the right decisions at that time.

You described the four years negotiating with Mandela as "torturous" at one point. What were the biggest couple of hurdles that the two of you had to get over, and were there moments when you thought the wheels were coming off?

Well, firstly, it would be a generalization to say the negotiations were, per se, torturous. Much of it was positive and, in a broader sense of the word, it was a spiritually enhancing experience, I think, for everybody who participated. One learned that one should not trust the stereotypes that you have created about your political enemies. Because in politics stereotypes are bull. And we learned in the negotiation that we agreed on more things than we differed about.

And our method was therefore to start formulating what do we agree upon, and then to define our differences. In the next phase we concentrated on resolving the less complicated and less serious differences. And thus, the body of issues that we agreed upon grew and the list of differences shrunk. That brought us to a point of no return, where really we just had to agree upon the outstanding issues because so much had been achieved already.

What was torturous was, more specifically, the issue of continuing violence and the ending of all forms of political violence. And it was this which caused, at times, rifts and great tension between me and Mandela. He was accusing the government of being continuously involved in undermining this political process, in instigating political violence. And I was asking for evidence, which he never produced.

I then appointed the Goldstone Commission and it established that elements in the security forces were acting against my policies, against my instructions, notwithstanding the fact that I had halted almost all forms of covert activities which had been developed in the years when the ANC was still using terrorist methods in order to overthrow the government by violence—they continued with this. This resulted in my firing and putting on early retirement and suspending a big number of very highly placed officers, generals, colonels in the Defense Force.

On the other hand, some of the elements in the ANC were continuing underground activities against their agreements. The ANC dragged their feet on opening up their arms caches, which was part of the agreements we had reached. The cold-blooded assassinations continued for senior figures in the Inkatha Freedom Party, a primarily Zulu party, which in the '94 election turned out as the third biggest party. About 400 of their top people were assassinated in cold blood, so this was the torturous aspect.

When we launched CODESA, which was what we called our negotiation forum, this almost derailed the process right at the beginning, because I was forced to make a very strong attack on their failure to live up to their agreements.

Mr. Mandela was to be forewarned that I would be making this attack. The people who should have told him I was going to do it did not tell him. He thought I was misusing the forum, and he got very cross. It resulted in almost a breakup right at the beginning, but we mended the fences.

How did you do that? There had been shouting matches previously . . .

My speech was supposed to be the last speech, but he then took the microphone and attacked me very strongly. I had to be calmed down. I got very cross because I was under the impression he was forewarned. So, I got up and said, "Look, I reject this," but I did so very calmly, and added that, "I stand by what I said," and that we would sort it out between us.

Immediately afterward, when he cooled down, at a press conference where both of us sat—I must say, he was a wonderful man in also diffusing situations—he took my hand. So the negotiations started and really made good progress in most fields except this one of continuing political violence and tensions.

Then in about June or July of 1992, the left wing of the ANC felt that their own party under the leadership of Mandela was making too many concessions. And this resulted in so much pressure on the leadership of the ANC that they walked out of the negotiations and said they would now start rolling mass action, that they would make the country ungovernable.

This resulted in some massacres; it resulted in great economic harm to the country. But, in the end, we returned to the negotiation table in September 1992 and continued for two and a half or three months.

And that's also the point in when the third most dominant group in the nation, the Zulus and their Inkatha Freedom Party, walked out from the talks.

From the moment the ANC walked out, our two main negotiators, Cyril Ramaphosa from Mandela's side and Roelf Meyer from our side, continued to maintain contact. And in that sense of the word, contact was never broken off.

What, in the end, I think, brought about the return to the negotiation table was what happened in Bisho, where there was a black-on-black violent situation. The security forces were in no way involved. Bisho was the capital of one of the "homelands," as we used to call them, which had accepted independence at that stage. The ANC tried to protest and occupy the capital of this small, independent state called the Ciskei, and the armed forces shot and killed a number of people, thirty, I believe. Shortly after that, our main negotiators brought us together again, and Mandela and I thrashed out our differences.

And at moments like that, when the ANC or the Zulus pulled out, how did you deal with the stress of it all?

Without being arrogant, the stress never got the better of me. I have never lost sleep in the sense of having absolutely sleepless nights.

That's amazing.

I always found it possible to put my head on the pillow to sleep my six and a half, or seven hours. Stress I had. Two and a half years ago, I had a colon operation and I had a cancer removed successfully. But, the doctors diagnosed that the cancer started fourteen or fifteen years ago.

Must have been the result of the stress, but, really, I could cope with it. Yes, in my presidency I did play and I still do play golf. For four hours, you clear your mind of all other problems, and that little ball and you have this conflict with each other.

I also tried to create quality time with family, quality time where I could stand away from the problems. I have a gift in being able to compartmentalize problems. To put something in a drawer for twelve hours and say, "I will open this drawer again later." And that, I think, saved me.

The theme of luck has been coming up repeatedly. I wonder, are there a couple points that you can remember where you were baffled by your own luck, by things just working out absolutely fortuitously?

Well, I do not like the word "luck." The word luck reminds me of gambling. But historical events, turns in the tide, I believe, create opportunities for leaders. And the successful leader has an open eye for these turns in the tide, sees the window of opportunity when it comes, and uses it to best advantage.

The best example of such a turn in the tide that benefited me was the coming down of the Berlin Wall. It opened an opportunity for us to take a quantum leap. If that did not happen, I would have been forced to adopt a more gradual approach, but because of that, I could make that leap, which kick-started a new era in South Africa.

But, yes, if you want to call it luck in inverted commas, on other occasions it has helped me. And I think all leaders whether in business, or in government, or in any other field, luck comes across their lives. But, the challenge is to see the opportunity that is created and to grasp it.

The biggest theme that's evolving in my book is lessons in leadership. In the context of your current work with your Global Leadership Foundation, advising current leaders on the various challenges they're facing, I wonder if there are major themes that you have run across? If there are common ideas you find yourself reiterating?

The first requirement is, perhaps, to encourage leaders to abandon their ideological approaches and other illusions, and to assess the situation that confronts them as honestly and realistically as possible. It is then quite often fairly easy for leaders to see what they need to do. The problem is to ensure that they will be able to take their constituencies with them—particularly if the course they advocate is difficult and will require sacrifices, but that is really the essence of leadership.

Something that has been lost from your legacy is the issue of disarmament. Though it was your predecessor, President Botha, who went to the IAEA, it was you who effectively disarmed South Africa. It was the first time and only time that a nation has ever had a complete, organic, nuclear armament and given it up.

Yes. I had many portfolios in my career before I became president, but at one stage I became the Minister of Mineral and Energy Affairs in the early '80s, and I then had to be informed of this. It was on a need-to-know basis. I did not like it, but it was a fait accompli.

I then changed portfolios again and lost track, but always it was in my mind. The moment I became leader of the National Party, I asked to be briefed on where this stood because I never liked the idea. And I was given the information that we had six atom bombs completed and the seventh was in the process of completion.

I called together the relevant ministers, those who knew about it on a need-to-know basis, and said, "We must review this situation." Then, the Berlin Wall came down and the chief of the Defense Force and all the main security advisors agreed that the whole threat against South Africa had changed. The USSR was no longer this expansionist world power wanting to gain power over the whole of southern Africa, and that opened a window of opportunity. Firstly, in the political sense for me to unban the South Africa Communist Party, but, it also opened a window of opportunity to do something definite about our atomic armament capability. I made the decision that we would dismantle them, that we would sign the international agreement of the International Atomic Energy Agency, and I appointed a small committee to work out exactly how it should be done.

Yes, it was, I think, the first and only time when any country has done that. I did it out of conviction because I am anti–nuclear weapons. I am against the fact that a few countries, in terms of the present international agreements, are allowed to have them lawfully. I think that in itself is also wrong. History changes. The countries that were the top four in the world at that stage are no longer the top four.

As you rose through the ranks of the National Party, there must have been times where you had to support policies that you disapproved of?

I think in any dynamic party there are, quite often, disagreements about very important issues. But, in a system such as ours where party discipline is regarded as very important—and this we inherited from the British—you voice those disagreements in the inner circle, in caucus meetings when all the members of the National Party in Parliament, for instance, would meet weekly and had the right to speak out freely.

And the caucus was then divided in committees around labor, and finance, and the economy, and justice, and so on. There, as a young parliamentarian, you had the opportunity to, in a sense, take the minister by his shirt front and shake him and say, "I am not happy with this." But then the discipline was that in the end, if you failed to change the policies defined by the leaders in this process, you had to publicly defend whatever the official policy was.

Where, for instance, did you have to do that?

Yes. What I supported was the concept of bringing justice to all through the nation-state concept. And I was part of a group of young rebels in the National Party, at a certain stage, to say, "In defining the borders of the future Zulu state, and Xhosa states, and Tswana state, we should make it much more attractive to them. We should give them more land."

We went through months of rebelling against the decisions by the minister and the leaders of the party with regard to where borders should be drawn and said, "Be more generous."

We failed, in the end, and I think it is one of the reasons why this concept failed to attract more black support. The whites were too selfish, and they wanted to keep too much land for themselves.

Since you left office, what letter grade would you give the ANC?

On the economy, I will give them an A. On some other issues, I will give them a D or a D–. So I do not want to write out the whole report at the moment, but basically everything was not bad. And while I am critical of many things, I think their greatest failures can be categorized as follows—

They overdid affirmative action, and this led to the loss of too many experienced people in the civil service and in the security forces and, specifically, in the police. As a result of this, they have failed to deal effectively with crime. They now admit it. The new leadership there has made a promise to fundamentally revise the whole justice system in order to improve its effectiveness in fighting crime.

You're saying that the government, by disbanding the existing white police and judicial structure, weakened the rule of law?

Disbanding is part of what I am critical of, but they simply just lost detectives who had twenty years of experience. Because they were white, there was such pressure on them to take early retirement that a vacuum developed where high skills and good experience are really required. And those posts were filled with people who might be very good, and there is nothing racial in what I say, but who simply do not have the necessary experience. They should have rather adopted an in-service training situation and a more gradual approach in their affirmative action plans for the public service and the security forces.

Their second big failure lies in the time that they have lost with regard to HIV/AIDS. They went almost in total denial. Once again, there is now admission in the ANC that they have lost time, that they have made serious mistakes. There is a whole new regime with regard to dealing with the scourge of AIDS, and I welcome that. And the third big failure, to my mind, is this failure to drastically reduce the percentage of people living beneath the bread line.

You grew up, regardless of your family's personal views, in a hugely xenophobic, hate-filled period and climate. Your father Jan wrote many of the apartheid laws you found yourself working to repeal. I wonder why you ended up so open-minded when so many others did not?

Well, you see it is a simplification to say that the people of my time grew up as racists. We had a little farm to which we went on holidays, and we had a few people, black people, working for us. They were uneducated, they could not read. My father said to me, "You will show respect to this man. He is your senior. You must say 'Please' and you must say 'Thank you.' You must respect him as a fellow human being."

There are racists who look down upon people because of their color. But the house and the family in which I grew up never looked down on people because of their color and accepted fellow human beings irrespective of race or color.

The driving force [behind apartheid] was the loss of our self-determination in the Anglo-Boer War. We fought the first anti-colonial freedom war in modern history on African soil, from 1898 to 1902. Twenty-seven thousand women and children of my people and old men died in concentration camps erected by the British. I grew up fiercely anti-British as a youngster. Not anti-black, anti-British.

The whole focus of the National Party politics was to become a republic, to become totally free again. And that led to this restriction of freedom of movement, the restriction of freedom of where you can settle, and other hurtful, degrading apartheid measures.

For that, I have offered to the Truth and Reconciliation Commission a profound apology.

De Klerk managed to stay ahead of the wave, to remain a step in front of the massive forces he unleashed. Unlike Gorbachev, who was crushed beneath the weight of the wave of openness he allowed, de Klerk nimbly slipped between the currents. It would have been impossible if not for de Klerk's pragmatism and his iconic counterpart, Nelson Mandela, an adroit but reasonable negotiator consumed by the prospect of a peaceful future rather than vitriol over a violent past. "I think that the only person that I have thoroughly admired, and who is on the pedestal in my mind, is President Mandela," Martti Ahtisaari, the Finnish Nobel laureate told me when we met. "I have an extremely high regard for somebody who, after twenty-seven years of being jailed, doesn't have any bitterness in his heart, and genuinely so. I am willing to admit that I don't think I could adopt the same attitude, but he is an exceptional personality and leader."[11]

De Klerk shows the imperative of moving with the historical tide, regardless of one's ideology or political foothold. Nearly all the political giants of the last century moved against publics and constituencies that lagged behind; they had the courage to risk their careers for what they knew must be done. De Klerk, too, was an exceptional leader.

Gorbachev's reforms afforded Pretoria a rare moment of strategic still, a window to come in from the cold and build a durable, representative democracy. The same reforms gave Afghanistan and

Pakistan an hour of electric calm—just the sort of unnerving, idle energy that promises a torrent to come.

As Afghanistan slid into civil war and, a continent away, as de Klerk and his Afrikaners dismantled their nuclear arsenal, Pakistan was moving in the opposite direction, exporting its nuclear program to the world's fringe regimes.

Pervez Musharraf, when he took control of Islamabad in October 1999, found himself atop a hornets' nest, one the world's most reviled, sanctioned, and feared states.

Chapter Seven

THE GOOD GENERAL

PERVEZ MUSHARRAF

PRESIDENT OF PAKISTAN

2001–2008

ON DECEMBER 25, 2003, Shehba Musharraf was home at Army House, the white-columned, palatial residence of the Pakistani military chief, when two explosions ripped the air. She rushed to the porch and waited for her husband's motorcade to return, or for an aide-de-camp to arrive instead bearing horrendous news. Pervez appeared minutes later, his armored car riding on flattened rims. Blood and flesh were plastered over the car's dark paint, and a massive object was gored through the spider-webbed windshield. In his memoir, Musharraf would include a picture of the failed attacker's face, ripped from his head and left lifeless in the dirt. It was the second time in two weeks that he had returned home in such a state.

The general has dodged death an astounding number of times. I asked him, when we met in London, if he had kept count. "No," he replied with a disarming chuckle, "I just hope God hasn't given up on me." In addition to the two December attacks, Musharraf was scheduled to be aboard two planes and a helicopter that crashed; in each instance, everyone on board perished. He nearly broke his neck falling from a tree as a student and narrowly avoided death twice in the 1965 war with India. In one battle, he purportedly climbed atop a flame-engulfed artillery piece to remove three shells, using his shirt to protect his hands from the searing metal.

Musharraf is a smallish man; he wears gold-rimmed glasses, and gray tufts above his ears match a carefully groomed mustache. He has a round face and gentle demeanor, which belies his reputation as a somewhat rogue and accomplished commando in Pakistan's Special Services Group (SSG)—a piece of biography that he clearly revels in. We met at his new home, a three-bedroom flat that feels decidedly more Pottery Barn than Peshawar. A drill sat in the corner, alongside several pictures waiting to be hung.

He came to power by way of a peculiar coup. Prime Minister Nawaz Sharif, who had appointed Musharraf as his army chief only a year before, attempted to oust the general in October 1999, while Musharraf and his wife were visiting the head of the Sri Lankan armed forces. Sharif had selected Musharraf from relative obscurity within the general officer corps, hoping to breed loyalty through the favor. But by the time of the coup, tensions between the pair had been high for months. Musharraf's army had captured a strategic high ground in Kashmir, known as the Kargil, in February of that year, greatly escalating tensions with rival India. Musharraf insists that the advance was authorized by Sharif; Sharif holds he knew nothing of the provocation.

Musharraf and Sharif made overtures toward a mend in the relationship. Nonetheless, a month before the coup, Musharraf appointed a loyalist to head the 111th brigade, which is charged with security for the capital city, and met with his generals to discuss the possibility of an attempt to oust him. That October, after Musharraf's flight took off from Sri Lanka with 197 civilians on board, Sharif signed a directive sacking the general. He ordered fire trucks parked on the runway at the Karachi airport and the runway lights extinguished, hoping to force Musharraf's plane to reroute to India. As the flight neared Karachi, the captain was informed that he could not land in Pakistan; he summoned Musharraf to the cockpit, recognizing that the bizarre orders likely were a result of the general's presence on board.

As the plane ran low on fuel, the air controller began issuing contradictory orders. Musharraf's military guard attempted to confiscate weapons from air marshals traveling onboard; they resisted, but committed to backing the general if a firefight ensued on the ground. Below, Musharraf's military apparatus nimbly seized the prime minister's residence and airport, and the plane—with seven minutes of fuel remaining—touched down in Karachi. The general was furious, certain that Sharif had nearly killed a plane full of Pakistanis in order to settle their rivalry. Musharraf had cheated death once more, and his reward was the presidency.

THE PAKISTANI PUBLIC LARGELY welcomed Musharraf's rise. As president, he made strides to repair the defunct economy. He improved the failed tax system, the evasion of which had become a national pastime. He privatized a number of industries that had been nationalized under civilian rule, and annual economic growth approached 7 percent by the end of his tenure.

He overstretched his prerogative though, and stayed well beyond his welcome. The Supreme Court initially granted him authority to hold the presidency for three years, but Musharraf proved unwilling to relinquish power. When challenged by the court in 2007, Musharraf attempted to remove the nation's chief justice, Iftikhar Mohammed Chaudhry; the result was a massive and violent uprising of lawyers. It marked the beginning of the general's slide toward resignation.

In October 2007, amid Musharraf's unravelling, Benazir Bhutto, who had served two terms as prime minister, returned to challenge the general in the coming election. She was assassinated two months later as violence peaked. The circumstances around her death—she was killed following a political rally in Rawalpindi, the Army's headquarters—remain murky. Her husband, Asif Zardari, currently Pakistan's president, wouldn't allow an autopsy, and the crime scene was hosed down before an investigation could be launched. Scotland Yard, later asked by the Pakistani government to conduct an inquiry, concluded that the reverberations from two bomb blasts, not gunshots, killed Bhutto, as her head slammed against the sunroof of her vehicle.[1]

Musharraf stepped down in August 2008 as the country spiraled into unrest and the public demanded a return to democratic rule.

AFTER 9/11, MUSHARRAF MADE the momentous decision to ally with the United States rather than back Mullah Omar's Taliban government in Afghanistan. Previously, only Pakistan, Saudi Arabia, and the United Arab Emirates had officially recognized the ragtag Kabul regime. Prior to the attack, Pakistan had been heavily sanctioned, with the Clinton and second Bush administrations refusing to recognize the legitimacy of Musharraf's coup. Pakistan's pursuit of a nuclear weapon—successfully developed in the late seventies and early eighties and first tested in 1998—made it a pariah state and stifled all trade with the United States.[2]

In September 2001, the relationship changed dramatically. Pakistan moved into the inner circle of American allies; Musharraf's government became the recipient of billions in aid while ostensibly supporting US efforts in Afghanistan. The extent to which Musharraf's regime acted as a faithful ally has been debated. It is clear that at least some elements of its intelligence apparatus, the Inter-Services

Intelligence (ISI), maintained their allegiance to Taliban tribesmen forged over the previous two decades.

During the Soviet occupation of Afghanistan, from 1979 to 1989, the United States and the Saudi royal family funneled billions of dollars through neighboring Pakistan to train and equip Afghan refugees who had sought refuge in Pakistan's mountainous north-west corridor—largely lawless tribal territories situated between the two nations. Local Pashtun tribesmen, allied by ethnicity to many of the displaced, and between 20,000 and 30,000 foreign-born jihadis were also commissioned for the anti-Soviet insurgency. The decade of US- and Arab-funded war led several virulent strains of Islam to co-alesce; it brought the Egyptian extremists of the Muslim Brother-hood into contact with the rigid Salafi faith espoused by Osama bin Laden and his compatriots from the Gulf. It gave rise to the al-Qaeda ideology of global jihad aimed at toppling authoritarian rulers of the Middle East and the patrons of those regimes in the West, most no-tably the United States.

When the Soviet forces finally withdrew from Afghanistan in February 1989, the spigot of American aid abruptly went dry. Both nations, Afghanistan and Pakistan, maligned by war and massive population movements, would remember the abandonment bitterly. The rise of the Taliban, meaning "students" in Pashtu, specifically Koranic students, was driven by the Pakistani military. Recognizing the vacuum left by the rapid Soviet withdrawal and the strategic value of the Afghan territory should India ever launch a successful in-vasion, the Pakistani military leveraged relationships built over the previous decade to extend influence over much of the country. Musharraf, siding with the Americans in September 2001, faced a population far more apprehensive of Washington than the neigh-boring Taliban or Osama bin Laden. As the United States launched its offensive in Afghanistan with the Northern Alliance of Uzbeks, Hazaras, and some Pashtuns on its side, Pakistan's allegiances were largely contradictory, tethered to the Pashtun Taliban that had con-solidated control over the country in 1996.

TODAY, PAKISTAN IS AMONG the most volatile and dangerous states on earth. Nearly all of the militant groups formed to create stability in Afghanistan and undermine India's control over Kashmir have now turned their weapons on Pakistan itself. Most poignantly, in October 2009, as the Pakistani military prepared an offensive in South Waziristan, a Taliban stronghold in the country's northwest, militants launched a bloody, twenty-four-hour assault on the military headquarters in Rawalpindi. The installation is the equivalent of the American Pentagon. The event was an embarrassment for the nation, above all, its proud military. It underscored the extent of instability and raised serious concerns about nuclear security.

Pakistan's arsenal complicates the equation and greatly expands the number of nations troubled by its failings. Seymour Hersh, writing for the *New Yorker* in November 2009, reported that the US Department of Defense has a team—an amalgamation of intelligence, special forces operators, and weapons experts—ready to fly out of Andrews Air Force Base, Maryland, within four hours. It is tasked with extracting as many nuclear triggers—the sophisticated detonators crucial to employing warheads—as possible. Earlier that year, according to Hersh, a false alarm was credible enough that the team reached Dubai before standing down.[3]

In December of 2003, after the second time in two weeks that you were almost killed by terrorists, what did your family say to you?

The first time my wife was absolutely stable. The problem with my wife is that she behaves very, very strongly during a catastrophe, but when everything is over, then she starts crying.

She breaks down after that—and I tell her that "Everything is all right, why are you crying?" So on the second occasion, yes that was bad. When I reached the house, my car was in terrible shape. There was blood, and body parts on the car, and the windscreen was not smashed but something big had hit it. The rims were totally finished, we were driving on metal. It was in very bad shape.

You never worried that she would say, "You're simply bad luck."

Yes, but you would be surprised. My people think that I am good luck. They think that with me they'll be safe. "Nothing happens to him"—but no, they didn't say that. They were all really support-

ive, but they worried all right. I used to violate and break a lot of security rules. My security people always used to say, "You are really
careless about security. You must take extra care." But I used to tell
them, "Secrecy is the best security. Don't tell anyone."

What can I say? I think that I started believing in my own destiny. I am not such a great religious person, but I did start believing
in destiny, that maybe I am not destined to be killed as yet. I don't
know. With all these events, frankly, I got bolder.

*Is it accurate to say that the violence, which nearly killed you and
which Pakistan endures today, is the blowback from policies of supporting extremists in the 1980s in Afghanistan, and also supporting
them in Kashmir? Do you agree with that?*

To an extent, yes, because it brought this militancy into our region. About 25,000 to 30,000 *mujahideen* from all over the Islamic
world were brought here and armed. When we say "armed," I
mean the arming and training of Taliban used to be done through
our people—through our intelligence, through our military.

With the Kashmir struggle it was volunteers, most of them from
Pakistan, with sympathy for the Kashmiris. They really erupted,
these militant, mercenary organizations. Lashkar e Taiba, Josh e Mohammad, all this came about; there were so many names which I
have even forgotten—

Dozens.

Dozens. All independent organizations. Since I was from the
Special Services Group [SSG], I knew a few of my friends that were
in Afghanistan or in Kashmir. They were retired men but they were
fighting. I would say, "What are you doing?" But this brought militancy into our environment, into this society, into the cities of
Karachi and Lahore. These people used to recruit youngsters from
the public and send them to Kashmir.

From 1979 to 1989 we were encouraging the Taliban and all
that. Then, 1989 to 2001, for twelve years we were left high and
dry.

*One of the things I think most Americans don't understand is the
magnitude of anti-Americanism that developed after the Soviet*

withdrawal, specifically in the military ranks. Was that the most difficult obstacle you faced in trying to mobilize the Pakistani public after 9/11?

Yes, I think that was a major obstacle. We were left alone in 1984, totally alone. No resettlement, no rehabilitation for the 25,000 fighters who were there. The religious lobby could make me a scapegoat very easily—that I was Western oriented, American biased. And the people responded because of what they saw in those twelve years, the biased approach of the United States toward Pakistan in general, toward our nuclear plan. While India was being encouraged, we were being told to stop. They were not being told to stop.

I think it was in 1947 that we took a decision to be Western oriented. India took a decision to be on the side of the Soviets. So we were always in the Western camp. India was in the Eastern camp—for forty-two years we were the strategic ally of the United States.

We joined all kinds of organizations. People used to say that we are just an extension of the United States. In '89, the West reoriented themselves toward India. The enemy is now your friend—a strategic ally—and the friend is left high and dry. No help. You're all alone, Pakistan. So everyone thought we had been used. Even now, people ask me in Pakistan, "How do you know that you are not being used again?"

So if we were to jump back to the early 1990s, to the early Clinton years, what would being a good ally have meant after the Soviets left Afghanistan?

Certainly there should have been a rehabilitation, a mini-mini-Marshall Plan, to reconstruct the ravaging that had happened in Afghanistan, and some assistance to us. There were vast, vast dumps of ammunition and equipment left in the mountains.

American?

American and Soviet. Equipment, tanks, guns, aircraft, all in greased condition. Our people had done tunneling in the mountains. They were packed with ammunition, weapons, and all that stocked for the *mujahideen* who were fighting. All of that was abandoned—all those guns.

People could go to the border region and buy a rocket launcher on a handcart; you could buy armored personnel carriers. You could buy anything.

The conventional wisdom in America now is that after 9/11 your government said one thing, took American dollars, and did another. The thinking in Pakistan, is that you did too much—that you gave too much ground to the Americans. If you were to go back and sit in that seat again, what would you do differently, if anything?

First of all, the reality is, we didn't do whatever they wanted. It is a misperception that I agreed to whatever their demands were. Their demand was far more—they wanted to use our airspace; they wanted to use our air bases.

They wanted to control the whole country, use of all the seaports, the entire airspace and all the airports—"blanket overflight and landing rights."[4]

Yes. I said, "Not a chance." We gave a small air corridor which could be used. We gave them two air bases. One was in a godforsaken place in the desert that was a satellite air base. The infrastructure was there, but no aircraft, no establishment.

We didn't give any forces. So we negotiated—we asked, what would we get in return? Yes, one could have gotten more in return, but, frankly, I used to feel very, very embarrassed asking. I don't have whatever it is that you need to go and say, "How many billion dollars are you giving me?" and play the quid-pro-quo game.

I think back about that. A lot of people used to tell me to get money from Saudi Arabia, and Abu Dhabi. And, initially, I did, because we were in such dire straits. But later on, when our economy stabilized, when people used to suggest that, I said, "Don't be silly. I'm never going to ask that." It looks bad every time you go begging for something—asking for money or oil. We don't do that. We stand on our own feet. I believe that sovereignty of a country is very directly proportional to your dependence on another country. So the more you are dependent, the more you have compromised your sovereignty.

So I could have asked for more. I could have said: "These are the facilities. You are going to give me $5 billion, period. No, don't ask me"—which they do—"'Where is this going?' No micromanagement." For heaven's sake, what is this micromanagement going on?

I could have said, "Okay, this is the thing we are giving you, and we expect this money from you every year, and there are no questions. That is all."

When we talk about that $10 billion or $12 billion that the US gave Pakistan in 2002, observers say that you took the money and spent it on forces that were really designed to fight with India, as opposed to using it in the west in the fight against al-Qaeda and the Taliban.

Yeah, now that is what people don't understand—how our army is organized, what is our modus operandi. We have an army of nineteen infantry divisions, two armored divisions. Now, the army moves. The units keep moving. They are not stagnant. Every three to five years, every unit which is a regiment—a regiment of 700 or 800 people—tank regiments, artillery regiments, infantry, they move, and they move everywhere. They can move to the western front. They can move to the frontier, Baluchistan. They can go to Sind, they can be in Punjab, they can be in Kashmir.

We assess the threat. And according to the threat assessment, which is regularly done at the general headquarters, the distribution of forces is done. If the threat is more of the Taliban, the force will move there. If the threat comes from India, the force will go there. But they carry all their equipment. So the equipment is moving around. So this is what I've been explaining in the United States. For heaven's sake, there's no compartmentalization here.

So did you feel short-changed? Shafted in some way by the Americans?

No, I wouldn't say that. This was in our own interests too. Whatever we were doing was certainly in our own interests. We did not want Talibanization in our society. The majority of Pakistanis certainly thought these Taliban to be very obscure and illiterate people who were trying to impose their brand of Islam in the region and on us. We didn't want that.

So there was incredible pressure after 9/11, because the United States had to strike back. If we didn't join, they would have gone through India and violated our airspace with the Indians in the coalition. We would have been butchered and trampled in between. And our Kashmir, our nuclear capability, the things we most cherish and value in the world would be gone. So I evaluated all that.

It's important to understand that the vast majority of Pakistan is moderate. These Maulvis, these Taliban clerics in Pakistan were made fun of, even in the frontier. I know that, because we in the army have lived everywhere. The Maulvi were treated as lowly persons who came begging. You give them a little bit of food, and all right, they are happy. But then with this Afghanistan war, the Taliban, even in their tribal system in the frontier, the Maulvi had no place whatsoever.

It's the tribal leaders, the Maliks as they're known, and their descendants that have the power. But with the emergence of the Taliban, all this changed. The Maliks' authority broke down and went to the Taliban. What I used to tell the United States is that we need to wean away the population from the Taliban. "Don't treat all Pashtuns as Taliban." I meant it, and I used to tell them that there was a Malik system. Let us now get those Maliks. I'm really sure they're not happy with these Maulvis being in charge, they are taking their power from them.

This should have been done immediately after the Taliban were defeated. This was the British blunder, too—one of their greatest blunders—and I was telling the Americans all the time, you have come with the support of the Northern Alliance, the Uzbeks, and Hazaras. They are not the majority, though. The majority is Pashtun.

I used to tell them, "Leave the old strategy. Deal with the Pashtuns, they have always ruled Afghanistan. You are ruling Afghanistan through the wrong people."

So this is the blunder that we made, and we are suffering for it today.

It's interesting how much more public support Zardari has against Talibanization—

Zardari has public support for what?

For the campaign in the Swat Valley and South Waziristan and other Taliban strongholds, for a more aggressive tack against them. When you were leader, a lot of people said, "They live how they live, we live how we live, let's not mess with it."

Yes, I agree. But it's not Asif Zardari, it's the general atmosphere that has changed. Asif Zardari is a hated man, for heaven's sake. Not one man will say anything good about him. In my time, because of what we have discussed, I was considered to be a pro-American man. I was called Busharraf. ·

Busharraf?

B-U-S-H—Bush, extension of "Musharraf." I knew some articles here in the Western press had called me that. Which I was not. Ask President Bush how much I was in his pocket. I never agreed to anything that was against our national interests.

I never compromised on Pakistan's national interests. However, because of the dislike for the Americans, for what happened between 1989 and 9/11, you don't know all that happened—what the [Pakistani] people know.

For instance, our F-16s. The United States left us high and dry. We had paid about $600 million for thirty-six F-16s. They were not given to us. They were sanctioned in the Pressler Amendment—sanctioned and parked in the United States. This was before I came. And then when I came to power, the most preposterous thing was that we were forwarded a bill for damages and fees for our aircraft lying in your desert.

You were charged storage fees?

Yes, they were demanding that because our aircraft were taking up space. I said, "What the hell do you mean? Give us those aircraft. We want those aircraft." Why should we be paying you when we were not given the aircraft? It didn't finish there. Let me tell you— you must know these things. Since I got into their good graces after 9/11, now they said, "Okay, we can't give you the F-16s, but we will give you the equivalent in kind."

I said, "Okay, give the money back. We are in economic straits. Give us our money—$600 million is good money." They said, "No, we can't give you the money."

So I said, "What do you mean—?" They said, "We can give you in kind. We can give you wheat and oil." I said, "I'm going to refuse this," but my prime minister said, "We are in bad condition. We have to import oil. If we can get oil, it will save us money." Otherwise, I was going to say, "To hell with you, you will give me our money or nothing else." So I accepted the oil, but it didn't finish there.

We said, "Okay, we are going to hire ships to collect the oil." They said, "No, we will send our own ships. We'll deliver the oil there." The ship charges were, I think, about three times more than what we would have managed to pay. So this is what we suffered. The Pakistani people have seen this. The F-16s were a symbol. Every truck had F-16s painted on the behind. Every man knew it. The United States took our money and did not deliver our F-16s.

Then on our nuclear program, every effort was made to squeeze and sanction us. When I used to meet with Americans, I used to say, "Your policy is so incorrect. You should have stopped India. We would never have gone nuclear. And you're trying to stop us. We will not stop. No government, no president, no prime minister will ever stop." You should have known that, because there is a public demand.

When I was going after the Taliban, yes, there was a backlash. People thought that I was doing it on behalf of the United States. Then, when we moved the division into the Swat Valley, we held an election because we had pacified the district. Mawlana Fazlullah, the main Taliban leader, was on the run, so this was how we could hold elections in my time.

Then the army left after the elections, and these Taliban came back and they slaughtered and butchered all those people who supported us. So there was a big outcry.

This cutting and slitting of throats, suicide bombings—there was a wide outcry in the public of Pakistan. And the politicians and the media—the same politicians and media that used to malign me—said that we have to now do something about it. That is how the tide has changed now.

Kashmir, the warring princely state in southwest Asia, is comparable to Yosemite or Alaska in its insufferable beauty. It is the second front for which the Pakistani military has enlisted the *mujahideen* to do its bidding.

As Britain grappled with financial ruin after World War II, the empire was hastily liquidated. The Indian Independence Act, passed by the British Parliament and approved by the Queen in 1947, partitioned the Indian subcontinent. The northwest of the territory and a small foothold in the southeast, which would break away as Bangladesh in 1971, became the predominantly Muslim state of Pakistan. The remaining territory became present-day India. The colony had long been plagued by ethnic tension, and as Hindus and Sikhs fled east to India and Muslims sought refuge to the west, violence prevailed. Trains full of refugees were lit ablaze; entire towns were razed, their residents raped and hacked to death. Over 10 million people were displaced; as many as half a million were killed.

Kashmir and the other princely states—which had been under British sovereignty but effectively controlled by local royalty—were to choose which nation to join and, in some cases, retain independence. Both India and Pakistan began vying for the Hindu maharaja of Jammu and Kashmir, Gulab Singh, to assent to inclusion in their new nations. In October 1947, Afghan tribesmen, impelled by the Pakistani military, invaded the predominantly Muslim territory, driving the small Hindu elite into Indian arms. Singh quickly signed letters of accession with New Delhi in exchange for military protection. The first of three official wars between Pakistan and India was on.

While Kashmir receives far less media attention in the West than the Israeli-Palestinian dispute, a sister conflict also born from the dissolution of the British Empire, it is by far the more bloody of the pair. Since 1989, between 35,000 and 50,000 lives have been lost to the feud; the International Crisis Group believes that the conflict has orphaned 30,000 children.[5]

Today, India controls roughly two-thirds of Kashmir—the Hindu-dominated Jammu to the East, the plush Kashmir Valley, and the province's largest city, Srinagar. The territory has been plagued by perpetual guerrilla violence and Muslim uprisings, most recently in the summer of 2010. The Indian response has taken the form of indiscriminate paramilitary violence—a proven, if primitive and short-sighted, counterinsurgency tool. Pakistan holds the remaining third of the territory, the mountainous northern areas as well as the province's western strip, termed "Azad Kashmir," Free Kashmir.[6]

Strategically, the Indian military, if the two nations went to war, could advance easily through the Punjab plains and capture Lahore, a major population center, before rolling on to Islamabad, the capital city. As a result, the bulk of the Pakistani military remains tied up in the nation's heartland, rather than in the northwest corridor where al-Qaeda and the Taliban have found refuge amid lawlessness.

During his presidency, Musharraf and his Indian counterpart, Manmohan Singh, undertook an audacious peace initiative. The general sent a close college classmate, Tariq Aziz, as his negotiator to various secret meetings in hotel rooms from London to Bangkok.[7] He also slowed the pace of incursion by rebels into Indian-controlled Kashmir substantially. After Musharraf's failed bid to retain the presidency in 2008, the pace of infiltration resumed. Between April 2009 and March 2010, for instance, the Indian Defense Forces reported thirty-three attempts, slightly less than one per week.

Recently, details have emerged about the process Musharraf pursued, referred to as "the back channel." Pulitzer Prize–winning journalist Steve Coll has reported that Aziz seemed to live on a dangerous mix of adrenaline and tobacco, rarely carried a briefcase, and often resorted to taking notes on hotel stationery. Nonetheless, a substantial non-paper emerged from the discussions, an easily deniable document outlining a potential peace deal. Coll suggests that the deal progressed so far that selling the agreement to respective publics remained the largest hurdle.

Although Musharraf purportedly claimed in a February 2008 meeting with the prime minister of Pakistani-administered Kashmir that a solution to the conflict was "inevitable," he left power unable to secure a deal.[8]

In 1947, when you were four, you and your family took a train from Delhi to Karachi, and along the route were bodies of those that had been killed, tortured, and raped. You arrived in a brand new country called Pakistan. Where did you live?

There was a place called Jacob Lines. It's the heart of Karachi today. There were long barracks divided into two-room quarters that were allocated to families. My father got one of those. There were two rooms with a veranda in front with a wooden mesh divider, so it could be converted into three rooms. There was one toilet, one kitchen, one bathroom, and no flush system. At one time, there were 18 of us living in those two rooms. My auntie came and her children and my uncle. So they all joined us. But we were quite happy, the eighteen or nineteen of us in those two rooms. That's the way we lived.

And no one was killed? Miraculously, in your family—

Yes, in our family, no one was killed, because we came a little early. And some people stayed back. We had a lot of relatives, and a lot of reasonably close relatives that stayed.

It's been reported that you came quite close to peace with India. That there was a secret document that was down to semicolons for a peace deal on Kashmir. Is that accurate?

Yes, we were trying to finalize a document—a mutually accepted document—

And is it true that domestic politics got in the way? That if you and your partner, Manmohan Singh, had been in stronger positions domestically, a deal would have gone through?

It really should have gone through. The Indians wasted a lot of time. I was also moving forward with Atal Bihari Vajpayee, his predecessor. But then Mr. Vajpayee thought that holding early elections in India would result in a victory for his party. They lost. Before that, when their parliament was attacked—we were moving forward on the Kashmir issue—on all issues. When the parliament was attacked, they moved their forces to the border and things became very tense.

So for two-and-a-half years, what we had done was worthless. When I went to Katmandu I shook hands with him. That broke the ice, and we again started talking. As soon as we started talking, the government changed, so we lost another year.

I think about four years were lost on this. Then, with Prime Minister Manmohan Singh, yes indeed, he's a good man. We got along

very well. But, in 2007, he was supposed to come to Pakistan and return my visit. We had decided that when he was in Pakistan it would
be anticlimactic if we didn't sign some kind of agreement, whether it
was Kashmir, Siachin, Sir Creek, all three, or two—we'd just have
to do it. So we were moving again, and he agreed. But then there
were domestic events in Pakistan. He decided not to come.

*At one point you said that you thought peace was inevitable, that it
was on a track. Do you stand by that still?*

I still stand by that. It's very, very important. It is important
from an economic development point of view. It is beneficial to
both countries—

*But being a good thing economically is a very different thing from
being inevitable.*

Yes, okay, you are saying inevitable. I think it is inevitable, yes.
It has to—I am not understanding the difference—

*"Inevitable" means it will certainly happen—indisputably, within
your lifetime, there will be peace.*

Not easy.

Not easy.

Not easy, no. It needs leadership. It needs boldness in the leadership to take decisions, which may not be palatable to sections of the
public. My theory is that when you are trying to reach an accord, a
deal on a dispute, there's a give-and-take involved. It cannot be a
take-and-take. The give part is the difficult part, because it's going to
raise an outcry with the public. But that is where real bold leadership
comes in.

Knowing that it is in the interest of the country, and in the interest of the majority, and the majority will not be against it: That is
how you go and seal a deal.

A lot of people thought that Manmohan Singh might not be able
to do it because he is a Sikh. He is not a Hindu. Sonia Gandhi, the
leader of the party, is a Christian, an Italian, not a Hindu. Their party
is supposed to be a moderate party. For a Sikh and a Christian it may
be difficult to be that bold, because these Hindus are vicious. We
know that. *[laughter]* They are vicious.

Just to be clear about the deal that you were arranging, it would have provided autonomy for Kashmir, it would have had both militaries gradually pull back from the Line of Control—

Yes. The theory was graduated demilitarization, and I was insisting, to develop some confidence in the people, "why don't you withdraw your forces from inside the city of Srinagar? Just take them to the outskirts. Look at the comfort you'll give to the people. Look at the positive impact. Then go for Baramgala and one or two cities in the valley, where most of the population lives."

India wanted the Line of Control to become permanent; we cannot accept its permanence on the Pakistan side, because that is the heart of the dispute. So we thought that we could make it irrelevant. This was my idea. Let's make it irrelevant by gradually opening six crossing sites for people and for trade—free movement—and then opening more sites and allow freer movement. Then the line of control becomes irrelevant, gradually. Then for 15 years, that's the system—that we are doing self-governance on our side, and India is given self-governance on their side. There is trade and there is human interaction—the line of control becomes irrelevant.

Of course, the concern was always that if you went through with this, there would be saboteurs. People would stage bombings and try to doom the peace. This leads me to the question—did you ever feel like you didn't have full control of the military or the intelligence services? Both of the coups in December 2003 traced back to the military ranks.

No, not at all, never, never. They were all on board, and our military and ISI is manned by the military. It's a very disciplined system. They listen to the chief, and the chief follows whatever the government wants. Since I was lucky that I was the army chief as well as the president; that was a great advantage in going for peace and going for action.

I passed orders to the army. There was a unity of command. I understood the political dimension. I was in charge of the external dimension. I was in charge of the military, so I could execute things in a much better manner. All of them were on board. It's said that the army doesn't go for it. That the army is against peace is all Indian propaganda, humbug. The army is for peace. The army will go for peace. There is no doubt. Everyone would like to have peace, but with honor and dignity, no selling out.

You said in 2007 that your military uniform was like a second skin. Benazir Bhutto said she, as prime minister, never had control of the nuclear arsenal. Your successor as president, Asif Zardari, tried to pull the ISI into the interior ministry and failed. Can a civilian ever fully control the military in Pakistan, ever have that second skin?

Yes, absolutely. Again, please understand that the military has always followed the government instructions.

The West doesn't understand, they are so obsessed with democracy—or at least the election part. Have an election? You have elections in Egypt and you think there's a democracy in Egypt?

Let's be very frank, let's leave hypocrisy aside. The important thing is the country. The responsibility of the government is to ensure the security, progress, and development of the state and of the country, and the welfare and well-being of its people. Period. This is underlined ten times. This is it.

Now, if this is happening, I take it that human rights, civil liberties in democracy, that is all happening, because the people are happy. The people are progressing. People are getting richer. They have more resources. The country is prospering, so what more do you want? This is democracy. This is democracy for the people.

The army is the only institution which is alive, which is vibrant, and which is dynamic. They examine, they analyze things, what is happening, where the country is headed, why it is headed there—because there is no other organization in Pakistan.

Democracy, politics have not matured that much. The country used to suffer, so the army would intervene—not because the army was against the prime minister. Now today, Asif Zardari is in charge. Who likes him? But the army will go along with the orders that the government gives. The army is a disciplined force.

In regard to the Benazir Bhutto assassination, a number of press reports said that she was looking for foreign protection from Blackwater or perhaps British contractors—and that it was denied to her.

Was that denied by the US State Department or by your government in Pakistan?

Nobody asked us for that. But the second thing, if anyone would have asked me, I would have certainly refused. It's an insult and a humiliation for Pakistan, its police, its army. Nobody takes this humiliation that we have to get Blackwater and all—what the hell? Nobody enters—we look after her. It's an insult, I think. We are not a Banana Republic, a Rwanda, or Burundi, and these places.

This is Pakistan, which has 170 million people. It has got 600,000 military. It has second-line forces, the rangers. There is no question, why should anyone from outside come in?

As we parted, Musharraf's bridge partners began to arrive. They made their way past the Scotland Yard detail, one player carrying a bottle of Chivas Regal beneath his arm. The celebration of Pakistan's victory the day before in the World Twenty20 cricket championship would continue.

To take the measure of the man, one reads Musharraf as intensely resolved. There is conviction behind all that he has done, and an eagerness to stand steadfast behind that work. He is a military man with little affection for intellectualism or nuance. Orders and results; mistakes and reevaluation; tactics and strategy. The general seems a man at peace. He may not have shifted once while we spoke, anchored in the contented way one drifts into a couch after a massage or a long run. Yet, he's also quick with a laugh or to point to an absurdity. He seems as if he could entertain himself purely recalling memories by his lonesome.

From Musharraf, I take two lessons. The first suggests that it is best to leave power early, rather than overstay one's use. José María Aznar of Spain, a proud, wiry man with a meticulous mustache, who, despite his public's vehement opposition, supported the invasion of Iraq in 2003, spoke to the way he had changed over his eight years in office. "Patience. I'm far less patient now," he told me outside Madrid, "which I think is normal. When you take office, there are a lot of things that you know, but also a lot of things that you must learn. And as you master the questions around the exercise of government, you find out that it is impossible to move some things; it is possible to move others. But you know very well the key questions that cannot be dealt with, and the temptation is to be extremely concentrated on that, which is dangerous."

"I think that eight years was enough, because, with more time, you transform yourself into a mechanism of resistance against what's in place. And to be a good leader it's necessary always to promote new ideas, to promote change, and to have illusions about what can be done."[9]

Fernando Henrique Cardoso of Brazil also warned, "at some point in time, it's better to leave the office for another one." He told me, "As more time comes and goes, you believe that you know everything. And that's not true. If you don't understand that, it's better for you to leave the office to others: you become an obstacle."

Musharraf, when I asked if there were other leaders he admired, turned east. He noted that Jacques Chirac, of France, understood things well, but cited Zhao Ziyang of China as "a great economist and a great thinker," as well as Jiang Zemin, who deposed Zhao after Tiananmen, as "certainly a great thinker." His lauding of the Chinese general secretaries implies a respect for the system—authoritarian capitalism—that weighs economics supreme and thoroughly disregards the legitimacy of protest and human rights. It echoes an admission Musharraf made earlier in our conversation. Speaking about democracy, he said that the responsibility of government is threefold: first, to provide security; second, to ensure development; and third, to provide for the welfare of its citizens.

While one can easily argue that Pakistan is failing on each of these fronts, the more important argument—and the ideological divide beneath it—is much broader. A successful democratic system is not the same as a prospering economy, and the two don't necessarily go hand in hand. Musharraf's words betray a false understanding of liberal democracy—of the freedoms and provisions an empowered, voting public ought to possess—but simultaneously demonstrate the essence of a rising movement in global politics. The popularity of Vladimir Putin's United Russia Party's retreat from democratic values, the resurgence of China, and the economic rise of Lee Kuan Yew's Singapore all speak to this revival. It is, of course, the same rigid, industrial phenomenon that fueled both Japan and Germany and gave the world two global wars in the last century. If there is an assault on the consensus that emerged from the Cold War—that liberal democracy and capitalism are the best ways to organize politically and economically—surely authoritarian capitalism is the rising foe.

Less than two months after our meeting, Musharraf was indicted. His old rival, Chief Justice Iftikhar Chaudhry, leveled charges that the general had violated the constitution in 2007 when, as violence spiraled, Musharraf declared martial law. In February 2011, Pakistani courts issued a second warrant, with twelve charges related to the Bhutto assassination. It remains unclear if the tranquil Musharraf will face arrest upon his return to Pakistan; he has insisted publicly and privately that he is in London by choice, not in exile. He has announced the founding of a new political party, the All Pakistani Muslim League (APLM), and will undoubtedly return to contest the presidency.

When I met with Ehud Barak, the former Israeli prime minister, in Jerusalem, I raised the issue of Kashmir, as well as the parallels between Musharraf's biography and his own—as commandos and military chiefs, then as heads of state who sought peace with remarkable vigor. Barak shook his head solemnly. He recalled a dinner with a prominent Kashmiri-American businessman, Farooq Kathwari. "He told me all about the conflict," Barak said. "When I say that we might end up with a Bosnia or a Belfast, probably we should worry we will end up like Kashmir."[10]

One can't help but wonder what Pakistan, if its massive military was freed from guarding the Punjab, might be able to achieve in the volatile northwest, where al-Qaeda and Mullah Omar have found refuge. Kashmir is, quite simply, the most important conflict on earth today, even if among the least recognized.

Chapter Eight

THE HOROLOGIST

EHUD BARAK

PRIME MINISTER
OF ISRAEL
1999–2001

March and May 2010

ON JANUARY 2, 2000, a distinguished-looking Australian émigré with thin hair and a gap between his front teeth stood alongside the red carpet at Andrews Air Force Base, against the steady gray of Washington's winter. Martin Indyk, the former American ambassador to Israel, was waiting beside the runway for Ehud Barak. In addition to being the Israeli prime minister, the short and unimposing Barak was, at the time, the most decorated commando in his nation's history. He remains so today. At that moment, much of the political world—including Indyk himself—thought the Clinton Administration was poised to broker an elusive and historic peace between the dying Syrian dictator Hafez al-Assad and the Jewish state.

When the prime minister's old, white 707 arrived, the Israeli delegation filed off but Barak failed to emerge. Indyk climbed aboard and found him sitting alone. He took a seat on an armrest, conscious of the motorcade and security detail waiting anxiously below.

"I can't do it," Barak told him solemnly. "My political circumstances have changed."[1]

The peace had failed before the summit began, before Barak so much as set foot on American soil. There would be no deal between the Syrians and the Israelis, nor between the Israelis and the Palestinians months later. Barak, a soldier and warrior in nearly every sense, was destined to fail on his final two missions. But it didn't change the fact that he, as the tenth prime minister of Israel, went further than any of his predecessors—and, indeed, than either of his successors—in the name of peace.

EHUD BROG GREW UP on the Mishmar HaSharon kibbutz in northern Israel, a few kilometers from the Mediterranean Sea and, by car, roughly forty-five minutes north of Tel Aviv. As a boy, he was known for his talent as a pianist and knack for picking locks. He's alleged to have picked one hundred in a row in one contest.[2] In 1999, Bob Shrum, a noted American political consultant, convinced Barak—who's notoriously reclusive about his skill as a pianist—to play for a campaign advertisement. Barak reviewed the tape and noticed several missed notes; he refused to allow the spot to air.[3]

He was expelled from high school for discipline problems, and, at seventeen, he enlisted in the Israeli Defense Forces. Barak was initially assigned to an armored division but was quickly pulled into a new elite unit, called Sayeret Matkal. The group was formed in 1957 after a series of embarrassing intelligence and operational blunders by conventional forces. Somewhere in those years, he took the name "Barak," Hebrew for lightning. The unit, known for its selectivity, secrecy, and a somewhat cultish ethos, gained renown in the 1970s after several successful, high-profile missions. There was the night raid into Beirut by sea in 1973 to assassinate three Palestinian Liberation Organization leaders, later depicted in Steven Spielberg's film *Munich*. Barak led the mission dressed as a woman. In May 1972, a group of sixteen commandos, disguised as airplane mechanics and again led by Barak, convinced four Palestinian hijackers aboard a Belgian airliner that the plane needed repairs. They killed two terrorists, captured the others, and lost only one hostage. Barak kept a picture of himself and his unit mates dressed in white mechanic's overalls behind his desk for years.

The unit also boasted Benjamin (Bibi) Netanyahu, Israel's current conservative prime minister and Barak's long-time political adversary, as well as Bibi's two brothers. The eldest, Yonatan, who lived in the same apartment building as Barak and served as his deputy in the unit, was killed in one of Matkal's famous raids in 1976. It was Barak's first wife, Nava, who told Yonatan's girlfriend of his death.[4] Barak and Bibi's relationship is the quintessential example of the intertwined lives of Israel's political elite. Barak, who dismantles and reassembles clocks as a hobby, compared his political rival to a watch during the race for prime minister in 1999. After opponents on both the right and left assaulted Netanyahu's character, Barak said that Bibi was neither the superficial nor the malevolent force that he had been cast as. "I think of him as a high-quality mechanical watch with one small wheel turning the wrong way," Barak said.[5]

IN MARCH 2010, I WAITED for Barak in the lobby of the King David Hotel in Jerusalem. Barak is currently the Israeli defense minister, and, a few hours later, he was scheduled to fly with Prime Minister Benjamin Netanyahu to Washington, DC, to help stem fraying US-Israeli relations. The United States is Israel's only meaningful ally, and each year US taxpayers give Israel close to $3 billion in direct aid, in addition to exceedingly favorable defense procurement deals. Two weeks before we met, Vice President Joseph Biden had been humiliated in Jerusalem after traveling across the globe to try to jump-start the peace process. Just as he landed, the Israeli Interior Ministry announced that 1,600 new apartments would be built in East Jerusalem, the half of the city captured by the Israelis in the 1967 war, which Palestinians hope will one day be the capital of their sovereign state. Relations between the two allies was at its lowest trough in years, and the anxiety within the Israeli political establishment was palpable.

Today, Palestine is comprised of the West Bank, an area roughly the size of Delaware, and the narrow Gaza Strip set along the Mediterranean Sea. The West Bank remains occupied by the Israeli Defense Forces; Israeli forces pulled out of Gaza in 2005 under Ariel Sharon, and the territory is now controlled by Hamas, the perceptibly more violent of the two main Palestinian factions. The group won popular elections, recognized internationally as both free and fair, on a platform of reform and justice in January 2006. In 2007, amid escalating tensions in Gaza, Hamas usurped complete control in a bloody coup, killing numerous Fatah officials and supporters. Determining exactly how the violence began has proved difficult, as has identifying the extent to which Fatah and its American backers may have provoked the assault.[6]

The political chasm between Hamas and Fatah further complicates the peace process. The West Bank is now completely controlled by Fatah, led by Mahmoud Abbas—who's often called Abu Mazzen— and Gaza remains controlled by the disparate Hamas leadership. In effect, there are now two Palestines, led by warring groups with ostensibly different demands from Israel in exchange for peace.

IN 1999, BARAK RAN for prime minister largely on the promise of fulfilling the legacy of peace undertaken by his fallen commander,

Yitzhak Rabin. Rabin, twice prime minister, signed the historic Oslo Accords with Palestinian leader Yasser Arafat in 1993, made peace with neighboring Jordan in 1994, and was gunned down by a right-wing Israeli in 1995. Barak also crafted a comprehensive domestic platform; it spoke to concerns about the sluggish economy and re-dressed privileges afforded to the ultra-religious. But the importance of rhetoric and campaign promises were quickly cast aside as the commando drew up plans for a final offensive.

He formed a coalition government—as the fractious Israeli par-liamentary system demands—with the ultra-Orthodox Shas party, undercutting his promise to eliminate conscription exemptions for the ultra-religious and to cut funding for the separate Yeshiva schools. Barak was already abandoning a key pillar of his campaign, and would soon appear to be dashing headlong into peace talks, with little thought or time for anything else.

In reality, the economy improved measurably under his leader-ship, and redressing the relationship between Orthodox Jews and the state has proven an insurmountable test—one that has bested sev-eral successors. Barak also ran on the promise of withdrawing Israeli forces from southern Lebanon, which they had occupied since 1982. He delivered in May 2000. Nonetheless, the narrative of Barak chas-ing madly after peace took hold.

Barak found an equally ambitious partner in Bill Clinton, who genuinely grieved the death of Rabin. Clinton and Barak's first meet-ing in the Oval Office lasted three hours. Over four shared dinners and a retreat at Camp David, the pair forged a deep relationship and set to work first on the Syrian track, then the Palestinian equation. Both ended with failed, high-intensity summits. In the Syrian case, the Israelis, Syrians, and indeed the entire world, recognize that the final deal will have to include a return of the Golan Heights, the strategic high ground captured by the Israelis in the 1967 war, and Damascus's recognition of Israel as a legitimate state. Barak, though, found him-self out ahead of his public in the spring of 2000, traveling to the United States to cut a deal just as Israeli support for such a compro-mise waned, and as Ariel Sharon drove home the message that Barak's quest for peace had become reckless. Expecting he could burnish his credentials as a tough negotiator by failing to make concessions at a first summit—and rebut the pervasive view in Israel that he was a *freier* (a sucker), willing to make peace at any price—he misread the state of Assad's health and his character. The failed summit hardened the old dictator, and he died in June, before a deal could be reached.

In July 2000, Barak showed the world the blueprint for the final Palestinian-Israeli peace. The offer came, though, under the guise of American authorship, and at a point at which the talks were faltering. It outlined complete Palestinian sovereignty over both the Arab and Christian quarters of the Old City of Jerusalem, the full return of Gaza, and the return of over 90 percent of the West Bank, with some territorial swap as compensation for the land taken by Israel. The issues of control over Haram el-Sharif—the third holiest site in Islam and the home of the Western Wall, which Jews believe to be the last remnant of their faith's first temple—was suggested as a "permanent custodianship" for the Palestinians; Israel would retain control of the Wailing Wall. Barak refused to budge on Palestinian refugees' right of return to land and property in Israel: The outline only suggested that a "satisfactory solution" would be reached.[7]

Arafat, long unsettled by Barak's reputation as a masterful tactician and his friendship with Clinton, was wary that the offer might be a trap. It was an unprecedented gesture, one that Arafat was unprepared to hear, and that his public—like the Israeli public months before—was not yet ready to swallow. He chose to sit idle; not only did he refuse to engage with the proposal, he failed to even make a counteroffer. In September 2000, Palestinian youths took to the streets; the Second Intifada had begun. Four months later, amid worsening violence, Barak lost to Likud candidate Ariel Sharon and resigned as leader of the Labor party. Four years later, when violence finally calmed, over 5,000 Palestinians and 1,000 Israelis had died.

WHILE HE WAS PRIME MINISTER, a popular saying held that the "inner cabinet is between the left and right ears of Ehud Barak."[8] He has a tendency to begin forming answers, and even begin delivering those answers, before a question has been fully asked. He didn't trust the Labor party structure, so he built his own apparatus to run for prime minister, drawing heavily on old army friends and American politicos.

Barak, to the chagrin of those who work for him, is at times honest to a fault. While competing with Netanyahu for the prime ministership in 1999, he was asked what course his life might have taken if he were Palestinian. "If I was the right age, at some stage I would have entered one of the terror organizations and have fought from there," he responded.[9] In February 2010, weeks before we met, Barak said candidly, "as long as between the Jordan [River] and the sea there is only one political entity named Israel, it will end up being either non-Jewish or non-democratic. . . . If the Palestinians vote in elections, it is a bi-national state, and if they don't, it is an apartheid state." Both statements were insufferably honest; both ricocheted through international media channels; and both left his advisors pulling their hair.[10]

He has a genial, if not jovial, demeanor. Behind a heavy jowl and small dark eyes, something remains distinctly excitable about his character. Not surprisingly, though, he looked worn when we first sat down late in the day. The political row with the United States was two weeks old by that time and showed little hope of quieting.

We met in one of the King David's small meeting rooms, flags pompously propped behind us and some finger foods on the table between us. Barak set to work on the grapes; I thought to try to steer him away from politics.

"What is your favorite kind of clock?" I said. "Do you have a particular favorite to pull apart?"

"I only take the stupid ones apart," he said, glaring at the cluster. "I won't take a Breguet or a Patek Philippe and pull it apart, only the ones I don't really like. But, yes, sometimes I take apart the simplest one, just normal clocks, and try to rebuild them, but it takes quite a time. I have all the equipment." He chuckled, waving his hand. "You know, you need special instruments. I can't just pull them apart with my hands."

I want to ask you about Sayeret Matkal, the commando unit you led. I wonder, looking back, which was the diciest mission?

Well, there were too many. I don't know. I cannot—

There's not one that stands out as being particular? Was there ever a moment where you felt in your gut that you'd likely die, that things had gone miserably wrong?

There were many, many times. In fact, many of them were not operations, but full-fledged wars that we had. I have been there too many times in situations where I felt like that—what struck me as a young officer was the arbitrary way by which death chose its victims.

But of the very famous raids, the Belgian airliner, the raid into Lebanon—

You know, I was interviewed this morning. It was the thirty-eighth anniversary of the Sabena raid recently, so they interviewed me about it, together with the mother of a young woman that was killed during this raid, and one of the terrorists that was onboard.

What can I tell you? It was a kind of operation that we did not expect, did not prepare ourselves for. It was just a call of immediate urgency. I found myself at the headquarters of the elite unit, and we were just told there was a Sabena airplane with more than 100 passengers that had landed at Ben Gurion Airport.

In the actual raid, where were you? Do you remember where you stood?

I was with the first group, not the first man to enter because I had to have an overview of the operation. But I came from the left wing, and we had, symbolically enough, a young man named Bibi Netanyahu on the right wing. Another, later head of Mossad, came through the nose wheel into the cockpit. And it was stormed within 90 seconds.

And did you fire any shots?

Yes, I fired some shots, but mainly it was to avoid killing the passengers. Basically, we were disguised as mechanics who were supposed to prepare the airplane for takeoff.

You recalled former prime minister Menachem Begin's words a number of times when you were trying to make peace with Arafat, citing that only a third of Israelis supported returning the Sinai Peninsula to Egypt in exchange for a peace deal before an agreement was reached, but afterward, two-thirds supported the decision. Broadly speaking, do you think leaders today aren't bold enough? That they're not far enough out ahead of their publics to truly lead?

I don't think so. I think that leaders now are probably more constrained by the nature of public discourse, which is extremely transparent now, practically in real time. And that discourse is a little bit more shallow than it used to be a generation or two ago. So, in the case of Begin, for example, he basically prepared or let the whole thing cook underneath the surface, without anyone knowing about it. In meetings between General Moshe Dayan, his foreign minister, and 'Abd al-Hamid Karama, representing [Egyptian president Anwar] Sadat, they cooked the formative event of Sadat landing at Ben Gurion Airport and going to the Knesset to give a speech. That changed the whole attitude toward Egypt overnight in the minds of millions, but it did not suffice to convince them to give up the Sinai, which we thought for years should be a natural part of Israel. In the Bible it was given to us. And it's empty, though it's strategic if we were to be attacked.

So, it took the vision of Sadat, the courage of Begin, and the tenacity and determination of Carter to make it happen. Basically, at Camp David, the case that I referred to happened probably a year after Sadat landed in Israel. And yet when Begin went there, it was clear that he was going to negotiate. We had a few Israelis who believed that we would stay and hold the Sinai, but many who believed that we had to hold at least one-third of it, from El Arish to Sharm el-Sheikh, and—it's true—two-thirds of the public in the polls were against giving it back completely.

And then came Begin. He was isolated for two weeks at Camp David. No one could help; no one could follow in real time the ups and downs and moments that they were on the verge of breaking apart. And they ended up with an agreement; in fact, not an agreement, but a framework, and this framework-agreement was the item that the polls showed three weeks later had the support of two-thirds of the public. For me, it shows the shaping capacity of things once they are delivered.

It was a dramatic change, and it could not have happened unless it had been cooked to full ripeness far from the public eye; there were a lot of crises within the fences of Camp David, but they were far from the public eye. It took another year to complete the agreement and another three years to implement it, but that changed history. And that's the nature of certain steps that we have lacked. Even the Oslo Accords—years later—could not have succeeded unless it had started in the woods of Scandinavia, far from the scrutiny of public debate. And it was proposed to the government for approval as a quiet, ripe, concluded deal. It was short of a peace agreement, but it was a statement of intentions and brought the Palestinian leadership back from Tunisia.

Okay. So let's take this idea of how far out ahead of your public you are. And then also this idea of the baking time, the time it takes for leaders to reach an agreement, but also now, it's the time that the public has to wrap their minds around it. While you were at Camp David negotiating, the numbers that supported giving sovereignty over two quarters of Jerusalem to the Palestinians—something that was previously unconscionable—went from very low up to 45 percent. Given that we have to have these things play out in real time, how do you bake that pie? How do you create the atmosphere for peace?

I still think that in order to be successful there's a need for a discreet channel so that, amid any kind of event in the public arena, both sides can genuinely and sincerely probe each other's intentions and willingness to strike a deal. A secret back channel, not one which is announced, a *secret* channel cannot be established in the headlines; but a real back channel and a shaping, formative event are still necessary in a conflict like ours.

They are still required?

Yes, I think so. Beyond the prerequisite or the precondition that both sides should be interested in peace, that is. Now, my judgment is that leaders are ready to make tougher and more far-reaching decisions than their power bases and peoples believe. I said to Arafat once, in front of Clinton at the sixth anniversary of the Oslo Accords at the residence of the American ambassador in Norway, "The toughest decision you will have to make won't be facing me, it will be facing your own people. The toughest decision *I* will have to make will be facing my people, and not you." And we were probably on the fourth or fifth floor, and there was kind of a ledge by the window. I told him, "It's like we're going to jump from here with parachutes, but I'm holding the handle of your parachute and you're holding the handle of my parachute. We have to jump together." It's that kind of decision.

I think that leaders are ready to take it. I said the same sort of thing to Abu Mazzen with President Obama at the Waldorf-Astoria a few months ago, and I believe that that's the truth. But having said that, people are not necessarily making their decisions out of greatness. It's usually out of the tyranny of circumstances.

They are gradually brought by events into situations where the alternatives have gotten worse, and there is a need for a courageous decision, and only then are they ready to make it. Usually, when you try to negotiate under normal terms, the real question is not whether the leader will be ready to make the decision at the end. In many cases, he has the predisposition to be able to do it. It's about how he crosses the corridor to the door where he has to make the decision to open the door. He crosses it in front of his own public, exposed to all political vulnerabilities.

Take for example Netanyahu and Abu Mazzen. Abu Mazzen explicitly told me, "You know the Americans raised the bar. They left me on the tree very high, then they had second thoughts, and they took the ladder and left me there. *[laugh]* I cannot come down naked and go into the streets. I should be able to bring something with me in order to be able to tell our public that we're going to negotiate with Israel." And the same [goes] for Netanyahu; he cannot afford to just go naked in the streets. When he started as prime minister, he went to Egypt to see President [Hosni] Mubarak, and he shared some of his thoughts about how to move forward on the peace process with him. And immediately afterward, someone leaked it to a left-wing political operation here. There are people who were members of my cabinet, people who would sacrifice their lives to make peace, but who are suffering from the N.I.H.

(not invented here) syndrome—people who think, "we can do it better," or, "if we're not involved, then the hell with it."

So, this gets leaked to the media and someone comes to Netanyahu: "Is it true that behind the closed door with Mubarak you signaled readiness to consider a Palestinian capital in Jerusalem?"

"Oh, no, no, that's crazy, it can only be dealt with in negotiations," he has to say.

"Is it true that you talked about certain settlement block?"

"Oh, no, no."

And that's a great discovery, or a great rediscovery: Leaders, when they try to convince other leaders, sometimes say things behind closed doors that they cannot repeat in front of their people. Bibi cannot afford to end up like this *toro*, this bull in the arena with all these matadors and arrows on his back—you can be killed before you reach a place where you can actually make the decisions, and political leaders do not tend to commit suicide.

To come back to the Israeli public, wouldn't you agree that they voted with their feet when they elected you with the mandate of peace, and, today, that they voted with their feet when they elected Bibi, who has said "we will never divide Jerusalem"?

I don't think so. I keep telling my colleagues in the government that, unlike what they feel—that people voted for *them*—they didn't vote right or left. The public tries to be realistic, and as long as there is no real deal in sight, they prefer to be right wing. The moment we come into substantial negotiations and a peace will be seen over the horizon, they will immediately find that we cannot hold together as a coalition without widening it, and I believe it should be widened. But we cannot hold together politically as a government with heavy weight on the right. I believe, and I can tell you, that half of Likud and three-quarters of Yisrael Beiteinu, which is a right-wing party headed by [Foreign Minister Avigdor] Lieberman, and 90 percent of Kadima, which is in opposition now, will be of my position rather than theirs. I believe that the distribution of positions in the public is much closer to my position than to what appeals at the Knesset. The Knesset is much more nationalist, or right wing, than the public.

The public wants to get rid of it [the West Bank], and they expect it to be done by people who are responsible and who will not give up our security or rightful interests. But, basically, they do not agree with the deep—or what I call extreme—left that believes that we should make peace at any price or yield to the Palestinians' wishes. But I think that underneath the surface they are much more ready for the deal than the results of the voting for the Knesset reflect.

When you came back to politics, you wrote a letter in 2007 announcing your return that said, "I made my share of mistakes and my inexperience hurt me." In my view, you were tremendously experienced. You had been defense minister, you had been foreign minister. What job do you wish you had held?

I don't remember the exact wording, but I believe that the meaning of the letter was kind of an attempt to draw the attention to the fact that I was coming back, and to somehow provide an explanation. It was something saying, "Okay, I think that I did the right thing for the country. I do not look at what I've done with regret or feel uneasy about what I've done, but I know that the public interpretation or public reading of it is different, and am aware of the fact that I need to provide certain logos or explanation for this."

I didn't mean that I was an inexperienced human being. I was less experienced in politics. I had been in almost every kind of role: I was a commander in the armed forces and head of the intelligence community, head of planning and commander of the whole armed forces. The minister of interior, minister of foreign affairs, and a member of Knesset. But I didn't bring political experience with me, knowledge about how to hold groups of political people together. I was brought up in a kind of culture in which the unity of purpose counts for something. You don't have to consider it; it's self-evident, it's there. You don't ask, you assume that others are doing their best, that the common purpose will be achieved.

I was brought up in a unit. The first formative years of my experience as a young officer, you didn't even have to look back to see whether people were charging behind you. You could take it for granted that even if they were isolated or taking on a complicated mission, that everyone would do his best in a skillful manner.

Later on, there is some politics in the higher echelons of the armed forces, but it is totally naïve and simplistic compared to what you find in a civilian kind of party politics and gang politics. In terms of time consumption, the military hierarchy is a very effective organ because you don't have to invest so much time—

Convincing people? You tell them, you give orders.

Yes. You don't have to convince them. Those who join are those who are ready to accept this framework and they are predisposed to follow whatever you say, and, of course, you can exchange views with them. They are likely to perform more accurately if you have an opportunity to discuss things with them, but it's not a precondition. Here, you have the situation where people probably think of themselves, even subconsciously, before they think of the common purpose of the state of Israel.

That's something that takes time to recognize, and to understand the importance of the question, "What have you done for me lately?" The human nature, human weaknesses, human needs, all of this is a major part of statesmanship and the capacity to effectively run a government, especially in our system.

The one question I'm asking in all these interviews is, If you had one free card, if you could right one regret, one mistake that nags at you, what would it be?

I probably would have invested much more time in dealing with what I called the "human nature" around government. To keep a group of politicians, under our system, moving together is a precondition to come to power here and to accomplish anything that will endure.

I think I would have invested, from day one, much more in nurturing these human commitments, human attention, human reciprocity or sense of being a part of everything that happens. That probably would have enabled me, in my experience as a prime minister, to stay there for longer and do more. What I do not regret is the very choice that I made in trying to make peace, unlike most of my predecessors and probably like Rabin.

I once, as head of intelligence, sat down with Yitzhak Shamir, who was prime minister, and whom I liked very much. And he was kind of falling asleep during my briefing on these issues that he had to make a decision about, that could be critical for him and for the nation. I said, "Look, Yitzhak, you are the most successful player in politics in Israel." I told him, "You are now on top of the pyramid. It seems to me that you invest 80 percent of your energy just to stay there. You don't have enough energy to do the things for which you wanted to climb to the top."

Most prime ministers, as a matter of fact, want to stay there as long as possible. Shamir did it, Sharon did it until a certain point; most of them have had this strategy. Rabin, and I dare to say, myself, we thought differently. We thought that there was no meaning to sitting in the prime minister's chair if you were not ready to do what is needed in order to change reality for the better—even if changing reality means, under certain circumstances, taking risks that could cost you longevity of tenure. So, in his case, it ended tragically; in my case, it ended in something that caused me a certain kind of disappointment, but not tragic by any measure. Basically that was my attitude.

People ask me, "Couldn't you predict that putting the stakes so high or trying to tackle both the Syrian and Palestinian track would cost you your position?" I say, "I don't see another reason to be here. It's too important for the country." In advance of those summits, as I sought election even, I said that we were sailing toward an iceberg, and we must muster our forces to try to turn. Even if it fails, we have to try.

But, I think it could have been more effective if I would have invested more in human beings.

You've said that we know what the final peace is going be, that it will take a magnifying glass to see the difference between what you suggested at Camp David and what the final agreement will look like. If the Palestinians are hugely reliant upon European aid and Arab aid, if the United States gives $3 billion a year to Israel, and if the cost of inaction is perhaps thousands of lives, why shouldn't the world, together, those who sell you both arms, who support you both, why shouldn't we try to force this peace?

First of all, because the possibility of enforcing it is not as practical as you might assume, and because it will not hold together if it is forced. We have to go into the details to see how complicated it is to force it. I prefer to find the innate energies from within to go for it.

I talked to the [UN] secretary-general earlier today, and to Tony Blair and George Mitchell, and I told all three of them, "The time has come for you, for the world community, to convince the other side, something else must happen here." The world becomes more and more sympathetic to the Palestinian cause, the tide is more with the Gazans and the Palestinians than it is with Israel, and instead of seizing the opportunity and moving toward striking a deal—the behavior I would have expected from Abu Mazzen—it turns out he sits idle, feeling better probably.

Instead of trying to find the ideal point of equilibrium, assuming both sides are trying to go into it, put the energy into bringing the two sides to the negotiating room. We will know better who is the party that is unready to make the painful decision that way.

Talk to me about the differences you've found between what's required of a Matkal leader and a political leader, and the head of a military?

I think there is a certain changing element in leadership along this kind of ladder. At the lower level, it's much more physical, it's reflex-like. It's more about physical courage, about the capacity to withstand the sites and events, the collapsing people, and the material and physical destruction around you, without losing sight of what has to be achieved; a certain kind of a swift, split-second judgment about realities, the capacity to act amid these immense psychological pressures, staying effective and [remaining] capable of moving people around you almost physically by your example.

The common element, both on the battlefield as a commander—and I remember now the toughest, most bitter moments of crossing the canal in the Yom Kippur War as a tank battalion commander, and later on as prime minister or as a minister of defense—in all cases, you need a certain inner detachment—when you're both an active player, and, simultaneously, an observer of the whole thing.

I remember feeling on the battlefield that, even at the toughest moment, that I was so cool. And you pull this trigger of your weapon or throw a hand grenade, but, at the same time, you have to watch the rest of your battalion, to keep in mind the need to identify what happens, what has changed, what should be done—to give orders and to make sure that they are followed. And then to see, immediately, how it changes the situation. You have to keep the cycle of what's the situation, what should be done about it, orders and making sure that they're followed, and then another strike.

Without this sense of detachment, the capacity to see, at the same time, the whole picture and understand the relationship between the whole picture and the slightest details, you cannot operate in the battlefield.

And, on another level, you need some attributes of character even at the highest reaches of strategy. You need to understand solely different levels of sight, not the enemy tanks or units, but your geo-strategy and policy and politics and sometimes the other culture—trying to understand the other side as well, what they have in mind. Why are they acting the way they're acting?

You need these three elements. An overall kind of panoramic deep feeling of reality, without losing grip of the slightest details, which are the substantive metals of any diplomacy or leadership or moving a nation.

And, at the same time, with all ups, downs and zigzagging—when you're sailing against the wind you have to zigzag, so to speak, in order to keep direction—there is a need never to lose sight of where are you heading. What's the essence of it? What are you trying to achieve? And it's in all these triangular elements that leadership—both in the battlefield and in politics or any crisis management—is based. Overview of details, contacts with the objective, and a certain mental detachment—the capacity to look at it from the outside or from the inside simultaneously. I feel that that's the element of leadership.

When [Charles] de Gaulle once was asked what's more important in leadership, the IQ or the character, he said, "clearly character."

Barak, it is important to note, is not popular in Israel today. His return to the Labor Party in 2005 was met with a tepid response, and, although he now serves as defense minister to Benjamin Netanyahu, his party won only thirteen Knesset seats in the February 2009 vote, half of the twenty-six his coalition won to make him prime minister ten years earlier.

The right wing charges that he was reckless in his dash for peace, that his brash attempt came at the cost of thousands of lives. They argue that his precipitous withdrawal from southern Lebanon in 2000, his decision to relinquish a portion of the West Bank in the lead-up to the Camp David summit, and his provisions for expanded safe-passage permits for Palestinians to travel between Gaza and the West Bank, fueled the violent uprising that followed.

The left wing of the Israeli political establishment, in the words of one member of Rabin's Oslo delegation, feels that Barak "hijacked" the peace movement, and "crashed it into a fiery wreck." In January 2011, after peace talks abruptly began and ended, pressure mounted for Barak's Labor Party to leave Netanyahu's governing coalition. Barak instead resigned from the party to remain in Netanyahu's cabinet.

It is intriguing how close the two generals, Barak and Musharraf, came to building peace. When we sat down in Hamburg, I asked Helmut Schmidt, the former Nazi artilleryman, about the impact of military careers on leaders. "If you have been in the war, or if you have seen the war only from the outside, it makes an enormous difference," he said. "Jack Kennedy had known the war, Eisenhower had known the war. Jimmy Carter had not; Bush Jr. had not. It can make a great difference, people who don't know what the war really means, who have never smelled human corpses burning, who have never seen heavily wounded people who will die that same afternoon—it can make a difference if a person has to take severe decisions."

From Barak one takes a keen appreciation of the distance those who know war will travel beneath the banner of peace. There also comes a lesson on the personal fabric of leaders: Above all, politics remains an art of managing egos and interests, insecurities and fears. Barak recognizes that, as prime minister, he failed to concentrate on the emotional aspect of leadership. But his language intones that he—

despite having diagnosed the problem—may still lack a remedy. "He still speaks of people like tools to be manipulated," an Israeli political analyst noted after reading the conversation.

Bill Clinton sat at the negotiating table with Barak and Arafat in 2000. He is the modern leader who perhaps understands the human component of leadership better than any other.

Chapter Nine

THE NATURAL

WILLIAM JEFFERSON CLINTON

PRESIDENT OF
THE UNITED STATES

1993–2001

THE OFFICE WHERE I met Bill Clinton high in the UN headquarters building belongs to another era. It is an institution built for a world of the past—one based on Cold War rivalries and the last century's balance of power. It was Clinton's first day in the cramped space, and his entourage of bodyguards and assistants were stumbling over one another in the confines. The Secret Service men dispatched a young press aide to inquire why so many UN staffers were loitering near the elevators, though it was clear that they were simply trying to catch a glimpse of the ex-president.

"Is this the office?" an exhausted Clinton asked after shaking my hand. I nodded, as did most of the swarm that followed him. The entire place felt as if it hadn't been touched since the early fifties when the building was raised, a lone skyscraper above an otherwise flat block on the East Side of Manhattan. I heard him chuckle to a staffer as he stepped inside, "You know what"— "wahut," the final word came out—"It kinda reminds me of *Mad Men*. Have you seen that show yet?" Floor plants sit in brushed gold planters and, above the windows looking out toward Queens, there's a clock, likely identical to one from your grade school classroom, slightly askew. Pictures from various corners of the globe, dry mounted and warped with age, hang from the walls or sit on the floor below where they ought to be hanging. For a man who's often asked if he would like to be secretary-general one day—a question which he expertly navigates without answer—taking the office must be a bizarre feeling.

A YEAR AND A HALF before Clinton and I sat down, he was cast as a villain, an overbearing spouse allegedly eliciting racism[1] to propel his ambitious wife forward to the presidency and, conceivably, to reclaim a good deal of power himself. The Democratic presidential primary of 2008 muddled, if not sullied, the esteem that had ballooned during eight years of gaffes and incompetence by his successor in the Oval Office. During that span, Clinton largely redefined the post-presidential years; he circled the globe as a nimble, intrepid freelancer, leveraging charisma and a seemingly limitless Rolodex for both the broader good and personal gain.

He was only a year old when construction began on the UN complex, and though he has now been pulled into its bureaucracy as a special envoy for Haiti, the success of his post-presidency holds a mirror to the cumbersome body. "Clinton is a nonprofit conglomerate," says one former advisor and long-time friend. It's not an inaccurate characterization. His work fittingly mirrors the rise of social networking and the Internet, a two-point-zero version of previous post-presidential benevolence.

Among his most important accomplishments is his success drastically reducing the cost of life-saving anti-retroviral treatment for AIDS victims around the world. The latest round of deals with pharmaceutical companies—on the heels of others that have helped two million people access treatment—drops the cost of second-line regimens, for those whose illnesses have overcome first-line drugs, by 60 percent. Commitments to charitable work made each year by individuals and corporations attending the Clinton Global Initiative conference reach into the billions of dollars. He launched a ten-year $100 million campaign against extreme poverty in Rwanda and Malawi and, in 2005, raised over a $120 million following Hurricane Katrina with George H. W. Bush.

AS PRESIDENT, HIS ACHIEVEMENTS were matched by equally notable shortfalls. He presided over a massive expansion of economic growth, generating surpluses of $122 billion and $230 billion during his last two years in office; he waged a successful campaign to stem genocide in Kosovo, and greatly expanded free trade and global commerce. But his failure to intervene in Rwanda, where some 800,000 were massacred, or to move effectively to stop genocide in Bosnia, or to advance Middle East peace, marked high-profile failures. Domestically, he was unable to pass comprehensive health care reform and ambitious campaign finance reforms. He signed the repeal of the Glass-Steagall Act in 1999, which had raised a wall between the speculative trading and underwriting of investment banks and the more traditional lending of commercial, depository banks. The law had been in place since the 1930s. Its elimination helped inflate the massive bubble that burst in the 2008 financial collapse, and meant commercial institutions, like Bank of America and Citibank, were allowed to assume massive risk in the form of housing market credit derivatives. They had to be bailed out to protect the broader economy. "I think they were wrong," he told ABC in April 2010, referring to his economic advisors, "and I think I was wrong to take [their advice]."[2] The Monica Lewinsky scandal and a myriad of other sex-related allegations forever scarred his legacy and remain the first thought for many when his name is invoked.

But for most of those who've had the chance to interact with Clinton, his warmth and intelligence overpower the more lurid details that special prosecutor Ken Starr seared into the American conscience. Clinton is surprisingly tender in person, a gentle handshake matches the soft white hair and the unmistakable bulb nose. He has been called the Michael Jordan of politics, an apt comparison in terms of both talent and intensity. Stan Greenberg, who worked as a consultant for both of Clinton's bids for the White House, recalled Clinton's rage at a Ross Perot attack in the closing days of the 1992 campaign: "They are attacking my character and we must attack Perot's character." He went on, speaking over the phone with aides after a long day of campaigning, "We need to take a meat axe to his brain, cut his head open." He demanded a response that was "red meat and passion, no more pussy ads."[3]

WILLIAM JEFFERSON BLYTHE III never met his father, a traveling salesman who died in a car accident three months before Bill was born. He took the name Clinton from his hard-drinking and abusive stepfather, Roger, who Bill, at fourteen, demanded never hit his mother again. He hid the abuse from most people in his life. As a junior at Georgetown University, though, he shuttled back and forth to Durham, North Carolina, on weekends to make peace with his dying stepfather as he underwent cancer treatments.[4]

Clinton almost never drinks; he sleeps little and speaks without reprieve. On the day that we met, the topics of his endless seminar ranged from the evolution of the light bulb to early twentieth-century American film to the beauty of Colombia's Aburrá Valley and Medellín.

Perhaps the most interesting dimension of his character is the pace at which he lives. "He had said to everybody over and over and over again," Chelsea Clinton has said, "that none of the men in his family live past sixty, or much past."[5] As a result, he has always moved at a rather reckless pace, trying to accomplish as much as possible before a short clock—either real, imagined, or prophetically self-fulfilling—ticks to a stop.

There's a story about your campaigning for governor almost literally in the middle of the night. You supposedly met a woman who said that she was going to vote for you, but had changed her mind after seeing that you were crazy enough to be out at that hour. Is that a true story?

That was the earliest factory opening in the state, the Campbell Soup factory. They all had to be at work by five and they started showing up at three-thirty, so I went up there and met them.

After graduating from Georgetown, you were home in Arkansas before going off to Oxford and went to a campaign rally for Jim Johnson, a segregationist who was running for the US Senate. You confronted him and told him how ashamed you were to be from the same state, and the thing that shocked you most was how calm he remained in the face of your assault.[6] Was it difficult for you to learn that skill yourself as a candidate?

Well, when you're young you wear your passions like a badge of honor. When you're older, you try to mete them out. I actually am very good at it, except when I'm tired. I noticed an interesting thing after I had my heart surgery, which is that 90 percent of the time I feel more calm and serene than I did before I had it; but it changed my biochemistry in some way so that now when I am supertired, I'm more irritable and less likely to conceal what I'm really thinking or feeling. I really do think it's a combination of the mental and psychological, almost an emotional discipline and literally biochemistry. Some people do better in some circumstances than others, and everybody needs to know that. But in general, feelings need to be measured and meted out in politics. Because if you allow your personal feelings to overwhelm your communications with others, then you're neglecting your public responsibilities; because it's not about you, it's about the people you were hired to represent.

For example, Henry Hyde, who managed the totally bogus impeachment process against me, was in the White House, in the Oval Office, on some mission that he and some other House members wanted me to help him with, a week after the whole thing was over, and as far as Henry Hyde knew, I did not remember what happened [in the impeachment proceedings]. Why? Because it didn't have anything to do with my obligation that day to get up and make good decisions either for or against his entreaty, based on what was best for the American people. You just have to develop that, you have to keep purging yourself of your feelings. But some days it's easier than others. And for me, at this point in my life, it's almost 100 percent, I'm sad to say, a function of how much sleep I've had.

John Major, a former conservative British prime minister, told me that a leader should always have a quantum of doubt in their mind at the end of the day on the decisions they're forced to make, and that those who don't are the ones who lead nations into absolute disaster.

I admire John Major. He had a very tenuous three-vote margin in Parliament, which depended on the Irish Unionist Protestants when he started that whole Irish peace process in December of 1992, before I got in and tried to help him close the deal. Look—Tony Blair was a great partner when he was prime minister, he was great in the Irish peace process, but he always had the votes in Parliament to support what he was trying to do. Major really, literally risked having the whole damn government fall, and so I never thought he got the credit he deserved in history. Because when a person sticks his or her neck out, you have to ask yourself not only what do they get, but what do they have to lose.

Any time you're in unchartered territory or using extraordinary power, humility should lead to doubt. Keep in mind that in our moment, the most egregious examples of abuse of power normally are those we associate with terrorism. Well, how do you justify blowing up a train in Madrid, never mind the World Trade Center or a hotel in Bali or all those things? You believe that you are so right, that your view of the truth is so absolute, that anyone who disagrees with you is of a lesser order and you have the right to take their life. That shows you the hazards of exercising power.

President Václav Havel of the Czech Republic, for example, would be very sensitive to this, because in the Soviet-style systems in the Warsaw Pact communist satellites, the Russian totalitarianism, the autocracy of it sort of had a built-in abuse of power. There was no free speech, no free movement, no freedom of religion, no public debates, and they lived day-in and day-out with the adverse consequences in their own lives and in their societies. So, anybody that has ever lived in a system of abuse of power would be likely to tell you, "You ought to go to bed with doubt every night."

For me, it was different. When I was president, I used [doubt] mostly in military situations—when we were fighting with Saddam Hussein about opening more sites to inspections. On more than one occasion in my eight years when we were thinking of doing air strikes, people would say, "You know, you simply can't put this off or people are going to think you're weak."

And every time somebody said that to me for eight years, I'd look at them and ask them one question, "Can I kill them tomorrow?" If the answer is, yes, then by definition neither I nor my nation is weak. But can I bring them back to life tomorrow if I kill them today?

Therefore, whenever possible, if you know you're by definition not weak, just like going to bed with doubt, keep your finger off the trigger as long as you can. If you can kill them tomorrow, you're still strong. And I think that there needs to be a certain humility in the exercise of all authority because it's inherently corrosive. In 1918, the great German Christian democrat, Max Weber, wrote a 100-page essay called "Politics as a Vocation," which basically said that anyone who aspires to exercise political power must be willing to put his own self at risk because it was inherently corrosive.

If we take that notion, that power is corrosive, how did you feel it corroding yourself?

When Saddam tried to assassinate President Bush and I bombed his intelligence building, I tried to do it in the middle of the night so I wouldn't kill anybody, but three of the missiles killed eight totally innocent Iraqis in an upper-class neighborhood near the building. When we were trying to save lives in Kosovo—where Milosevic's henchmen had already murdered 10,000 people and had driven nearly a million to become refugees—we hit a bridge that we thought was a major transit point for his crowd and there was a whole school bus full of our people who were trying to help Kosovo's Albanians. All of them died. We bombed what a CIA map said was a big intelligence center in Belgrade but it had become the Chinese embassy and three totally innocent Chinese were killed. And they were rioting against me in Beijing after they loved me because I was trying to help China get in the World Trade Organization.

So you just have to be prepared to live with all that. If you don't want to run the risk of making errors with other people's lives—and if you kill them, they're irreversible errors—then you should not run for president, and you should not take the oath of office.

On the other hand, you should be more humble than the crowd that was just in [office]. None of us have perfect knowledge and none of us are free of the vagaries of luck and fortune. But, no, I never was paralyzed by it, because I had lived long enough and studied long enough to know that if I ever had to start pulling triggers, bad things could happen. That's why I didn't like to pull many of them.

David Leopoulos, a childhood friend, used to joke with friends that if they were bored, they could always go and watch you read.[7] Is that insatiable curiosity critical to being a good leader? And as a student of politics, what other things have you noticed that are absolutely fundamental to all the political giants?

Well, I think that insatiable curiosity is important in a time dominated by complexity and dynamism, because you have so many things you need to understand. You have to be able to juggle more than one ball in the air at one time. So certainly, for the last twenty years, insatiable curiosity has been really important. I think it was Isaiah Berlin who wrote the book *The Hedgehog and the Fox.* The hedgehog knows one big thing, the fox knows many little things—

and I think it's a bogus dynamic. I think in order to do one or two big things, you have to know many little things. I think it's also important in a complex time with a lot of dynamism to be able to relate to all different kinds of people, because, in the end, most political power depends more on persuasion rather than coercion.

So I think being able to talk to different kinds of people, reconcile different interests, and be curious not just in an aggressive way, but curious enough to ask questions and to listen, that's important. And then I think you have to be able to reconcile the complexities and order them in a pattern. For a lot of people who just follow the evening news or read the morning paper, it's like the political equivalent of chaos theory in physics.

But your job, if you're a leader, is to take superficially random events and organize them into patterns that tell you what you should do to maximize an opportunity or head off the problem. Being decisive in the face of complexity and ambiguity is important. Being able to make a call, to decide to act, and then figuring out how to act to support that decision.

Yes, be curious; yes, appreciate the complexity and ambiguity; but then organize into patterns and decide what you're going to do and execute. I think that's extremely important.

After you lost your reelection bid for governor of Arkansas in 1980, you gave a guest lecture to a friend's class at the law school in Little Rock. You said, "great politicians don't give a rip about public opinion."[8] Does that still ring true?

Yes. Well, that's not always true, but you have to know when it matters and when it doesn't. Public opinion is highly dynamic and fluid. And so whenever possible, you have to decide what you think is right and then try to sell it. But if you're going to do something controversial, then it's arrogant not to care about public opinion. It is arrogant not to have a strategy to try to get the people on your side, because otherwise they'll throw you out.

All polls, except elections, are pictures of horse races that are not completed. People hire you to deliver. You can't be paralyzed by public opinion. I'll give you some examples from my presidency. When I loaned money to Mexico to help them out of financial crisis, the public opinion was 81 to 19 against me, but I never gave a second thought about it. I knew absolutely that it was the right thing to do. And we had just lost the Congress, so the young people working for me thought I was really nuts. "Well, let me ask you this," I said. "You concede that if we don't loan this money, their economy is going to collapse."

"Yes."

"And if their economy collapses, they'll have more illegal drug trafficking and we'll have another million illegal immigrants." I said, "So, in a year from now when people ask me, 'Why, Mr. President, did you allow another million illegal immigrants, and why did you follow policies that promoted more drug trafficking?' When I answer, 'Well, I did it because you were eighty-one to nineteen against me doing what would fix the problem,'" do you think I'll look like a leader?

Then we went into Kosovo and Bosnia, and the majority was against that. When I went into Haiti, it was like 58 percent against [it]. But in every one of those cases, the people had hired me to win for America and to do the right thing. And if I had just been paralyzed by opinion, it'd be wrong.

But, on the other hand, these decisions aren't all free. And losing a controversial decision hurts you much more than winning one helps you. So you can do all kinds of unpopular things, but you need to be able to fight for it and you need to deliver. You get hired to do what's right over the long run. That's the point I was trying to make in Diane Blair's class.

As members of my generation look around the world today, we see climate change on the rise and nothing in the way of a successor for the Kyoto Protocol, the proliferation of nuclear weapons still unabated, Millennium Development Goals we're still well short of. I wonder if you worry that you and this post–Cold War generation of leaders will be judged harshly by history?

No. I think that's a cheap trick. I mean, all of this "the greatest generation is World War II"?—it just happens that they're the most horrible parents in human history, right? If all of us baby boomers were so bad, then our parents were terrible; they failed. And if we were so bad, how come our kids are so great? We were hellaciously good parents.

I think it's phony as a $3 bill. I think they had a chance to win World War II and it was clear. These are much more complex things [now]. We have no idea if the World War II generation would have made the decisions they should make on climate change if they thought doing so would bring an end to their economic prosperity.

The real problem in climate change is that we're paying for our past success. The established order has too many self-protecting economic entities, and not enough people who yet understand what it takes to change. The World War II generation was thrown into a war by a madman, Hitler, and an expansionist empire in Japan, and we did what we had to do. Look, I admire the World War II generation; I'm just trying to make a point here. I don't think there are defective generations. There are times and struggles and they present different challenges.

I believe the United States will pass reasonably good climate change legislation, and I believe we will get a successor that will be better than Kyoto, and I think that we're in a race against time and circumstance.

The end of the last ice age and the warming of the planet actually permitted the sustained, stable colonization of the whole earth. It was a good thing because the world was too cold to make the most of it before. This will be calamitous if we don't do something about it, and the population of the earth will drop hugely over the next 1,000 years, maybe over the next 200 years, if we don't do something about it.

But my focus is not on making these judgments from the sidelines. I'm trying to demonstrate to people that it's good economics to save the planet, and once we convince the core number of people that it's good economics, then we'll get what we need. We're really in a race against time. But I believe that the United States is way better than it was politically in '92 and way better than it was in 2000 when Al Gore didn't win by enough to stay out of the Supreme Court.

I think we were too sympathetic to the right-wing group that was controlling the Republican Party after 9/11, because we just wanted to be united and we were worried about security. But I think we're pretty much back staggering in the right direction now. I think history is a relay race and you just got to keep handing off and making things happen. I'm basically pretty optimistic.

Where the intersection of science and politics is on climate change, I'd leave to others. We might lose. Our minds may not be able to expand enough collectively to avert the worst. I think most people are more literal and they learn things in a serial fashion. Just the very thing you said about curiosity when we were talking about how leaders have to be able to organize it all. Most people have all they can do to keep body and soul together—even before this economic collapse—raise their kids, pay their taxes, worry about how to pay for college, deal with their mother's health, and everything.

One of the reasons I think Barack Obama was well suited to be president now is he's obviously got a curious mind and he can keep a lot of balls in the air at once, because I do think you have to be able to make patterns.

It just takes time to change the mindset, but we're a much more communitarian country and a much more communitarian world than we were twenty years ago. I basically think you've got to get people's attitudes right, and then they have to have a general analysis that's right, and you have to organize for action. And you just have to stumble in the right direction. I'm pretty upbeat about it. When you're my age, you're dealing with a different set of problems. There'll always be problems, but that's what I hope will happen.

Bill Clinton's and Ehud Barak's insights build to a critical realization on public opinion. Nearly all of these leaders lament how transfixed their successors have become with opinion polls and, indeed, the amount of time their own advisors spent consumed by them. Publics follow leaders who move decisively, who can explain their renovations, and who refuse to balk at opposition. Citizens are, above all, wary of indecision, of leaders who seem uncertain of exactly what they want—but their perceptions are malleable, particularly in the face of daunting problems.

Barak's recollection of Menachem Begin winning two-thirds of his public's support to return the vast Sinai Desert to Egypt in exchange for a peace deal—a proposition that only a third of Israelis supported before the agreement was signed—is emblematic of the fluid nature of opinion and of the fruits of decisive execution.

There is an important distinction between support for a leader and public opinion on a specific issue. While public support for leaders themselves matters a great deal, opinion on individual issues often does not. In an era of scarcity; in years in which the world will become more anarchic and further dominated by dynamism, we cannot afford presidents and prime ministers who are paralyzed by pollsters' results. We need men and women eager to shape opinion themselves.

Jimmy Carter, who shepherded the Israelis and Egyptians to peace at Camp David in 1979, understands that distinction as well as anyone.

Chapter Ten

A GOOD AND
DECENT AMERICAN

JAMES EARL
CARTER JR.

PRESIDENT OF
THE UNITED STATES
1977–1981

THE GREATEST DISPARAGEMENT OF the Carter presidency is the argument that it was, at its core, a fluke. That an unremarkable governor from the South ran for president at a moment when the nation, ashamed and disheartened by the Nixon years, was in search of something good and decent. That an ambitious man from a small town who reminded us what was great about our country started his bid in Iowa, and campaigned there for nearly a year, in the same election cycle that the national media first began paying attention to the caucus system. While other candidates remained preoccupied with the more traditional New Hampshire primary, Carter pulled almost 30 percent of caucus-goers in Iowa, enough to place second, nine points behind "undecided." He captured national headlines. The field of Democratic candidates would never catch him. His Republican opponent, the incumbent Gerald Ford, was no match for the history he was stacked against. Carter won the presidency with hardly a single policy proposal.

As president, Carter, a peanut farmer from Georgia who had graduated from the Naval Academy and, later, served aboard nuclear submarines, was seen as ineffectual, unwilling to play by Washington's rules and thus rendered impotent. James Fallows, who served as a speechwriter in the early years of the Carter administration, wrote an eviscerating essay for *The Atlantic Monthly* upon resigning. It was titled "The Passionless Presidency." It sketched a president who thought he could run the White House the same way he had run Georgia, a president who decided not to appoint a chief of staff and tasked himself with controlling the south lawn's tennis court schedule.[1]

The Iranian Revolution in 1979 set an energy crisis in motion, and the capture of fifty-three American hostages at the US embassy in Tehran further weakened Carter. Unable to secure their release until the final hours of his presidency, his administration crumbled.

Carter was, however, the first president to make strides toward peace in the Middle East, brokering an Egyptian-Israeli agreement at Camp David in 1979. He has since become an outspoken supporter of Palestinian rights; his 2006 book, *Palestine: Peace Not Apartheid,* proved controversial but is increasingly recognized as an accurate, balanced interpretation of the dispute. During his presidency, he opened diplomatic relations with China, and Deng Xiaoping, the great liberalizer of the communist economy, made the first visit by a Chinese premier to Washington. Carter created two new federal departments, energy and education, and signed the SALT II treaty with Soviet premier Leonid Brezhnev. Carter had told the UN General Assembly that he hoped both nations would reduce their nuclear stockpiles by 50 percent; the treaty proved more modest than Carter had hoped and was never taken up by the US Senate on account of the Soviet invasion of Afghanistan. Nonetheless, it was the first treaty to move beyond merely stemming the production of weapons and toward eliminating them altogether.

CARTER, AS THE GOVERNOR of Georgia, had a line-item veto over the state's budget. He brought a deep loathing of deficits with him to Washington. He tried far harder than any modern president to smother the superfluous spending that is the lifeblood and political currency of the Capitol. He opposed Senator Ted Kennedy's proposed health reforms on the grounds that they were too expensive; his opposition compelled Kennedy to challenge him in 1980.

Perhaps most important, Carter offered a prescient understanding of America's overconsumption and foreign oil addiction. He installed solar panels on the White House roof, which Reagan later removed, instituted tax breaks for wind energy and new standards for auto fuel efficiency. As a result, fuel efficiency for cars doubled, from 13.5 miles per gallon to 27.5, between 1975 and 1985.[2]

"I am asking for the most massive peacetime commitment of funds and resources in our nation's history to develop America's own alternative sources of fuel," he told the nation from the Oval Office in his July 1979 "Crisis of Confidence" speech. "From now on, every new addition to our demand for energy will be met from our own production and our own conservation. The generation-long growth in our dependence on foreign oil will be stopped dead in its tracks right now and then reversed as we move through the 1980s."

"Too many of us now tend to worship self-indulgence and consumption," he told the nation. "Human identity is no longer defined by what one does, but by what one owns."

The speech gave Carter an 11-point bounce in approval rating, a figure that's almost unimaginable as the result of a single address today.[3] But the electorate would reject Carter's assessment a year later, instead choosing to heed Reagan's words: "I find no national malaise. I find nothing wrong with the American people."

WE MET AT THE Carter Center in Atlanta, a decidedly circular set of buildings—round rooms, round hallways, round columns—that makes a rather ironic home for Carter and his library, given the dominant narrative that his presidency went nowhere.

When I walked into the office at exactly the scheduled meeting time—Carter has a notorious affection for punctuality—the old president was standing at a tall window, his hands burrowed in the pockets of brown wool pants as he looked out over a small pond and grove at the center of the compound. He wore a collared blue cotton shirt and sat on a hand-carved double rocker as we spoke. Across from us was a full-size replica of the intricately carved Kennedy desk from the Oval Office. It looks a bit out of place in Carter's quaint and tranquil office, perhaps in the same way Carter was once a touch out of place in the desk's more natural abode.

What's the single decision you made as president that you most regret?

I would say the hostage rescue effort in Iran in April of 1980. It was a perfectly planned, highly secret, somewhat complex procedure that everybody agreed to do. And in order to extract all of the hostages plus all the rescue team from Iran, we had to have six functioning helicopters. So I ordered eight helicopters and two of them had to fly from an aircraft carrier about 600 miles across areas of Iran and Oman and land in a desert, which we had already explored.

One of the helicopters, with no reasonable explanation since then, turned back to the aircraft carrier, which left us seven. Another one was forced down in the desert by an unexpected sandstorm, which left us six, which was fine. And so our whole rescue operation assembled there in the desert. And then one of the helicopters developed a hydraulic leak and couldn't fly. So I had to abort the rescue operation. We couldn't have afforded to extract five-sixths of our people and leave one-sixth of our people in Iran to be executed, so we had to terminate the exercise.

So it was not sending a large enough squad of helicopters?

If I'd sent one more helicopter, there's no doubt in my mind we would have had a successful operation. The Iranians never knew we were there until after we all left. But we would have had the hostages rescued, I would probably have been reelected, and so forth. So that was a bit of a turning point.

Gary Sick, your national security advisor for the Middle East, and a number of others have written convincingly that Reagan's campaign staff were conspiring against you to keep the hostages held for fear you'd win reelection if they were released. Do you believe that? Does that resonate with you?

I never have taken a position on that because I don't know the facts. I've seen both sides. I've seen the explanations that were made by George H. W. Bush and the Reagan people, and I've read Gary Sick's book and talked to him. I don't really know.

The thing that I do know is that after they [the Iranians] decided to hold the hostages until after the election, I did everything I could to get them extracted, and the last three days I was president, I never went to bed at all. I stayed up the whole time in the Oval Office to negotiate this extremely complex arrangement to get the hostages removed and to deal with $12 billion in Iranian cash and gold. And I completed everything by six o'clock on the morning that I was supposed to go out of office. All the hostages were transferred to airplanes and they were waiting in the airplanes. I knew this—so they were ready to take off—and I went to the reviewing stand when Reagan became president. Five minutes after he was president, the planes took off. They could have left three or four hours earlier.

But what, if any, influence was used on the Ayatollah to wait until I was out of office, I don't know.

At your eighty-fifth birthday celebration and the reopening of the Carter Library, you mentioned a list of challenges—eighteen challenges I think it was—that the current president faces and that you also faced. I wonder if you see something in the American system or something in the American national character that's keeping us stagnant or holding us back on these challenges?

I don't think that stagnation would be the right word. But I understand there is a sort of intransigence. In dealing with the Middle East peace process, for instance, I made a major step forward when I removed Israel's only real military threat—that was in Egypt. In the previous twenty-five years, Egypt had led the Muslim attack on Israel four times. I removed that threat, and now there is no Arab country that can really threaten Israel's mighty armada of weapons. But still, the succeeding presidents have not done what I did. They never made any progress on Mideast peace. Obama is still working on it, but that's something that carried over now for twenty-five years.

So I don't think it's a matter of lethargy on the part of the United States. It's a matter of some constantly changing circumstances in which the United States has to decide how strong a role to play or how much to let regional decisions be made without our involvement. Since I left office, some people—not me—have quantified about one hundred times that the American president has authorized military action in trouble spots around the world. A hundred different times.

That's an amazing number.

Yeah. I didn't do it. I went four years without doing it. But that doesn't mean that I'm criticizing my successors, because, sometimes, it's been justified.

I want to go to the "Crisis of Confidence" speech that you delivered to the nation in July of 1979. And the first question is, do you feel vindicated? And secondly, it seems to me that in 1980, the voters made a choice between your assessment that outlined making sacrifice and moving this nation down one path toward energy independence and living more humbly, and another path that said we can

continue this, that there's nothing wrong with the American way of
life. Are we particularly bad as a nation at making the right decisions
that are hard?

Yes. We are bad about making difficult decisions that everybody
knows are right. I don't know how to talk to you frankly without
being so self-defensive, but of the major decisions that I made as president, I would say none of them were politically attractive or positive.
I harassed the American people constantly about doing something
about energy conservation, and we were remarkably successful in
getting laws passed and putting other things in the hands of future
presidents.

Reagan, unfortunately, reversed those energy conservation measures over which the president has a lot of control, like mandatory
efficiency of automobiles and the allocation of support for renewable energy sources, photovoltaic cells, windmills. He reversed all
that because his premise was that America was self-sufficient, that
there was no shortage of energy. We had a right to use what we
wanted—not what we needed, but what we wanted—and we
shouldn't be insinuating that our country was so weak that Americans had to make a sacrifice to face the future. And that attitude
was totally different from what I had, and it was pretty well adopted
by Reagan's successors. I think that some of these things are coming back to haunt us.

But even if we just look at consumption in terms of living the way we
want versus the way we need—

I know. Now, Obama is beginning to see that some of these
things need to be resurrected.

Right. But why won't he fall in that same trap? Why won't he speak
honestly?

He hasn't done that yet.

But if he were to, wouldn't he be undercut—?

Yeah. Well, I don't know.

By an opposition that says we can continue our present course with-
out making sacrifices?

I'm not sure. That wasn't the reason for my failure to be re-elected. It was a relatively minor position. The main reason was, we didn't have the hostages back. And the Democratic Party was split, and Iraq attacked Iran and cut off about 20 percent of the world's oil supply, which created a 21 percent inflation rate in Europe. Well, Kennedy split the Democratic Party so that I lost by 10 percent of the Democratic vote. But I have always felt that I didn't need to be justified, to answer your first question.

I never have felt that I made a mistake in going to the American people and saying, "This is what we must do to show our resolve and we're capable of doing it," with the so-called malaise speech, which was a phrase that you know I never used. I never had any doubt about the accuracy of that speech and the necessity for that speech, so I didn't need to be justified.

Does that distance concern you? that distance between what is right and what needs to be done.?

Yeah, it concerns me.

And what the American people are willing to give?

Yeah, it concerns me greatly.

Could it—is it likely that will be our undoing, that this is the flaw of our nation?

Well, I wouldn't want to predict that America is going to be undone, so I'm not agreeing with that premise of yours.

But I think it does harm to our country in not being willing to face the facts as espoused from the White House about the threat of global warming and the substantive things we need to do to make sacrifices on a temporary basis to resolve the long-term threat. And the same thing applies to health care. The same thing applies to Middle East peace. The same thing applies to control of nuclear weapons and other major issues that are in the forefront of headlines today.

How do we do better with that? In your 1979 speech, you said nearly two-thirds of people don't vote; we're around half, at best. Do you have any idea how we conquer it?

When I was asked what advice I would give to the president, my advice was, "Tell the truth no matter how much it hurts."

In our case, we did that for four years. We never lied to the American public. We never made a misleading statement to the American public that we knew about. And we faced the facts. We told the truth. We obeyed the law, kept the peace. And that's a very difficult thing to do in these days because the American people don't want to hear unpleasant facts.

And, it's much more difficult now than it was when I was in office. I only had three TV stations to worry about, CBS, ABC, and NBC. CNN came into being in 1980, my last year in the White House. Back then you were really on, I would say, a one-hour cycle per day, and that was the evening news broadcast from the three major networks. Obviously, you had the morning newspapers too, I'm not ignoring that, but what reached the 30 million Americans every day was what Walter Cronkite said in the evening or what was said on NBC or ABC.

But it's different now. You have these highly biased news sources, with Fox on the right and MSNBC on the left, 24 hours a day with a little—I would say—less concern about the facts or accuracy than existed back in the Walter Cronkite days. So I had a kind of a halcyon opportunity to tell the truth and get away with it better than you would now. If I was in office right now and I wanted to be reelected, I'm not sure how much different I would be than I was thirty years ago. I have to say that what I did was quite often not what my wife wanted me to do. Or what my political advisors wanted me to do.

You cannot imagine now the influence and commitment of the so-called Taiwan lobby. Taiwan and Chiang Kai-shek had been our friend. And for me to decide we're going to abandon Taiwan and cast our lot with Red China—that was the only phrase used—was a step that my advisors advised me to take in my second term.

And I wouldn't go down to details, but the fact is that we made those decisions and they turned out—most of them—to be okay. But I'm not criticizing my successors, because it is a different environment now. And almost everybody is much more concerned about getting reelected than I was.

Speaking of elections and what candidates do to get elected, I want to ask you about 1970 in Georgia.[4] In your acceptance speech, you made it quite clear where you stood on segregation. But politicians— to get elected, to play this game—have to make friends with people they don't like, often with people you disagree with.

Sure. And I did.

But my question is, was it difficult or nerve-racking for you to have to do that, to sidestep principle? Because the fear is that if you give an inch, that's when you begin to slide. Did you have that fear that this was a dangerous, slippery road?

I ran against a former governor under whom I had served as a state senator and I supported his programs: His name is Carl Sanders. He became a very rich, powerful lawyer in Atlanta. He was originally from Augusta, Georgia. And he was looked upon as very progressive, and legitimately so. I ran as a peanut farmer from South Georgia, and South Georgia was looked upon then as fairly conservative on all issues. I came out of an environment, though, that separated me from my neighbors on the race issue. I grew up in the only white family in a black community. I was immersed in the black culture, and my mother paid no attention to racial divisions. My father was a segregationist, as was everyone else.

When I ran against Carl Sanders, I didn't have to take a stand on that issue because Sanders had threatened Senator Dick Russell, who was a patriarch of Georgia politics and very conservative on the race issue but a hero in Georgia. And Sanders alienated the right-wing segregationists who came to me automatically, not because of me or anything I said, but to try to beat Sanders.

So I accepted their support without having to take any position on the race issue. So I finessed, you might say, the race issue and I beat Sanders very badly. But in private meetings when the issue of race came up, I was very frank.

And when I made my acceptance speech, which was very brief, in January 1971 and I said, "I've traveled the state more than any other person in history and I say to you quite frankly that the time for racial discrimination is over. Never again should a black child be deprived of an equal right to health care, education, or the other privileges of society." That was basically it—that was pretty late.

So, I don't know if I've answered your question or not, but I was not a bold endorser of racial integration. I didn't have to be. And I capitalized on that issue by remaining mute, which may not have been the most courageous thing to do.

The question I have is, did having those racists and segregationists as your supporters bother you, or make you nervous in some ways?

Not really because it was open and there is no way to have their support without everybody in Georgia knowing about it. The Atlanta newspapers were intensely interested in my defeat. They were supportive of Carl Sanders.

What shocked you most when you first came to the White House?

I would say the independence and autonomy of the Congress. I had dealt with the legislature as a governor—that's one advantage governors have in going to the White House: They have dealt with legislatures and they're not dictators and so forth. But that was the biggest surprise, although I had some forewarning about what it was. But in Georgia, I was almost a dictator as governor. The Georgia governor, among all the fifty states, is the most powerful: I was the most powerful governor in America. I'll give you two or three quick reasons. One is the Georgia legislature is prohibited from serving more than 35 working days in one year and 45 working days the next year by the Georgia Constitution, whereas the Massachusetts legislature serves 270 days a year if they want to.

Also, the Georgia governor has line-item veto on the budget items. So I could present my budget proposals to the legislature. They could change it as much as they wanted to. I could just go down a line and just veto anything they put in there that I didn't like.

The third thing is that I didn't have to ask for a bill from the legislature until ten days after the legislature went home. So if I had a bill to veto that I didn't want to have overridden, I would just wait until the legislature went home and then veto it.

So I had great power as governor. And when I got to Washington—it wasn't like that at all. So that was a change. That was my biggest surprise. Truman said he found that when he got into the White House, when he gave an order, nobody paid any attention to it.

And did you makes mistakes in that regard, whether it was not having a chief of staff or appointing a congressional liaison that had barely seen the Congress? If you had to do it again, what would you have done differently?

If you take all the presidents since Roosevelt, the only president that had a better batting average with the Congress was Lyndon Johnson. Mine was better than [John F.] Kennedy's or anyone else's. And I had extremely good bipartisan support, Democrats and Republicans. My main problem was with the Liberal Democrats.

The first year I was in office, Kennedy supported me more than any other US senator. Then he decided to run against me and he became my worst thorn in the side. He tried to sabotage—that may be too harsh a word—he was against a lot of the things that I proposed that previously he had supported because he wanted me to fail so he could replace me in the White House. And in the fall of 1979, in some polls, he was 3 to 1 against me. And when we actually got started in the campaign itself, when he publicly announced, he was 2 to 1 ahead of me. Ultimately I beat him 2 to 1 [in the primary]. But that permeated the last part of my administration so I got increasingly good support from Republicans and conservative Democrats as Kennedy became more and more affiliated with the left-wing Democrats. And so I had a remarkable bipartisan support.

Having watched the post–Cold War generation, and seeing this incredible moment in terms of a hinge in history—with the opportunity to make leaps on nonproliferation, to build a more balanced global economy, to recognize and tackle climate change—do you think this generation will be judged harshly?

I think so. I don't know what's going to happen in the near future, but I served under a totally different umbrella of the Cold War where the utmost issue always in my mind was nuclear holocaust, where I never knew if the Soviets were going to launch an attack against us. They could destroy our country. I could have destroyed the Soviet Union in a response from one submarine. I never knew when that would happen.

So everything I did on an international basis, I did with the concern about how it would affect Brezhnev. I didn't accommodate him, but I would come in my office early in the morning and sit next to a globe—now, I don't mean every morning, but sometimes—I would turn that globe to Moscow and I would try to put myself in Brezhnev's shoes. What is it that might cause that paranoid nation to resort to a military attack on America in order not be embarrassed or not to have their top priorities aborted? I was always concerned about that. And we implemented some things that may have helped cause the downfall of the Soviet Union when Gorbachev took over. But I don't think that we've taken advantage of that potential global peace that could have come with a friendly accommodation between Moscow and Washington.

And not just relations between the two nations—it was a chance to reimagine many relations.

It was. It was. That's true. You have to remember that back in those days, almost every country on earth I'm talking about—was defined by this. All the Asian countries, including China, was affected by US-Soviet competition.

And Soviet-Chinese competition too.

Yeah. Ethiopia, South Africa, Rhodesia, every country or a lot of them in South America were wooed assiduously by the Soviets with their ally Cuba, so that they could have better strategic relationships, better trade relationships with Moscow than they did with the US. So I was competing with them all the time. But that all disappeared when the Soviet Union collapsed under Gorbachev's influence. And we didn't ever take a long strategic look at what can we do to capitalize on this. And I've already told you how many times American presidents have authorized military action since then.

I think if the United States had become the world's acknowledged champion of peace, of human rights, of environmental quality, of the alleviation of suffering, of democracy and freedom, our world would be in a different place now.

Just take the president of Botswana. If he had faced a civil war, a war with one of his neighbors in southern Africa, if his first thought was, "Why don't I go to Washington because Washington stands for peace; or Washington stands for human rights; or Washington stands for democracy, freedom? Washington is the foremost leader on earth being generous to people in need"—it would be a different world.

There's a tradition of leaving a letter to the successor on the desk in the Oval Office. If you were to draft such a letter to the next generation of leaders, you've spoken about the importance of the truth, speaking truth. What else would you include in that letter?

I was in Wales at what I think is the largest book fair on earth, and I was asked by the editor of the *Guardian* newspaper, "What can the next US president do in the first 100 days to change the image of America around the world?"

And in a somewhat brash moment, I said, "He can do it in ten minutes." And there were about 1,200 people in the audience, big crowd. And the editor kind of scoffed at me. He said, "What do you mean ten minutes?" I said, "In his inaugural address, he can say the United States will never torture another person. The United States will abide by international law. The United States will not initiate a nuclear attack on another country." And so I went down the list—"If he could say that in the first ten minutes, the image of America would be transformed in the world." And Obama, I would say, has said some of those things. That's why he got the Nobel Peace Prize.

Now to carry through on that is a more difficult thing.

Carter, on July 4, 1979, cancelled a national address and retreated from public view for ten days. Amid the hiatus, which concluded with the "Crisis of Confidence" speech, he holed up at Camp David, hosted a string of prominent figures—businessmen, diplomats, governors, and clergymen—and tried to diagnose the problem with his presidency. During 1978 his public support had crashed to levels nearing Nixon's during the Watergate scandal. But the nation felt abandoned with the president's absence, which further undermined him. The press was locked out of the ad hoc summit's first seven days and

mused that there was likely something wrong with the president—a
health problem, perhaps even a psychological one.

Carter could hardly stomach the critique that his guests delivered. He wrote in his diary, "It's not easy for me to accept criticism
and to reassess my way of doing things." When he heard criticism,
his jaw clenched and he scribbled on a legal pad furiously.[5] Great
leaders take criticism well; they seek it and value it. Carter was averse
to it in all forms.

Machiavelli in his discourse on power, *The Prince,* toyed with
the question of love and fear; as a leader, is it better to be loved or
feared? Both, he concluded, are quite useful. Today, above all, it is
best to be listened to.

When Carter gave his first speech in the face of the energy crisis
in April 1977, 80 million people watched; two years later, in April
1979, when he delivered a far more aggressive call to arms by suggesting the "moral equivalent of war" was needed to build an en-
ergy-independent America, only 30 million heard him.[6]

Richard Neustadt, a scholar of the American presidency and a
former aide to President Harry Truman, noted that "presidential
power is the power to persuade."[7] A prerequisite is the capacity to
be heard, to command attention—whether through fear or love or,
simply, respect. Carter quickly lost that.

While public opinion on a given issue may matter far less than
most leaders believe—as Ehud Barak and Bill Clinton hold—support
for leaders themselves and confidence in their capacity to lead remains crucial.

Carter's West German counterpart, Helmut Schmidt, an irritable
intellectual and former Nazi artilleryman, held that Carter "was just
not big enough for the game."[8] Carter wrote in his presidential diary
that "Schmidt seems to go up and down in his psychological attitude.
I guess women aren't the only ones that have periods."[9] The relationship started on rocky ground in 1973, when Carter, then the governor of Georgia, traveled to Germany and asked Schmidt, then the
West German finance minister, to consider building a Volkswagen
plant in Georgia. Schmidt preferred to discuss the Watergate scandal.

The relationship never warmed.

Chapter Eleven

SCHMIDT SCHNAUZE

HELMUT HEINRICH WALDEMAR SCHMIDT

CHANCELLOR OF WEST GERMANY 1974–1982

March 2010

HELMUT SCHMIDT, AT AGE ninety-one, did not hesitate to snap when I asked for a favorite memory from his chancellorship thirty years prior. "I've never thought of that," the former Nazi artilleryman snarled, a white cigarette pressed backwards between his lips. What—I found myself wondering—is the proper etiquette when a renowned but aging statesman is prepared to light the wrong end of a Reyno?

He had raised the cigarette to his lips with a trembling hand, and it now dangled there precariously. As I tried to craft a diplomatic warning and moved my hand closer to his, he shakily lifted a lighter and—in an almost transcendent moment—deftly flipped the cigarette and clicked the lighter to life. He turned and looked at me with a cool smile.

This is Schmidt. *Schmidt Schnauze*, Schmidt the Lip, as he was dubbed by political adversaries who charged that he had "learned his socialism in the officers' mess."[1] This is the chancellor who berated his American counterpart, and who, popular belief holds, usurped power during Hamburg's 1962 flood while he was a minister for Interior Affairs, telling the mayor, "Mr. Mayor, you're in my way here." Schmidt insists the story is folklore. He holds that he respected the mayor a great deal, and never would have berated Paul Nevermann in front of others.[2] The anecdote sounds exactly like Schmidt, though. He is at once prescient and antagonistic, disarmingly forward but now also gentle in his old age.

Though in a wheelchair and nearly deaf, the hefty Schmidt was, as recently as his ninetieth birthday, polled as the most popular politician in Germany. He wore a dark suit, blue suspenders, and a pink pocket square on the day that we met, and pushed himself in and out from the table incessantly, as if trying to expend an excess of energy. His face is heavy now, but the shade of a boyish smile remains, particularly when he is playing the contrarian. Schmidt burns through three or four packs of cigarettes each day, roughly one every seven minutes. His doctors have allegedly told him not to stop for fear it will kill him.

IRONICALLY, SCHMIDT IS ONE-QUARTER Jewish. His father was the il-
legitimate son of a Jewish banker, a fact Helmut only learned as the
family scrambled to hide its heritage. The Schmidts were practicing
Lutherans and managed to forge the necessary papers to escape the
Third Reich's category of *Mischlinge,* mixed parentage, which would
have guaranteed discrimination if not the fate of full-blooded and practicing Jews. Helmut was pulled into Hitler's war machine at seventeen,
three years after his rowing club was taken over by the Nazi Youth. He
was suspended from the club that year for, among other transgres-
sions, painting a boathouse tapestry with the lyrics: "Freedom is the
fire, brightly shining; as long as it is burning, the world is not too
small."[3] The words come from a Nazi propaganda song, but Schmidt,
as his coaches recognized, chose them for their particular irony.

He is representative of what he has called a "generation between
generations," a portion of German society that is often overlooked:
those who did not sympathize with the views of the Third Reich, but
who were either too young or too non-ideological to choose a life of
dissent. At *Stunde Null*—zero hour, the German term for the moment the war ended—Schmidt walked from Belgium back to Hamburg. He had spent the previous five months in a British prison camp.
He and his contemporaries had gone from schoolboys to soldiers,
with literally nothing in between. They found their nation carved
into zones of occupation and reduced to a skeleton of itself. More important, they faced confirmation of the horrors that many had witnessed and most had suspected, and that gave birth to the unyielding
and likely eternal question within the German psyche: What about
this nation—this advanced, historied society—had allowed for *this*?

As chancellor, Schmidt spoke at the Cologne Synagogue in November 1978, forty years after the Final Solution was set in motion
on the Night of Broken Glass. Standing beneath the eternal flame
and a latticed wood mosaic of the Star of David, dressed in a dark
suit and wearing a yarmulke, he said, "The truth is that a great many
Germans disapproved of the crimes and wrongs; by the same token,
there were a great many others who learned nothing or almost nothing at the time." He continued, "The truth is that all this, nevertheless, came to pass before the eyes of a large number of German

citizens, and that another large number of them gained direct knowledge of the events. The truth is that most people, faint of heart, kept their silence." He closed, quoting German-Jewish philosopher Martin Buber, "This heart of mine, well aware of the frailty of man, refuses to condemn my neighbor because he failed to find the strength to become a martyr."[4]

AS A BOY, SCHMIDT DREW artistic inclinations from his mother, who organized weekly madrigal singing at their home and took her children to museums and concerts, and Prussian discipline from his father, a teacher. Both traits remain visible in Schmidt's character: He is a talented pianist and has released recordings of both Bach and Mozart concertos, most recently on the occasion of his ninetieth birthday. He enjoyed drawing as a child and harbored ambitions to become an architect or city planner.

As chancellor, Schmidt found himself, like other European leaders, a tenuous middleman in a game of giants. The divided Germany was the first fissure that would rip open if the Cold War came to arms. Among the many difficulties between Jimmy Carter and Schmidt, perhaps the conflict over the neutron bomb is the most emblematic. Carter balked when fiscal appropriations for the bomb were suddenly made public, first wavering then committing to its development and deployment in Western Europe. The bomb decreased the physical blast of detonation but greatly increased the radiation released. If deployed, it would kill large swaths of population without reducing buildings and infrastructure. Strategic planners in Western Europe and the Pentagon were interested in the weapon for its deterrent capacity—more precisely, its ability to kill Soviet troops in tanks and armored personnel carriers.

As soon as Schmidt had gained political ground and public support for the weapons, Carter reneged.

The German economy remains the engine of Europe amid this current financial collapse. It assumed that mantle again quite quickly after World War II, within just a few decades, despite being deci-

mated. You've suggested that one of the great strengths of the German system rests with the role and strength of unions. The United States today lacks a comparably strong labor movement, and I wonder what you think of the viability of capitalism without such a force?

In the main, citizens of the United States speak of their country as capitalist. Nobody would do so in Germany; nobody will in France either. These are welfare states, totally different from the United States. To give you an example, out of a hundred people who are living in Germany—whether with their babies or elderly gentlemen like myself, almost ninety-two years of age—from this whole population, out of a hundred, twenty-five are living on state pensions. Unbelievable for the United States.

And it's more or less the same, too, for all of Scandinavia, the Netherlands, almost throughout France, and even the newcomers like Poland and the Czech Republic are trying to follow that example.

For instance, you have something between 30 and 40 million people who do not have any insurance. This is unthinkable in Europe, absolutely unthinkable. The European democracies would break into pieces if everyone would change their systems and adopt the American way. It would lose the confidence of the masses.

You said recently that the United States will need to follow that European lead—

I didn't say they will need to; I predicted that they will follow the European example by the middle of the century. By the middle of the century, the Hispanics and the Afro-Americans, these two minorities together, on the one hand they will form a majority of the electorate, and on the other hand they will demand social security for themselves. They will demand access to colleges and to universities and to positions higher up in the economy and the society. It may come in fifty years, maybe twenty to thirty-five. It takes a long time because it goes against basic instincts of the white Anglo-Saxon population.

And right now, a portion of that population at least is very angry and becoming somewhat violent. Do you think America will be volatile in those forty years if such a transition is to take place?

Not necessarily big trouble, but some trouble, yes. But certainly nothing of the quality of the fight in the middle of the nineteenth century, the fight for the abolition of slavery—nothing of that scale, much more harmless.

When you were captured at the end of World War II, you stayed up late at night in the prison camp in discussion with your fellow prisoners about the future Germany that you wanted to build. Do you remember those conversations?

The discussions, in the main, were dealing with the immediate past, with the crimes that had happened during the Nazi period, the mistakes that had been made. And, to a much smaller degree, these discussions were about the immediate future. There was almost nobody who had any concept for the immediate future of Germany. Germany, at that time, was in the process of being divided into four zones of occupation. The Russians didn't behave nicely in their zone; the British did behave much more humanely but not very nicely, the same goes for the French. It appeared a bit later that the Americans behaved rather naively, but on the other hand more benignly, and sometimes too much under the influence of Jewish immigrants who had left Germany after 1933 and 1934.

And what did you think of the future at the moment? Did you think it was possible that Germany would be where it was when you were a chancellor?

No, I didn't. I was also convinced that later, rather than sooner, the German nation would be reunified once again. I did know enough about the history of Europe over the last 400 years or so, about the enormous changes in the power structure inside Europe— the power structure between Britain and France or between Britain and Holland or between Portugal and Spain—to know that the power structure had changed at least once in every century, sometimes more. And from that knowledge it was easy to derive that the next time would open a chance for the Germans to get together under one roof once again. I didn't expect this to happen in the twentieth century, but I did expect it to happen in the twenty-first century. So, I was mistaken by ten years.

It still makes you an optimist.

No, no. This is a typical American interpretation. It has nothing to do with optimism. It was insights into the European realities.

Speaking about insight into realities, right now the world is thinking about nuclear weapons—

Not enough.

Certainly not enough, and when we talk about the reductions in nuclear arsenals, the new START treaty will still only reduce the totals by a very small amount. Instead of reducing by 80 percent or 90 percent, we're talking about using tricky numbers and really only cutting deployed warheads by about a thousand, when there are still ten thousand devices for each superpower. Why is this so hard?

Because the leaders of the world powers—or the leaders of Russia and the United States much more so than the leaders in China or France or Britain—are profoundly prejudiced by what they have been thinking during the first parts of their lives. And during the first parts of their lives, they were educated by the previous generation, the strategic planners at the Pentagon or in the Kremlin. Both are being educated by the leaders in the Cold War and they still think, quite frankly, in the categories of the Cold War. Or, to use a different expression, in the categories of friend or foe, in the categories of competition and power.

If one generation teaches that thinking to the next, won't that problem always remain, or will my generation shed that? Does it become a self-perpetuating way of thought, or will time dilute it?

You might say that Barack Obama is part of your generation. He is a bit older than you, but he is a part of a younger generation. Great idealistic speeches, and what has he accomplished so far? Almost nothing. Neither did he make an end to Guantanamo. Nor did he bring about a Non-First-Use Treaty for nuclear weapons. He believes in what he says but he can't do what he's saying.

In that sense, he reminds me of Jimmy Carter.

Not necessarily—because Jimmy Carter had a majority in Congress and his majority, Obama's majority, is questionable.

But they both are smart. Nobody thinks they're stupid men. They both speak beautifully, and they both have a good moral compass. And they both may fail to get much done, it seems.

Yes.

What did they lack? Is it a lack of aggression? You were called "Schmidt the Lip," and were known to raise your voice and muscle people around on occasion, and neither Carter nor Obama seems to like to do that very much. You said Jimmy Carter was not big enough for the game—

Yes. This is still my belief, and there's a great difference between Carter and Obama. Both of them seem to appear to me as honest human beings. What they say is what they really think, yes. But Jimmy Carter changes his thinking from time to time.

As Obama has, particularly with regard to Guantanamo, on having trials in New York, on whether they ought to be military tribunals or civilian trials.

I don't know whether he has changed his mind on Guantanamo. Maybe he has underrated the difficulties. He is not enough of a realist; he is really too much of an optimist. Jimmy Carter also was an optimist, but Jimmy Carter changed his mind rather too often.

So, besides changing his mind too much, what could have made Carter bigger? What could have made him a better leader? And I ask this not because—

I will not answer that question. Why should I criticize that man?

I understand. But in more general terms, not about Jimmy Carter, but American presidents in general, what could make them more successful? This superpower often seems impotent, unable to meet its ideals.

It has less to do with the superpower and more to do with the way in which the American nation chooses its presidents. It is rather the exception that you choose a candidate from the political class. It is rather the majority of cases in which you choose a candidate for president from the fifty or fifty-one governors of states.

But for the first 200 years of your history, you had a coherent political class called the Old East Coast Elite. This has withered away during my lifetime. This elite is gone and nowadays you choose your presidents from southern states or for some other popular reasons. You might even choose that woman from Alaska—Mrs. Palin. You might.

So, what you're really arguing that they're not experienced enough. Besides George Bush Sr., most of our modern presidents haven't had the political education that you had.

The last president who had the necessary international experience was Bush's father. But international experience doesn't really matter for the American electorate. It doesn't really matter to them. They want to have somebody who is honest, or makes the impression of being honest, and who is likable.

Then there is this weakness in the American Constitution. You are very proud of the checks and balances and the fabric of the Constitution, but you do not really understand that the Constitution does heap too much responsibility on one person. It is the people who elect that one person, as opposed to the parliament. The United States and its democracy differs from any other democracy in the world in that way. Every other democracy has made the president, to a higher degree, dependent on the parliament. You may argue that this is a great advantage. I say, yes, it is an advantage, but it's a danger as well. And in some other so-called democracies, the president has turned into a dictator—it could as well happen in the United States. You were close to it under Franklin Roosevelt. He was a great president, no doubt about it. And his morale was absolutely okay but if he had lived another four years, he might have become some kind of a predominant president, not necessarily a dictator, but something on the way toward dictatorship.

In his memoirs, Senator Chuck Hagel recalls sitting with you in his Senate office and listening to you lament that there are no great leaders on the world stage today. Why is that?

Because the challenges are smaller. Or rather, the challenges which the present leaders do understand do appear to them as being smaller. They are not really smaller, but they have an insufficient understanding of the challenges. I will mention three of them.

One is the banking crisis which, in the course of winter 2008 until 2009, almost sent the globe into depression. It has been avoided partially due to the leaders, but it still hasn't been overcome. And it's not as yet to be excluded that we may see some kind of recurrence of the whole thing. This they have not understood. That does include the American Congress, does include the political class in Britain, and does include more or less the political classes on the European continent, but not as severely as in Britain and not as severely as in the United States.

The second example is namely the danger of the general clash between the fifty or so states of Islamic impregnation on the one side and the West as a whole on the other side. There are 200 states in the world, one-quarter of them are Islamically impregnated, and none of them is a democracy.

The third example is the build-up of mutual distrust and envy and possibly enmity between the West led by the United States and the People's Republic of China. These are the three great problems of today and the political classes of the West are not up to them.

There are a couple other great challenges. Population growth is a huge challenge; climate change is a terrific challenge.

Yes, climate change and the scarcity of water and the competition for oil, and all that. In my view, these are important challenges, but they're second-rate challenges.

So, the problem that you're really describing is our capacity to understand. That for leaders, as well as for broader populations, these challenges have become very complex and we don't really grasp them.

Well, for a democracy it is normal for an administration or an elected body like the House of Representatives or the US Senate to think about the future limited to the next four years, at the utmost, six. So, that means you are tempted to limit yourselves to tactical gains, and not to understanding a strategic problem.

You mentioned three strategic problems that I could have added to the three of mine—namely, overpopulation, water, the growth of CO_2 in the atmosphere. None of the political classes are really considering these as problems for the next couple of decades, and therefore they don't treat them as immediate challenges.

So, then aren't we doomed? Doesn't that mean we don't have a chance of rising to face these challenges?

Not necessarily. It need not necessarily lead to pessimism, but at least it should lead you to understand one of the decisive shortcomings of every democracy. I mean, it's been limited to a certain period, a rather short period of years.

But, if what you're saying is that democracy inherently can't deal with these challenges—

I'm not saying democracy cannot deal with it, I'm saying it should deal with it.

But it would be fair to say you're not optimistic.

I have never allowed myself neither pessimism nor optimism, never ever. A normal American is an optimist. It helps them to some degree; to some degree it also leads them to make mistakes. My preference always has been to be as little optimistic as possible and to be as little pessimistic as possible and to be as realistic as possible.

What advice would you leave to future generations grappling with this intransigence about leadership?

I've never thought about it. I'm a typical European as compared to you. You believe in the American mission; I don't. I don't even believe in the European mission.

Is it dangerous to believe in this American mission?

It does have its weaknesses. It does have its dangers, yes. It does also have its advantages, but it's typically American to have a vision and to tell the rest of the world that this is the right vision also for them. For instance, human rights is one of your visions. You have no idea of the Chinese civilization, although it's 4,000 years old. You have no idea of the Islamic civilization, although it's at least more than 1,000 years old, but you tell them your vision is the right one. This is the weakness of the United States, always to tell the rest of the world that "we know better than you."

If you were to go back to being chancellor once more—

I would never go back.

But is there one mistake that stands out?

You never can remake a mistake.

Well, I guess the question is, which one troubles you most?

Nothing really troubles me.

Does it worry you that nearly half of East Germans in polls have said that Soviet East Germany, the GDR, had more good sides than bad?

No, that's not right. This is the consequence of the wrong questions being asked in the public opinion poll. Poorly articulated questions. The majority of the East Germans do believe in democracy nowadays, though they didn't do so twenty years ago.

The BBC did a poll on the twentieth anniversary of the fall of the Berlin Wall that showed globally an incredible tide against capitalism, likely the result of the financial collapse—

It would be a great advantage for the rest of the world and for the faith in democracy if we did away with any kind of public opinion polls. Any kind of public opinion polls falsify the real situation.

Because of the Internet, it's not just polls that are influencing elected officials, though. Publics have all kinds of spin coming at them from new mediums and the capacity, in turn, to terrorize their representatives. And I think that has made it much harder for democracies to function well. Do you see that phenomenon?

It is the fate of any democracy that people who do vote don't know what they are doing.

Nonetheless, you believe in democracy?

Yes.

And that's not a paradox? There's not a contradiction there?

No it's not a paradox. It's like Winston Churchill said, it does have enormous weaknesses, but still it's better than any other system that we have tried from time to time.

Schmidt's frustration with Jimmy Carter centered upon equivocation. It posits a critical lesson: Leaders must stay committed to the decisions they make and recognize that one's cabinet members, party colleagues, and fellow heads of state have postured themselves ac-cordingly. Perhaps nothing undermines a leader more than indeci-siveness and retraction.

Schmidt's argument that the American system heaps too much responsibility on the president is well taken, as is his recognition of the danger posed by publics selecting presidential candidates rather than the political elites. The system greatly expands the risk posed by populists and unqualified leaders, as we see today.

Schmidt also agreed emphatically that liberal democracies are, by and large, failing to deal with the challenges of this century. It is a reality that has made many quietly jealous of the concentrated power of authoritarian capitalist states. Many in the developing world, too, find themselves envious of the rapidly increasing living standards in states like China and Singapore.

Goh Chok's tiny island has become one of the world's most ag-gressive economies, and the memoir of his predecessor, Lee Kuan Yew, is given out by the World Bank to new heads of state around the developing world.

Chapter Twelve

WOODEN TIGER

GOH CHOK TONG

PRIME MINISTER
OF SINGAPORE
1990–2004

THE ISTANA IN SINGAPORE is among the world's most bizarre presidential palaces. First, there is the fact that the tiny island it governs feels like the collision of an industrial park and a shopping mall, albeit with the thermostat cranked to ninety and the humidity elevated beyond the index. Second, despite its square, columned, and colonial white exterior, the inside of the palace—or at least the bit of it I see—feels more like a staid airport lounge than any presidential abode. And, finally, it sits atop the island's plushest plot of land, "a welcome green lung within the city," according to the official description, as well as a nine-hole golf course.[1] It is one of the few reminders, save the humidity, of what Singapore probably felt like before the concrete took hold.

There's a single elevator from the portico, and, as I waited to see Goh Chok Tong, the depth and pace of aides doubled several times. We squeezed onto the lift, which has a forest green carpet that has certainly seen better days. As the meeting began, a seating chart was thrust in front of me.

Moments before, one of the affable and intelligent young men working for the senior minister—the title Goh inherited after stepping down as prime minister in 2004—asked whether I had found many of the former leaders I interviewed consumed by themselves. The truth, I said, was that it seemed to vary, usually based on how many people they were still surrounded by and how much their current lives resembled the experience and pace of the presidency. At this point, I should note, the aide was the only one around; the half-dozen others in light blue oxfords had yet to amass. His face fell a bit when I suggested this.

So, when the double doors of Goh's office were thrown open and I immediately broke ranks by—accidentally—sitting in the wrong seat, I was surprised to find that Goh is, perhaps, the most ego-less of all these figures. He's tall, a bit more than six feet, but seems larger alongside his short countrymen, and has the languid grace of a willow.

In our conversation, when I asked for a greatest regret or a mistake he had made while prime minister, he struggled to think of one;

he noted that major decisions were typically made by the cabinet, often by consensus. He turned, with a sly smile, to three aides in blue sitting alongside us in maroon leather chairs. "Can you think of any?" he goaded them.

The aides looked to one another cautiously. "Come on, you look the other way," he said, slapping his knee. "Come on! He can't say this former head of state never made a single mistake—no one will believe him."

TINY SINGAPORE, THE CITY-STATE hoof beneath the horse-legged peninsula of Malaysia, achieved the impossible in the second half of the twentieth century. It catapulted itself from "squalid colonial backwater," as the cliché now holds, to the ranks of first-world states.

It is often said that China, as it weighed its future, looked to Russia for what *not* to do, and to Singapore for what to imitate. Although there's a gap in that chronology—Chinese premier Deng Xiaoping began his reforms in the late 1970s, years before the Russian collapse was fully evident—the adage still holds. The Chinese sought to create what one of Deng's most important advisors called "a birdcage economy,"[2] a world with enough air for entrepreneurs and business to take life, but not so much freedom as to run wild— a society strikingly similar to what Singapore's leaders were crafting. The island's worship of free trade and its single-party dominance are also the hallmarks of China's rise, and Beijing is undoubtedly envious of the clean, orderly society that Singapore has built atop the Confucian values both nations share. Beijing has sent envoys to study Singapore's retirement and welfare system, and most of the developed world has noted its health care system.

Singapore's phenomenal success has made it the envy of developing nations around the world. Upon gaining independence from Britain in 1965, the nation was devastatingly poor and backwards, an amalgamation of races that seemed destined to be either swallowed up by a regional power or ripped apart by ethnic clashes within—divisions between the dominant Chinese and the minority Malays and Indians.

But that sense of fatalism became a potent catalyst, a David complex. The nation's first leaders—most notably Lee Kuan Yew, Goh's predecessor as prime minister—leveraged the British education system, Singapore's premier ports, and the nation's collective anxiety to build a roaring Asian Tiger economy.

The Jurong port swelled with traffic, becoming a hub of global commerce and a major oil refinery, then a dominant petrochemicals center. When space ran short, small islands in the bay were physically expanded and coalesced into one. When leaders recognized that the economy was bleeding hundreds of millions of dollars when citizens traveled abroad to gamble, they built their own gaming industry and brought in revenues from around the region. And when the nation faced a problem of excessive garbage, incinerated trash was molded into a manmade island. It became a nature preserve. Politically, in 1995 the government recognized the difficulty of competing for talent with its own vibrant private sector and pegged government wages at two-thirds of comparable private sector wages.[3]

The Singapore model is predominantly a cut-and-paste operation. Its leaders have constantly sought the most effective models from elsewhere in the world and then replicated them, with necessary adjustments, on the island. Above all, Singapore made itself attractive to foreign capital. It signed free trade deals with the European Union, United States, and Australia, and carried the strict sense of societal order into business law. Its leaders keenly eliminated the red tape and corruption that make wealthy foreign firms hesitant to manufacture overseas. They built factory shells that businesses could quickly slide their manufacturing equipment into and ensured that no labor unions formed. The government acted as a partner rather than an obstacle to new entities and kept the island's tax rates exceedingly low. In 1969, Texas Instruments, the leading calculator manufacturer, was the first major American company to set up in Singapore; its first product left the factory three months after negotiations began.[4] Other major tech producers followed; during the 1990s, more than 55 percent of computer hard drives were made on the island.

But Singapore's leaders were not satisfied as a global manufacturing hub. They recognized that as the society gained wealth and wages rose, manufacturing would move elsewhere, where labor remained cheap. Government-led corporations moved into biomedical industries; Singapore Airlines became world class; the regime focused on banking and attracted some of the most proven venture capital talent from Silicon Valley.

SINGAPORE SIMPLY WORKS. One can have a suit tailored nearly overnight; there are orderly queues for taxis inside malls or buildings to save one from the stifling humidity. All business is conducted in English, the only language taught in Singapore's schools; foreigners can drink tap water without concern; public transit is clean and efficient. The government sells affordable and respectable homes at manageable prices, having recognized—from the model of the United States—that home ownership engenders stability.

The price of that affluent and stable society is a rather paternal state, which the vast majority of Singaporeans seem willing to accept, particularly alongside much poorer neighbors Malaysia and Indonesia. Chewing gum is illegal without a medical prescription; the fine for eating or drinking on the subway is close to 300 dollars; the state controls the media and disallows a number of foreign publications, like *Playboy*—though they relented and allowed sales of *Cosmopolitan* in 2004 and, the same year, allowed a censored version of *Sex and the City* to air on TV.[5]

Most Americans' first introduction to the state came in 1994, when a diplomatic row played out over the caning of Michael P. Fay, then eighteen. Fay, an American citizen who was living in Singapore with his stepfather, faced charges of vandalism and theft, and received four strokes, or lashes, with a rattan cane. The punishment is employed as a penalty for a number of crimes in Singapore, and, for many foreigners, it is the most symbolic expression of the government's authoritarian tendencies. Nonetheless, Singapore doesn't feel like a police state. There are not gunmen on each corner, as one finds in Cairo, and Singaporeans do not retreat to hushed tones when griping about the government, as many must in domineering states.

The People's Action Party (PAP) is the sole political force on the island. Through a system of gerrymandering, personality assault, and co-option, the regime manages to retain complete political dominance. There are regular elections, in which the PAP typically wins 60 to 70 percent of the vote, and laws put in place under Goh guarantee that there are at least several members of the opposition in Parliament. Goh also encouraged more criticism from backbenchers within the party in Parliament, though the measures were later walked back.

After Goh amended the constitution to establish a presidency alongside his own prime ministership in 1993, the first PAP deputy to assume the post resigned with a letter denouncing the office for lacking legitimate power. His successor, a career civil servant, assumed the office without even an election.

Those who challenge the PAP politically are often assaulted legally, slapped with libel suits intended to bankrupt, thus disqualifying them from a role in government. Foreign publications, too, often find themselves under legal barrage: the *International Herald Tribune, The Wall Street Journal, The Economist,* and *Time* have all found themselves on the losing end of lawsuits. Not surprisingly, the government has never lost a case, according to Stuart Karl, a former counsel for the *Journal.*[6]

GOH CHOK TONG WAS the first of five children; when he was nine, his father died of tuberculosis. The widowed family squeezed into a single room in Goh's grandmother's home. At one point, there were twenty people living in the house, with a single bucket toilet. Goh had perfect school attendance and captained the swim team. Using state loans, he studied economics at the national university, then topped his master's degree course at Williams College in Massachusetts. I asked Goh about protests that year, the tumultuous 1967. He recalled watching demonstrators marching on campus. "They just kept going around and around." He was officially on leave from the government's Administrative Service at that time, and was barred from political activity, but, at a professor's urging, he "took one lap with them. There was no YouTube then," he laughed.

When he returned to Singapore, he resumed a position with the government. Lee Kuan Yew, the island's founding statesman, had made a practice of "helicoptering up" young talent within the party, to prevent paths to the highest rungs from becoming staid and patron-prone. Lee sought to hire Goh as a principal private secretary to work at his side, but Goh maneuvered away from the offer, seizing the opportunity to work instead in the Economic Planning Unit, then later in the shipping industry.

Years later, Lee was disappointed when Goh was anointed as his successor. Lee had left the decision to a group of second-generation PAP leaders, and, after the announcement in 1984, he described Goh as "wooden." He said Goh might have to see a psychiatrist for help with the problem.[7]

Nonetheless, Goh assumed power in 1990. Though the elections are not true political contests, they have become a kind of referendum on the ruling party's proposals. Goh quickly called elections and positioned himself as a modernizer, intent to open the society and relax the paternal state. The platform was rejected; the PAP won only seventy-seven of eighty-one seats, the opposition's largest gain ever. Ironically, the loss should have vindicated Goh's view that the society indeed sought more openness and freedom, but the defeat forced him to temper his ambition. Years later, Goh weighed splitting the party to create a viable opposition, but the plans were never enacted.

FOR ALL THAT SINGAPORE has achieved, where it goes next remains a looming question. Despite pouring immense resources into technology venture capital, genuine innovation has been slow to take root—again, like China, which has also had difficulty spurring homegrown quantum leaps. Beijing's crash 863 program, launched in 1986 to encourage green-tech growth, has proved more adroit at improving upon German windmills and American solar panels than achieving organic innovation, such as the lofty goal of carbon sequestration, also referred to as clean coal.[8]

Observers often note that the great American tech giants— Zuckerberg, Gates, Jobs—are societal malcontents, dropouts who relied on cultures of risk and intuition to build their empires. They, quite simply, might never have succeeded in the rigid, risk-averse societies of China and Singapore. As an editorial in *Nature* magazine noted in July 2008, "An even deeper question is whether a truly vibrant scientific culture is possible without a more widespread societal commitment to free expression. The right to challenge authority, and to doubt everything, is central to scientific enquiry."[9] One of the most intriguing questions of our era centers on the viability of central, domineering regimes atop free markets.

Many countries hope to emulate Singapore, to make massive strides in only several decades. More often than not, leaders find themselves making very hard decisions about how to allocate limited resources. You put a tremendous emphasis on education and rule of law. If you had to choose between those options which would you select? Which is the more important of the two in your eyes?

I would choose education. Assuming I've got to choose, I would go for education, because with that would come the rule of law. If people are educated, you want to be ruled by honest people, able people, and, of course, you want the rule of law. If you only have just the rule of law and you are not emphasizing education, then what would be the result? A very illiterate population. The people haven't got the skills to move the country forward. But, fortunately, we are not required to choose just between two of these issues. You need both.

If we talk about moving decisively, we need to iron out these huge economic imbalances, we need to move on climate change. These are things that make me hugely envious when I look at Singapore, when I look at China. If there's something the government wants, it can act quickly. It can retrofit plants overnight. It can pass emission standards without political wrangling and interest groups interfering. And, it seems to me, that may be the biggest flaw with liberal democracies—that you have to spend a tremendous amount of energy fighting with one another rather than working constructively.

I think that's too simplistic a statement. Even China must take into account the feelings, expectations of the people, especially in today's context where you have the Internet. The Internet's voting power is tremendous in China. The Chinese people may not be allowed to vote, but the Chinese leadership has to recognize the voting power of the Internet constituency.

Explain that to me. Even if you don't have the right to vote, you still have power.

Yes. Let's say the Chinese government decided to move very quickly with implementation of measures on climate change and the rest of the world is not doing so; there is an immediate cost to the economy, shutting down polluting factories, and so on. People are unemployed. There is social dislocation. You're going to get the Internet generation just blaming the government.

You notice that whenever they had a quarrel with their neighbors—say, for example, Japan—they had to be very mindful of how they handle the dispute. Because if it's uncontrolled, that same kind of a nationalistic feeling amongst the people expressed through the Internet could, in time, be diverted to be expressed against the government over certain policies. So they have to handle it very carefully.

They are very, very mindful of this. If you watch President Hu Jintao or Premier Wen Jiabao, whenever there is an earthquake or natural disaster, they will be there for you; just like Bill Clinton, he feels your pain. In the past, they could maybe delay two, three days before appearing. Now, they cannot, not with YouTube. Therefore, even with a centrally controlled country, I do not think they could just push through policies if they are not going to have beneficial results for the population.

And, on your other question, I don't think democracy is unable to push through issues like climate change. It's a bit more difficult in the sense that you have to go through a certain process. Look at Norway. Look at the EU. Those are democracies. But they have the political will. They recognize the long-term impact of climate change and they are taking steps now. In the United States, of course, you have an automobile society. It is hard to cut back. Petrol prices are too cheap. So you need the political will, I think, to get the process through. Political will is most important.

If your children or grandchildren were to come to you and ask, "Should I enter public life? Should I be a politician?" What would you say?

I would say, "Know thyself." You must get to know yourself. If you are able to do it, it's something you like to do, it is a tremendous job because you make a difference in other people's lives, and if you get tremendous satisfaction out of that, then proceed. But you must do this because you want to do good for other people, not to advance your own career. If you go into politics because you need the limelight and speaking to cameras and so on, or you walk with a swagger, don't do it. The public is not stupid. The public can see through you very quickly. And anyway, this is not the purpose of getting into politics. It's to make the society better, not to make your own career better.

If you look at this region of the world, what keeps you awake at night? What keeps you tossing and turning?

I think the issue would generally be the economic competitiveness of Singapore. And, of course, there are always issues such as security, terrorism, and what can go wrong with the whole region. I mean you've got to plan for it. But the economy is key. If you don't have a growing economy, challenging jobs, well-paying jobs, people will emigrate. Talent won't come. Your own talent will disappear and then the whole place will collapse. And even the security will be affected. And we worry about that because we have an aging population, which means you've got to bring in foreign workers, immigrants, permanent residents, to help give vitality to the workforce. But that creates its own dynamics. Sweden is now facing it; we are facing it; immigrants create unhappiness in the local population. So this issue worries us, getting the economy going and then dealing with the consequences of having immigrants coming in.

The climate change summit in Copenhagen in December 2009 was really the first time leaders were getting together to divvy up suffering. We're heading into a world that's resource poor. Because of that, there seems to be a shift that we have to make away from consumptive societies to something else. I wonder how you think we go about telling publics that they can't live as well as they did before the bubble collapsed, that all of that was financed on debt? And how do we go about reassessing the compact between governments and people that each generation will live better than the last?

I agree that in the democratic system in which people have to be elected, all too often they will tend to look at what will satisfy the people. Make sure of good growth, happy voters, and so on. At the same time, I think you would come across leaders who would say, "Look, this is important but it is not what is going to hold up a whole society." The society needs certain values. We need to change.

If you take Mrs. Margaret Thatcher—at one time she was going to change the whole system, get people to work hard. Or even in Europe, some leaders were coming to reassess the welfare system, saying you've got to change it. Of course, some succeeded better than others because the systems are so entrenched. But in the case of consumerism, I think that is something which we are aware of.

So, speaking about our own case, Singapore is a very consumerist society. People spend more. So from time to time, we have to remind them of the basic values that we must have. And the values would include, you've got to have skills. Education is important. Skills-training is for a lifetime, train and retrain. Secondly, you've got to work hard. We used to have the message that we should be very frugal; but that message now wouldn't appeal to anyone. I mean the old finance minister (Dr. Goh Keng Swee) was very frugal. He passed away recently. Lee Kuan Yew, too, was very frugal. I would say especially Lee Kuan Yew. In the prime minister's office he had a wooden chair and a cushion with a cover for visitors. That was it. So he emphasized these values.

What else did he impart to you in terms of values?

Oh, I mean not directly to me, but he said it all the time to the ministers. Integrity. Integrity. He said we have been in power for so long because we have not gone corrupt. So the day the PAP goes corrupt, that's the day when we will fall as a party. And, hopefully, there will be a good party coming in to take our place. If there isn't, then the whole place is gone. So he emphasized integrity again and again.

By integrity, he also meant your lifestyle. Don't live in a manner where the local population will say, "Oh, you are just flamboyant," and all kinds of behavior which the public would not be happy with. So just go around modestly. Nowadays, it's not so bad. We can drive our cars down to the constituency.

Frugal Lee wouldn't have that.

In the old days, he would say, "Look, if you must drive a car, please buy a small one if you go down to the constituency." Because you've got the poor there.

And you're a tall guy. Small cars are not fun.

Small cars would be quite funny for me. But my very first car was an Austin Mini Minor, because that was all I could afford.

Those are great cars.

Yes, a great car. It's all I could afford. People would think, "Such a tall guy for a small car." They were amazed when they saw me get out of the car.

In the years that you, as a younger member of his party, watched Lee Kuan Yew, do you recall a time that he did something when you disagreed with him?

There was something which he did. As a young man, I will not say I disagreed with him, but I would say I was taken aback by what he wanted to do and the boldness of it, when he was trying to address the question of [college] graduate mothers not having enough children. And he was a believer that you've got to have talent, and talent bringing forth more talent.

Basically, the idea was to have the best educated marry one another, and reproduce other intelligent people, so there would be more talent.

That's right. That was his basic argument. So we were all taken aback. Then he explained the reasons why. But, of course, I couldn't totally accept that theory. I mean, he believed in genetics, so two bright people will end up with a bright kid. But it's not proven. So that was a policy where we had tremendous debate. And I will say, not all agreed. I was more in the middle ground; I was not fully persuaded at the time. So he introduced a Social Development Unit, which is actually a government-sponsored matchmaking agency, but it was only for graduates.

A dating service?

Of course, a dating service, but only for graduates. This sparked controversy. I was at the time uncomfortable with this; it had political implications. If we do that, a number of nongraduates would be most unhappy. But he said, "No, if you want to be in charge, don't worry about politics, do things right." And so we started the Social Development Unit. It was quite worrying.

So this is a policy which took me by surprise and was unsettling, but when there is a trend that you worry about for the country, you have to tackle it. You have to solve it. You cannot just say, "Oh, this is too tricky, too sensitive politically. Don't do it." So you've got to do it. But in trying to do this, you must know that you have to have the political strength. He knew he had the strength. He knew the votes would come back, and he knew that twenty years down the road, we would say he was right. So that's the kind of lesson you learn.

One of the most striking things about Singapore is that your ruling party, the PAP, even if people know that it's going to remain in power, they still come out and vote by a fairly large margin for opposition candidates. They may only get two, three, four seats in the Parliament, but they'll still come out on the order of 35 to 40 percent of votes for the opposition.

Yes.

Isn't that disconcerting? In the United States, for instance, if you get 40 percent of the vote, you'd be president. In Israel you might be prime minister with even less. That's a considerable piece of your population.

Well, of course, I think we would like to have more votes. It's an indication of whether we are doing well or not. But we accept 30, 40 percent in the population voting against us as a given, because, at any one time, you must have in a society a core group unhappy with any government—whether it's over a problem with the transport system, or over immigration—and the people express their dissatisfaction with those policies. That doesn't mean the votes won't come back to us.

Take me back to that election night in 1991, when you ran on a platform of relaxing the paternalism of the state, and you did not do as well as you expected with the voters. How did Lee Kuan Yew treat you?

He accepted the results. Well, I mean you have got to admire the man. When he decided to hand over power, he gave it to me; he very wisely stepped back. And, then, if he had to give you some of his own observations or advice, then he would do it in a wise way, but he would always leave you with the thought, "If you are in charge, you decide. This is how I see things as somebody who has gone through the same path."

So his advice actually prior to my taking over—when I became minister and was chosen by my colleagues to be the leader—was, "You've got to govern Singapore very firmly. This is an Asian society. This is a conventional society so you've got to be firm in your governance." And he actually gave me a book by Machiavelli, *The Prince*. That was also before I became prime minister.

You said he made a worrier out of you.

Yes, yes.

And you came to support that view more often.

Worrier in the sense that you begin to understand that, as prime minister, you are always looking long term, looking for storms ahead, and so on. So in that sense, when you assumed the mantle of governance, you began to worry.

So, he made a worrier out of me because I've learned that in order to succeed, you have got to think not just in the short term, immediate gratification of the voters, but with a longer view. So you began to figure out how to communicate with the 30 percent of the people who don't agree with you.

The primary concern that comes from the West is that to have such a small group in control of power, historically speaking, one of three things happens: it becomes impossibly corrupt, or it becomes complacent, or it becomes warlike. Really, throughout modern history, that's what we've seen from groups on top of affluent societies run without opposition. What makes you different?

It's the political philosophy or culture, and the practice of it, which is important. And I would give full credit to Lee Kuan Yew, because he is the one who has run the system and he taught us about the necessity of keeping the system open to allow opposition. In other words, he wanted a group to be in charge but to never shut out the competition. So in case this group goes wrong, somebody else can dislodge us. We compete on abilities, compete on character, on integrity. The other way of keeping ourselves in position is our humility. So if you go to any office, you won't see the prime minister's photograph. You do not see Lee Kuan Yew's photograph.

And, in terms of our party headquarters, we rent a place as our headquarters. We're way out in the suburbs. You will have difficulty finding it. You will lose your way going there.

So, be very modest. We had a Chinese leader who came to study our system and spent some time over here and he commented, "The People's Action Party is everywhere but nowhere to be seen."

What is most interesting is the dynamic inside the party. Basically, like the fight that played out between communism and capitalism, any time you have true competition, you get better ideas and more energetic people. How do you keep competition existing within that monolith, and how do you keep power from getting too consolidated behind one person or idea?

Well, I think each time after an election, we look around for people to come and join the party. If there is somebody new and considered very good in terms of his intelligence, but has expressed views against us from time to time, we ask: Is that person pro-Singapore and just against us on some issues, or is he just anti-us all the time? If you got somebody who is critical, we try to co-opt that person and then get the person to understand that in Singapore, whoever is in charge has got to deal with these problems. It's just a small country, situated in a place that was not geographically stable all the time in the past. So we get them to understand the problems, to try and bring them in.

We try to institutionalize the system so that we don't have a bad government being returned through a freak election result.

Meaning another party? So you would reject that?

No, we cannot reject it. We've got to accept it. Over time, can we carry on, maintaining this high-quality system? We have an elected presidency, which I introduced when I became prime minister. Basically, before this, the president did not have discretionary power. He had to act on the advice of the cabinet. But we made a change so that he is vested with discretionary powers in two areas. One is the protection of reserves not accumulated by the present government. After an election, all the surpluses we have in the budget will go into reserves so the next government cannot use it, even if it's the same party, even if it's the same prime minister. You've got to start all over again to generate your revenue, your surpluses, to fund your present programs, to protect your reserves. This is to prevent a government, whether it's the same People's Action Party or a new government, from using populist policies to win votes. Because it is too tempting to just use populist policies to win votes, but can you sustain the policies? What will be the consequence? So the president we hope, being elected by the people, would say, "No, you can't use the reserves to fund your populist policies."

Secondly, in the employment of key people in the civil service, the members of the Public Service Commission were responsible for careful identification of people for recruitment and for promotion in a professional, objective way. The members would have to be approved by the president. The chief of the armed forces plus other service chiefs must be approved by the president. Chief of police, auditor-general, accountant-general, judges, all these key appointments have to be approved by the president. So we have put in place a system to ensure that as much as possible, the government will remain good.

But even in choosing those who can run for president, there is, to some extent, a selection process. And it doesn't change the fact that both you and Lee, as prime ministers, could have simply stayed and nobody would have had the power to challenge you and say, "No, it's time to leave."

That is true, Lee could have stayed.

You couldn't have?

I could have stayed but I could be challenged. Supposing I stayed too long, I think the deputy prime minister could have challenged me. Supposing I overstayed, he might have that power. But had Lee decided to stay, I do not think I would have at that time the necessary political strength to challenge him. We are speaking frankly here. Let's recognize that he was a founder of Singapore.

He is a strong, wise man. It's difficult to challenge him, even if I had wanted to. And the older generations recognize his contribution to Singapore; so a debt of gratitude is there. So it's not easy.

Let me ask you a question about the economy. Obviously, you guys have done an incredible job, built an unbelievable economy that's very stable and multifaceted. One of the staples though remains manufacturing. And having achieved what you've achieved to become a first-world state, you have the unenviable task of competing with Germany, Japan, the United States, and that inevitably means you need to innovate, right?

Yes, correct.

Speaking with a number of business people here, and others involved in venture capital, they're amazed at the amount of money that is going in and the lack of results that have come out. And part of the argument they make is that societies in which you see great innovation, a lot of those innovators are rebels. They are people that wouldn't succeed in a place like Singapore. Does that worry you?

No. There are two types of innovation. I think one type is not so much by the rebels. This is where you have the R&D in biomedical sciences, the people in the laboratory looking at small things, peering through microscopes and so on. Those are not rebels. Those are researchers. They may discover new things. I think we encourage spending a lot of money in that sector.

So the question you ask, does it worry us, meaning will we lose power because people think out of the box? I say no. I think we need such people and we encourage them.

But do you agree with the assessment that a lot of times, those people come from the fringes? They're inherently people that sometimes don't finish college and, often, wouldn't get great jobs and would only succeed in a place that has a culture of risk?

I agree. In the US society where many people can't make it to university, many often succeed as entrepreneurs. Or like Bill Gates.

Everybody says he is a university dropout but he decided to do so to go into IT, risking a lot. That culture is not quite here, I will grant you that. We still tend to place more emphasis on the traditional route of education. You go to university. You get a good degree. You get a good job. Maybe partly because the market is too small in Singapore. In the United States, if you take risks and succeed, the market is huge. So this is an area where we should do more and I think the present government is trying to find out how we can do more in terms of innovation and creativity.

And, I could add, it is partly for this reason that we actually liberalized the arts scene. In the old days, humanities were soft subjects. They say, "Better study, invest in engineering, and so on. Arts, literature—ahh, what a waste of time." That was twenty years ago. Then you realize that you've got to move into this kind of innovative society. You have to move in that direction for Singapore. You need people with a certain creative flair who look at things differently. So we began to put more funds into the arts, both to create a softer environment for people working here, a more enjoyable environment, but also because you begin to recognize that you need people who think differently from us.

Just as Pervez Musharraf argues, for billions living in the developing world, political rights and democracy are second-tier concerns compared with financial well-being. Though 40 percent of the public in Singapore may vote against the PAP in an election, the vote is, for many citizens, merely a referendum on specific policies, a grandiose poll on the ruling party's work. Nearly all of the observers I spoke with agree that the nation, if faced with an authentic vote to keep or dislodge the PAP, would support the party by an even larger margin. The stability and advancement many of us in the West take for granted is decidedly less certain to Singaporeans—particularly those who lived through the nation's ascent—and its continuity matters above all else.

But, in the words of Harvard economist Dani Rodrik, "For every Lee Kuan Yew of Singapore, there are many like Mobutu Sese Seko of the Congo."[10] Though liberal, open democracy has proven frustratingly slow to lift populations out of poverty, authoritarians have rarely proven adroit. Singapore has been the exception rather than the rule, and both the island and China face a volatile future as growth wanes in coming decades.

From Goh, I take a lesson on the division of power. He compared himself to an excellent doubles player and echoed what others have suggested about the diffuse nature of great leadership. Several of these figures, particularly those who have also served in cabinet posts, noted that the legwork of translating doctrine into policy rests with ministerial heads. Presidents and prime ministers must craft that vision and inspire their appointees, but, more often than not, the labor of implementation resides with finance ministers and foreign ministers, secretaries of defense and education. John Edwards, an Australian journalist and former economic advisor to Prime Minister Paul Keating, noted in his book that his boss—like his three predecessors—"discovered that having the top job in the cabinet gave him some influence over all his ministers but control over none."[11]

Gro Brundtland urged leaders to trust their cabinet colleagues and not to avoid difficult decisions, as doing so stifles the entire bureaucracy beneath. The sheer number of choices a leader must make in a single day can be staggering; George W. Bush often called himself "the decider." Former White House chief of staff Rahm Emanuel said that, by December 2009, less than a year into the presidency, he and President Obama simply "didn't want to make another decision, or choice, or judgment." The pair joked that when it was all over, they would open a shop facing the beach in Hawaii and sell only one type of T-shirt. They took to opening staff meetings with Obama saying "white," and Emanuel replying "medium."[12]

Lee Kuan Yew, in the 1980s, said that Australia was fated to become the "poor white trash of Asia." Its economy was, in Paul Keating's words, an "industrial museum." Nonetheless, amid the global financial collapse, Australia and its government in Canberra found itself largely inured. "This is boomtown right now," one former Labor Party economist told me in Sydney during July 2010, "even if nobody realizes it." Unemployment was at 5.5 percent and falling;

interest rates on three-month treasury bills were at a robust 4.95 percent. Australia, tucked away in its own little corner of the globe, had managed to escape the avalanche of global financial collapse.

More than anyone else, Paul Keating bears responsibility for that success.

Chapter Thirteen

CANBERRA'S MAESTRO

PAUL JOHN KEATING

PRIME MINISTER
OF AUSTRALIA
1991–1996

July 2010

PAUL KEATING, THE AUSTRALIAN treasurer, launched his coup on a dreary Thursday evening, May 30, 1991. Hours before, he took questions from reporters in an anteroom of the Parliament, most all of them on economic forecasts, which had been released at 3 P.M. that day and suggested growth would resume after three years of recession. None of the journalists inquired about the unusual timing of the figures' release. As he waited to see Bob Hawke, the prime minister he intended to depose, he paced furiously, slapping his palm with a ruler. He knew that the story would break on the evening news at 6 P.M. and he needed to reach the prime minister before then, but Hawke was tied up in meetings. As Laurie Brereton, one of Keating's advisors, urged him to barge into the prime minister's office, the phone on Keating's desk rang. "Mate," came Hawke's raspy voice on the line. Keating walked down the hall to his office. "I always told you I'd let you know when I was going to come at you," Keating told him, "and now it's on." He continued, "We have been the strength of the show, but now the wheels have fallen off."[1]

THERE IS SOMETHING INTENSELY falcon-like about Keating, both in appearance and demeanor. He is tall, with an angular face that is mirrored by the wide and peaked lapels of his preferred double-breasted Zegna suits. He is part hustler, part blue-collar tinkerer; as treasurer, he pulled apart a Jaguar E-type engine and reassembled it.

In the early eighties, he and Hawke had worked together near seamlessly, fusing Hawke's popularity with Keating's vision for reform. "It was difficult to tell where one ended and where the other began," a former aide noted. Keating would often approach Hawke with half-baked ideas, to which Hawke's enthusiasm would quickly adhere. Together, they liberalized the economy and pulled it into the modern era. In 1983 they freed the currency from state control over valuation; in 1984 they deregulated the banking industry. They slashed the budget and the economy boomed as debt became cheap, precariously doubling compared with GDP in the second half of the 1980s.[2]

But beneath the surface—then later clearly above board—a Shakespearean drama was at play. As the economic boom of the mid-1980s withered to recession, so too did the rapport between the pair, who, despite being political allies, had never become personal friends.

Keating has always shown reverence for the sophisticated and old. He found refuge in Christie's auction catalogs as treasurer and prime minister, and his home and office are filled with antiques. He has a particular affection for Regency clocks and furniture from the neo-classical period of the early nineteenth century.[3] For years, he has blocked off Saturday afternoons to listen to classical music; Gustav Mahler and Richard Strauss and the conductor Otto Klemperer are favorites. When he was twenty-four and engulfed in what he would later call the hardest campaign of his life, and then later, when canvassing the constituency, he would return home and listen to Chopin. "I'd come back, I would sometimes think I was amongst savages," he recalled, "and I'd put this on. Next thing I'm in the world, the wonderful world of music."[4]

Hawke, on the other hand, was a hard-drinking and womanizing Aussie's Aussie. He once held the Guinness Book record for the fastest consumption of a yard glass of beer—roughly two and a half pints in eleven seconds. The relationship with Keating was complicated by Hawke's affair with his biographer, a journalist named Blanche d'Alpuget, that began in the late 1970s and rekindled in his years at the prime minister's Lodge in Canberra. It was further stressed in 1984, when Hawke's pregnant daughter was diagnosed as a heroin addict.

BY 1988, THE TWO were at war. Hawke suggested publicly that his treasurer was replaceable, then walked back on the statement; Keating threatened to leave, only for Hawke, with two witnesses present, to promise to retire after the 1990 election. That never happened. Only Annita Keating, Paul's wife, a Dutch flight attendant he had courted around the world and brought back to Canberra, had doubted the prime minister at his word.

By 1991, Keating, after eight and half years in the "engine room" of government, had grown restless. His coup in May of that year failed. He lost by 22 votes in the 110-member caucus and retreated to the backbenches of Parliament, where he spent the next six months. He drew inspiration from Winston Churchill. In his memoir, John Edwards, an economics advisor, recalls that Keating would flop into a chair in his sunny office and cite bits from the Churchill biography he was reading: "He was there so long" on the backbenches, Keating said of Churchill, "that a new generation of Tories came in and laughed at him when he spoke." He continued on about how the British conservatives hated Churchill for liking Jews and for not admiring Hitler: "I don't have any heroes, because when you get to my age you realize they all have flaws, but if anything Churchill was a hero, the way he fought his party for seven years," Keating told Edwards.[5]

Without Keating as its backbone, the Labor Party stumbled. The government quickly burned through two treasurers, and as a Conservative takeover appeared plausible, more of the Labor Party turned back to Paul, and his sharp elbows. "No one could chew up the opposition like Keating," Don Watson wrote. "The colleagues could complain, mutter that he was a liability, but no-one made them feel better than Keating on the attack."[6] There's an entire website devoted to Keating's best quips from parliamentary debate, and though he left office before the YouTube era dawned, a number of clips have found their way to the Internet. He called the opposition "pansies," and referred to the Conservative shadow treasurer as "Rosy," a jab at his boyishly blush cheeks.[7] "His performance is like being flogged with a warm lettuce," he famously said of an opponent, and he referred to John Howard as the "brain-dead leader of the opposition."[8]

Biographer Paul Kelly wrote, "Keating ran free from the party but the party could not afford to lose Keating. So Keating dared it to follow."[9] Keating again challenged Hawke in December 1991 and won by five votes. Hawke's parting advice was twofold: First, give your ministers room to run, and, second, get close to the electorate. "I had those characteristics," Hawke noted to the press. "Paul will have to learn to acquire them."[10]

ALONGSIDE HIS TALENT COMES profound confidence, extending often to arrogance. In 1986, amid the economic reforms, he told reporters, "You will never live through—while ever you are in parliament I'm sure—changes greater in magnitude and quality than you are reporting now." Nonetheless, one is drawn to Keating. An ego that should be reviling is instead intriguing, perhaps diluted by quirkiness and wit and an affable front.

Beneath the haughty words, many feel, lies insecurity. Keating left school at fifteen; when he entered the parliament at twenty-five he found himself surrounded by a political elite. Keating was always in the top third of his class at school, but often just barely. As a young member of the Labor Party, he took to spending time with Jack Lang, a fiery and egotistical former governor of New South Wales who had been struck down during the Depression years. Lang had divided the Labor Party and was one of the least popular politicians in the nation, but the pair lunched together twice a week as Keating culled Lang's mind for political insight and history. Lang explained that it was critical to own both policy and proposal, and told the young Keating that "some politicians were people of weight and substance and some were skyrockets who issued a great shower of sparks but 'a dead stick always fell to the ground.'"[11] The words stuck with Keating.

IN THE WEEKS BEFORE we met, Keating's relationship with Hawke devolved still further. A made-for-TV biopic aired, largely redacting Keating from the political triumphs of the 1980s. Hawke, who left his wife, Hazel, beloved by the Australian public, to marry mistress Blanche d'Alpuget in 1995, was a consultant for the film and worked through the script line by line.

Keating now keeps a quiet office just above Elizabeth Bay, on a tree-lined street in Sydney's eastern suburbs. The building was raised in the 1830s, and the dark floorboards feel solid and satisfyingly antiquated beneath one's loafers. The loft is remote; so removed, in fact, that when I asked a nearby shopkeeper for directions, she did not know where to find the address, nor that Keating kept an office in the area.

I'd like to start by asking about the imbalances in the global economy, because one can't really speak about the rise of Asia or other challenges of the day without addressing it.

Well, I think we're in a new paradigm. We're in the paradigm where everyone is deleveraging. Individuals are deleveraging, companies are deleveraging, banks are lending less, and now governments are deleveraging. The question is who's going to be spending, and the answer is many fewer people. So this is going to bring us into a new normal, and that new normal is going to be a much slower-growth world.

Europe is about 18 or 19 trillion of GDP. It's going to grow at under 1 percent, so its net contribution to world wealth may be 150 billion this year. The United States is—what, 14 trillion? It will be growing at less than its trend, right at 2.5 percent, probably 2, which will be 280 billion, call it 250 billion or 300 billion. China is 6 trillion but growing at 10 percent, so its contribution is going to be twice that; it will be 600 billion of new wealth but, fundamentally, I don't believe that it's sustainable. And Japan, of course, will grow at probably 1.5 or 1 percent which is another 60 billion in new wealth.

So if you look at Europe with a small contribution to world growth, US diminished contribution to world growth, China, large for the moment, Japan pretty ordinary. What's all this mean? Diminished demand everywhere. What does this suggest? It suggests we need a new global financial settlement. It suggests we need to see the savings countries spending more and saving less, and we need the borrower countries—the US, Britain, Australia, Spain, countries like that—we need them saving more and spending less. But, to date, there's been no fundamental shift in the underlying forces of the global imbalances that brought on the crisis. That is, the saver countries are still saving—Germany, Japan, China, the Middle East. The borrower countries are still spending, but the spending is now being done by governments, not individuals or companies, and that can't continue.

So the question becomes, how do you iron that out, how do we start even addressing this?

This is called leadership. This is why you have politicians. Politicians run your life from the cradle to the grave, and this is why the G20 matters for the first time. We've got the debtor and the creditor nations sitting together. What we have to do, though, is induce a change. See, what the natural savers do—Germany and Japan—and, now, the unnatural savers—China—what they do is they vendor-finance their exports. They outsource their demand to the industrial countries. Demand should be satisfied at home. So they're like giant high-purchase companies. They sell the goods and they give you the credit to go with it, except that the borrowing cannot continue because of the general indebtedness of the communities of the industrial states. So we're going to reach a point when the stimulus has wound down and governments can't take up the demand that was formerly there from individuals and companies. That's crunch time.

We're close to that moment.

That's not far away.

So if you're in the Oval Office, half the country says we need austerity, half says we need stimulus. Where to from here?

I think there's another commentary worth making, and that is, from the time that conservatives started depressing American real wages, which is like thirty-odd years ago, we started seeing the portents of this crisis because, particularly through the 1990s, the great leap in productivity in the United States, a paradigm shift in productivity, none of it went to wages. It all went to profits. It went to the top 10 percent of the community, and 60 percent of that went to the top 1 percent of the community.

So working Americans have had to indebt themselves to maintain their living standards as housing prices have risen, as the cost of living has risen. And, it is to those people, finally, as a source of demand, that the big integrated investment banks turned to to sell mortgages. And those mortgages turned out to be mortgages that couldn't be serviced—now they have the title subprime. But why were they subprime? Why weren't these people able to pay a mortgage, why, in modern America, can't you buy a home and finance it out of wages? Because of the essential inequity that has entered the American distribution of income.

That is, I say, the strength of conservatism vis-à-vis unions, and the ability of unions to garner a high share of national income for their members, and in many respects, the failure of the Democratic

Party. For instance, in Australia with the Labor Party, we've had, in the same period—it was since 1992—a 30 percent real increase in wages. So Australian working people had 30 percent more wages. That's why here they're wealthier.

So President Obama has inherited a problem that has been a long time in the making. The so-called great compression that arose out of the Roosevelt years and the Eisenhower and Nixon years—in which the highest incomes and lowest incomes were not that far apart, factors of ten or something—that great compression has been shattered. This leaves open a big question: Can America continue to go on like this? That is, can you build a cohesive, politically stable society in which the larger part of the population misses out, and the real jewel goes to the top 1 percent or top 10 percent? It's because of these underlying problems that President Obama is now inserting government demand into the equation to get America out of a recession. Because, in the end, there isn't the puff, the spending power, amongst the population. So he's been dealt a very tough hand.

But the question is, can he shift that now, or how does he attempt to shift it? That's one question. He has supported the development of the G20. This is a very great challenge. Before that, we had the shocking conceit that you can run the world from Western Europe, from the G8. Now, at least, it is a more representative world structure. Having got the representation in the world structure, we're now going to have to make that world structure work. And this does mean that the saver states—Germany, Japan, China, the Middle Eastern—have to induce more consumption in their societies or accept the fact that they're not going to be able to sell their vendor-finance goods, because American households, Australian households, British households can't take on more consumer debt to buy their products. So the endgame is coming. Better if President Obama's the steward for this change.

Let's go back to Australia and the subprime mortgage crisis, the toxic assets that poisoned banks around the world. You've mentioned before that you went from having 1 bank in the top 50 to 4 in the top 15. Was it something you built into the banking deregulation, or was it simply a better banker, a better mentality that was more averse to these financial instruments from the United States, that protected you when so many international banks fell prey to this?

I just would not fall for the nonsense, simple as that. The idea that I would let them join the casino, because I knew whenever they got into trouble, the moral hazard would end up with me. So I left banks in Australia to do what banks can do well enough, if they are limited to that, and that is, lend for housing and lend to corporations, mostly small ones. But I wouldn't let them lend their funds to hedge funds, wouldn't let them into proprietary trading. And I didn't allow any of them to take over one another.

So, therefore, because they were protected from takeover, the result was that managements did not try and do foolish things to grow by acquisition, because they legally couldn't take one another over. They had to grow organically. The end result was that we ended up with four solid commercial banks. And the managements at that time had fresh in their minds the recession of 1990, so there was some prudence on their part. But, basically, I rejected the plans to get bigger here to go out to the world.

I said to one of them, "So let me paraphrase your policy, you want to grow by acquisition at home, you want to be uncompetitive at home so you can be competitive abroad? Is that it? Did I get it right the first time?" I said, "What will happen, you will fatten up here and you will waddle out to the world and be slain, so don't give me the nonsense."

But, of the liberal democracies, you were about the only ones that—

I was the only one that understood to pierce through the screen of the financial market nonsense. You know, these guys are pretty ordinary, most of them. Give them an ordinary job to do and they go and do it. The moment commercial banks start to be clever, they start chewing the shareholders' wealth.

And did you ever have conversations with other heads of state about how precarious the path was?

No, but you expect people to have some real-world understanding. I mean, I was aghast when I heard Alan Greenspan in these congressional hearings say he was shocked to see the management of commercial banks and integrated investment banks were not doing as he thought they would do, to protect shareholders' wealth. Well, the thing is, if you are that unworldly wise, what are you doing running a central bank?

Let's shift gears—do you recall the most solemn moment of your career, the particularly lowest ebb?

Yeah, I think probably defeating Hawke, my predecessor. My predecessor had long run out of intellectual puff. And so in the end, I could have simply walked away, but to have done so was to sell myself out, and to let the system go on in a compromised way. And in the end, I thought, not just honor demands, but integrity demands, that this can't go on. Now, if the Labor Party made a choice, ultimately between two people—I mean I would've accepted that choice.

You did. And then the government fell apart.

Then it fell apart because my underlying assumption was right, that left to his own devices that it was not enough. He was not able to carry on, and we would have certainly been defeated at the following election. So that was probably the most solemn.

You have said before that you probably wouldn't write a book because "history takes care of itself whatever the participants might wish."[12]

I think that it's hard enough doing the work over a decade and a half without being required to write it down as well. That is, the energy required to do this stuff is so profound that it only, if you like, becomes legitimized if you actually write the book as well. Really? Should it be like that, really? Or should the work stand on its own account?

Now, what's happening with Hawke, I think, more driven by his wife perhaps than himself, is a need, nearly twenty years since his departure from office, to bring a new recap to events, relying on the fact that a lot of people's memories have sort of faded.

Well, that's all right if you can get away with it. The getting away with it is the hard part. See, I have written no books; I've had no essays. I've done none of this stuff, because there is a great coalescence between Hawke's instincts and my own, and I required of him mostly instinct rather than executive direction. And I was more or less happy to leave this opaque, but he was not happy to live with opaque.

After his daughter was recognized as being an addict in 1984, and he slumped into a depression, what did your relationship look like for the next three years?

Well, I think that Hawke was an alcoholic, and he famously gave up the alcohol for the prime ministership. But what makes someone an alcoholic? They become an alcoholic, I think, when they find it difficult to face life with all its complexities and pressures. So he had these periods in his life when he would, at the short hand, break down. The problem was that he broke down at The Lodge. It may have been his daughter's addiction, that may have been the trigger point—but it was not the reason for the breakdown. I think the reasons would be the underlying reason for earlier breakdowns.

And in the earlier breakdowns, Hawke would be cared for and put back together by his wife, Hazel. The problem was, in this breakdown I became the Hazel. And I was prepared to be quiet about it and not talk about it, as I am now—but he and his new wife are prepared to write the book about it, and they have to be honest about the period he wants to write about. That's all.

This must have been rather disconcerting at the time. Wasn't it alarming to see him discombobulated and dysfunctional?

Well, yes, but again, when we were in office he enjoyed enormous popularity, therefore the doer—and I thought I was—had a lot of drawdown rights on that popularity. In other words, there's a bank of public goodwill which you need to make the changes. So, what's the most important thing? Replacing the prime minister, or drawing down the public goodwill to continue to make the changes?

I mean, it was critical, from the 1983 currency float on—

From 1984 to 1988, through this period. So I took the latter choice; that is, I took the drawdown rights—it was the maintenance of Hawke as a prime minister with reasonable instincts and a lot of public support. That meant I was still able to do things, but I had then to get along with him and manage him.

You mentioned in one of your speeches about a year ago that you rec-
ognized that you had come to power in a moment of rare standstill.
Do you think that, in the longer run of history, this generation will
be judged harshly for not achieving more in that moment?

I think so. In the epiphany at the end of the twentieth century,
the end of the Cold War, the collapse of the Berlin Wall, there was the
great opportunity, the first since 1914, to recut the world into a more
cooperative, representative structure. Essentially, that opportunity
was missed. It was missed on four American presidential terms—the
two Clinton terms, the two Bush terms.

Liberal internationalism, which played so well for America during the Cold War years, virtually stopped in the early 1990s. President
Obama is returning to liberal internationalism and multilateralism
for the first time in 16 presidential years. That meant that all the opportunities of open regionalism, dealing with nuclear weapons and
nuclear proliferation, were broadly opportunities that were missed.

You might know that I set up a body called the Canberra Commission on the Elimination of Nuclear Weapons, and one of the
things I said at that time was—I'm talking about 1995—I said, "The
West gave the world nuclear weapons and the West is still in the position to take them away. But this won't remain." Because they're
now gone, that opportunity is gone. And how heartening it is to see
President Obama now take these issues up. Because one of the great
matters I can never quite ever understand was why the American
right, people who knew of America's predominance in weapons of
accuracy and conventional power and forward projection, would let
themselves be leveled down by any punk state with a cheap and dirty
nuclear weapon?

You see, there can be no nonproliferation without de-proliferation. You can't say we, the good guys of the Second World War, have
a right to have nuclear weapons, but all these other people do not.
That's not a policy.

So the only effective policy is to be rid of them: de-proliferation.
The cost of America not taking up that policy—of being rid of nukes
and having the moral authority to stop everybody, including North

Korea and Iran as well as, of course, the Pakistanis and the Indians and the Israelis—has been, we need to keep the deterrent capacity. But the deterrent capacity becomes a moot thing when you see, as we're doing this very day, American defense officials talking about the need to protect the United States' cities from a potential Iranian nuclear strike.

I mean deterrence only runs to a certain point. Far better to take nuclear weapons out of the calculation. That hasn't happened, but President Obama is now doing what he can to reinvigorate the Nuclear Nonproliferation Treaty and to stop their further proliferation, but there are a lot of horses that have left the gate.

There are a lot of horses that left the gate and we also see the limits of his power. The cuts with Russia are fairly modest when you get behind the numbers. It really only cuts 200 to 300 of the over 4,000 deployed weapons between the two countries.

Well, that's another, I think, mistake in policy. Gorbachev agreed to a united Germany in NATO; he agreed to the Wall coming down. He agreed to a united Germany in NATO. And within six years of his agreeing, the Clinton administration agreed to Poland and Hungary and the Czech Republic joining NATO. Given that 26 million Russians died establishing the *cordon sanitaire* between Germany and the Soviet Union, you can understand why many Russians saw this as a very hostile act.

I always said if you want to help Hungary, Poland, and the Czech Republic, let them join the European Union. But, at the time, because of the prairies of Poland and the common agriculture policy, nobody wanted to be subsidizing Polish grain in the EU, so they gave them the hand-me-down prize, the second prize of joining NATO.

Foreign policy realism demands that great states be accommodated. Russia is a great state. It has been a great state for most of the last 500 years. It has the biggest landmass in the world, it has an enormous mineral wealth, and it has its own national aspirations. Remembering that the Soviet Union was part of the victory in the Second World War over Nazism, a policy at the end of the Cold War should have included a place for Russia, but it didn't. As a consequence, we've had this sniping going on from the Russians. And then the idea of putting a missile shield in their backyard just made it worse.

The trick is to manage the world. I think with President Obama, his election was the last opportunity the United States had of getting a seat at the big table as the first amongst equals for the next fifty years, because it was reaching a point—by unilateralism and exceptionalism—where it was being pushed aside. By bringing the United States into the main flow of the world and in cooperative structures like the G20 and by reviving liberal internationalism, I think President Obama—in the nick of time—has put the United States back in the seat for the next half century.

But he can disappear as quickly as he came now.

Maybe.

The question that comes from all of this is: How do you move in such a way that you reach beyond what people think is really possible? One of the things that's phenomenal, I think, in reading books about you is that you were pushing hard steps. You weren't just giving out tax cuts. These are difficult things—

Just a complete remodeling. The Australian economy was completely remodeled.

But there's an adage in American politics that nobody gets elected by promising to raise taxes. It's very hard to sell people on painful decisions. What skill do you think you possess that enabled you to do that?

I had belief and energy and I have integrity. The worst that can happen in public life is you lose your job, so why conduct your life as a weakling? Why conduct your life as somebody who lives on polls? I believed that the better thing to do was a "policy streak" through the crowd. And the chances are the crowd would let you do it. But if you show you are afraid of them—or worse, that you are not really earnest—they then start reacting against that.

An informed community does want intelligent change. The political system underestimates the communities' general intelligence. That's what I think. One of the things I tried to do here was have a completely open conversation with the community about Australia's reasonably dire economic prospects in the 1980s as a rust-bucket industrial economy tucked away in the bottom of the southern hemisphere. You see, if you're in the middle of big markets, if we were Holland or Sweden, you pick up unearned commerce out of those markets. If you're Canada, you get the froth out of the United States. In Australia, this doesn't happen.

So we had to recognize that the day of reckoning was coming, and by taking the community into a long conversation—it really went for 13 years—the remedial changes were such that this is now one of the most supple economies in the world. The reason the Australian economy has gone through the global financial crisis without a recession is because of its flexibility and all of the industries' flexibility. The exchange rate, wages, the product markets are the result of the 1980s and 1990s changes. So these things can happen, but when the spin takes over then—i.e., the changes are not made—the public starts their long process of disenchantment.

It's a terrifying thing, and it's something that has come up again and again in these interviews: that spin fuels that disenchantment. That, in a paradoxical way, getting more information to people should have led to a more informed public and made democracy work better. But, in reality, it has probably made things harder. People get snippets. People think they understand issues, but it's very easy for them to be deceived.

I don't think so. I think they've got more information and they're better for it.

Really?

I think they're much smarter for it. The political system plays them as fools; this is a great mistake. They're not. They will respond if talked up to. You see, if you look at the disquiet about President Obama, it's not because he wanted to change health care, it's just because he wanted to do it and seemingly didn't know how, or backed off. If you look at Kevin Rudd, the outgoing prime minister here, it's not that people didn't believe in carbon remediation; it's just that they were supporting him and then he backed off. And, as a consequence, their confidence in the government dropped right away.

So I think that "the streak" is premium. You have the big policy and you keep on going through the crowd, and the moment you stop to wonder or look back, you end up like Lot's wife. This is a problem. So I think that the policies and the targets have got to be good ones, right? In other words, you take on a policy that has a beginning, a middle, and an end, that has completion, that can be executed. See, one of the things I think we could say about these changes here was that they were executed, they were actually done. They were taken on and done. That means when you begin to take them on, you've got to be able to see an endpoint where you can complete them. Once you have the endpoint in focus, the rest of it is simply getting there and taking the public with you, and taking other parts of the political system with you.

But politics is an ideas market; he who runs the ideas runs the market. So if a party or an individual has the ideas, they will have primacy. But they've got to want it. They've got to press ahead instead of looking at the second term or looking at the next parliament. See, in Australia the parliament is [elected for] three years, so if you want to be cautious, it means you never do anything.

But inevitably there had to have been moments when your ideas felt like they were too small, when you lost confidence in yourself.

Well, I think as a political leader, you need a large dose of unearned confidence. I had it and President Obama has it. What you hope to do is turn that bucket of unearned confidence into earned confidence. But if you don't have the confidence in the first place, you cannot win. You cannot win. So you have to keep building a stock of energy.

Let's look at that bucket for a moment. People posit that your confidence came from your mother and that it came from your ex-wife. Where do you think it came from?

I think in my case it probably came from my grandmother and mother. They'd say even if no one else thinks you're special, you are.

They said that?

No, but that's the essence of their message. Even if you may be uncertain, or no one thinks you are special, you are. And this is a different thing from ego; it's not about ego. It's about having a sense that the question about your inner soul doesn't have to be asked. You can go on and do other things in which a lot of people will doubt, will always be asking the question about inner strength or inner being. And I think from there on, one has to look for inspiration to build things.

You might have read that—if you're reading about me—I love music, you know.

When I had big things on, I would listen to music—mostly classical. And I'd start on—it might be—the Second Movement of Mendelssohn's violin concerto or something sweet, and then move up to—it might be—a song, one of the later songs by Strauss or Mahler. Then I'd move up to one of the symphonies, and then finally I'd be on Mahler's Sixth Symphony or No. 9 or something. And, of course, what it does is, it says: So great are these people, so extraordinarily great are these people, beyond the ability of all the rest of us, that you say, "what I'm doing is nothing compared to this. So I've got to do better. I must do better."

You see, I think what the music did for me was it made me do better. In other words, it does inspire, it does truly open up your head and do things. Whereas, if you are simply overtaken by the paper, that is, the briefings, the material, the staffing, if you are overtaken, then you cannot see the main battlefield. You cannot see the main game. I think you must be able to see the main game. So, I would—

So you've talked about writing things down, how this was your time to—

That's right. What happened—well, you must have read some—as I was listening, stuff would come to me and I'd write it out—because I'd feel better, because I'd be going, I'd be reaching. But, you see, a lot of people have never had a truly emotional experience with the arts.

You think so?

A lot of people, yeah. Normally, they'll support the arts or go to music, to concerts, to ballets, to operas, and they'll be entertained. But they don't have the deep, emotional contact. I think music is definitely the highest form of the arts. Don Watson once said to me, "I think that's debatable." I said, Don, if you think that's debatable, you've never had an emotional contact with the arts, truly, because you couldn't say that and say it's debatable. It's beyond debate.

I read a book about Einstein and Max Planck—and Planck invites Einstein around to dinner, and he says, "Now Einstein, tonight of course our guest here is Mahler, and I want you to be courteous to him, not speak across the table, not drown out the conversation because, Einstein, you and I are mere mathematicians, this man is with the gods." And this would be right. This is a notation taken down by his daughter. You see they understood the greatness. With all of the computing power in the world, with all the cleverness unleashed by it, who can write a Bruckner Eighth Symphony or a Mahler Ninth Symphony today?

And as you scan back through those years, can you tie specific ideas to pieces of music?

No, I don't think I can, but I had a set of ideas. You asked what got me on this, what sustains you. What sustains you is first of all the confidence, the inner belief in the work you are doing. But through the thicket of objections, there has to be a greater locomotive power, and, mostly, it's not within you. It's got to be in you, but it's got to come from somewhere else; you have to build it.

In my case, it was music and history and some literature. You've brought up something about Churchill; people are surprised I admire Churchill. Churchill was an Edwardian conservative, but he had a moral clarity about him that other people around him didn't have. Roosevelt in the same way remodeled the world and remodeled the United States. The power of one, you see, inner belief—Churchill became prime minister, was given the job by the British establishment. His job was to do a deal with Hitler, to recognize Hitler's hegemony over Western Europe, and he said, "no." And on that "no" went Western civilization.

So the inner being really matters, as core strengths really matter. And while remodeling the Australian economy of—at the time—15 million people is not like fighting the greatest army in Europe in the 1940s, nevertheless, the principles of leadership and policy clarity, moral clarities do matter. It's the energy you must have because, otherwise, the policy is phony. The attempt becomes phony because it ends up poll-driven or informed in some way.

The best leaders, in the mold of Churchill and Roosevelt, are often "bullies with a vision."[13] It is an apt description of Paul Keating, too.

Keating conveys a sense of the ferocity essential to succeed, but also the harmony essential to maintaining sanity. "If I were writing a letter, to a successor," former British prime minister John Major told me in London, "I would first say, keep a hinterland. Don't become so obsessed with politics. Not only will it affect you, it will affect your judgment. Keep a hinterland."[14]

Barack Obama, while running for president in July 2008, stopped in London on a trip to Kenya. A live microphone caught a private conversation between him and David Cameron, the current British prime minister. A Clinton official, Obama said, had told him that "the most important thing you need to do is to have big chunks of time during the day when all you're doing is thinking."

"These guys just chalk your diary up," Cameron replied. "We call it the dentist's waiting room."

"And, well, and you start making mistakes, or losing the picture," Obama said.[15]

The premium on a leader's time is magnificent, but keeping a hinterland, the place and room and energy to think, is absolutely critical. One wonders if Obama has managed to follow his own advice. Effective leadership is vision, judgment, and communication. The pace at which most leaders live clouds all three, sometimes damningly so.

CONCLUSION

At the hinge marked by the close of the Cold War, Francis Fukuyama wrote a wildly popular book—an expansion of a piece written for *Foreign Affairs*—titled *The End of History and the Last Man*. Rather than the sprawling communist utopia that Karl Marx had envisioned, the triumph of liberal democracy and the free market, Fukuyama argued, was the final phase of political evolution.

It was a false dawn. History did not end, nor did it slow much, either. We have since witnessed the resurgence of authoritarian capitalism, and managing the flow of capital and commerce between nations has proved a terrific challenge, as has striking a proper balance between regulation and openness. The economic integration of the European Union—an advance that Fukuyama thought might prove a model to be adopted more broadly—finds itself in a perilous moment, the debts and failings of weaker economies undermining the broader union.

Former West German chancellor Helmut Schmidt offered the contrarian's view: Historically, "one of the decisive shortcomings of every democracy," he noted, is its "being limited to a short period, a rather short period, of years." American hegemony might be an aberration, he suggested, as democracies have a tendency to slide toward authoritarianism or to be swallowed up by empires.

Although the Soviet collapse offered "a rare moment of strategic still," in Paul Keating's words, Washington noticed little idleness. There was the Gulf War, the Asian financial crisis, and the economic implosion of Russia; the Irish peace process and the Israeli-Palestinian peace process; conflicts in Bosnia and Kosovo and genocide in

Rwanda; the North Atlantic Free Trade Agreement and World Trade Organization negotiations; the first bombing of the World Trade Center and the Oklahoma City bombing. This is not meant to absolve those who failed to build more in that moment, but rather to suggest how difficult it is—in the modern era—to see over the horizon.

Except for Bill Clinton, who was the world's helmsman, and Goh Chok Tong, whose tiny Singapore could never have developed if not for the economic opening of the 1990s, all of the figures interviewed here agree that a tremendous opportunity was wasted. The economic liberalization that allowed China, Brazil, India, and others to hitch themselves to the American and European locomotives was too paltry an achievement to pull from that moment of still.

GREAT LEADERS ARE EXCEEDINGLY CURIOUS. They consume news voraciously and are, in particular, great students of history. "Almost nothing is new," the United Kingdom's John Major said when we met. "It may be freshly wrapped, but it isn't new. Someone has faced it before. See what happened and how people reacted, and you may be a long way along the road toward deciding how best to deal with it."

Political giants seek advice and criticism and listen carefully to both. They refuse to surround themselves with yes-men and make difficult decisions promptly—and judiciously—then stand beside their judgments, even if there remains a "quantum of doubt." Politics is an ideas market, and the best leaders sell their ideas, decisions, and accomplishments to their publics, rather than assuming that support will follow. They refuse to shrink in the face of shifting tides, even if it will cost them their positions. And history nearly always remembers their courage fondly.

The next generation of political giants will recognize that media overexposure does not exist in the digital era, but that publics tire quickly of repetitive and staid political-speak. They will grasp that scaring citizens with half-truths—citizens who, in turn, can terrify their representatives—has become damningly easy, while understanding policy remains tedious and difficult.

Vision and communication remain the bedrock of effective leadership. The capacity to listen, to feel—through the walls that often rise around leaders—undercurrents and anxieties that go unsaid, remains critical. They will also understand that citizens in the digital era are far more likely to notice a leader's mistakes, and that apologies resonate far louder than excuses.

Tremendous leaders understand that public support is key, but that polls are surprisingly fluid; they refuse to lead from the median of public opinion. Great leaders have an overarching vision they aim to realize and manage to maintain that vision even as confounding events cloud their field of view.

Barack Obama, speaking to the *Reno Gazette*'s editorial board in January 2008, noted that Ronald Reagan had been a transformational leader, regardless of how one felt about his politics. Nixon had not been, nor was Clinton, he said. He was right. Reagan had a distinct vision for limited government and massive deregulation and managed to execute the doctrine. His words—"government is not the solution to our problems, it is the problem"—remain seared in the American psyche, no matter how misguided.

Bill Clinton's vision for the post–Cold War world mirrored the freeing of markets and the rise of the Internet: the idea was to simply open the flow of commerce and information, to remain vaguely postured based on political values and the economic needs of the nation, but to let the innate power of freedom and information spring forth. The opening of the period created enormous wealth, and lifted hundreds of millions of people out of extreme poverty in China, India, and elsewhere in the developing world. But the bulk of that new wealth remained exceedingly concentrated, and massive bubbles of debt and speculation created a precariously imbalanced global economy. Fewer publics than expected rose up to demand democracy, and the system has failed to deliver for many of those that did.

Re-creating the world in the anarchic mold of the free market, Chilean Ricardo Lagos noted, reproduced all of the inequalities that exist in the market. In the wake of the financial collapse of 2008, we recognize that regulation and careful oversight are crucial. The broader globe, too, needs oversight and management, particularly to deal with the threats of climate change and dwindling resources. We have lacked that leadership and vision thus far into the century.

"WE HAVE IT IN OUR power to begin the world all over again," Thomas Paine wrote in 1775, amid the American Revolution. His words remain as inspiring and lyric two hundred years later.

There is consensus that Washington is broken. Every election cycle, pols of both the left and the right fume and rant, then, once elected, fail to take action.

There are three renovations this democracy desperately needs: a balanced and measured press concerned with news rather than entertainment; publicly funded elections and mandatory voting; and term limits for all elected officials.

Nearly all Americans agree that having candidates rely on campaign contributions from political action committee (PAC) slush funds, political parties, corporations, and bundlers—regardless of whether the millions come from Halliburton or George Soros—poisons our politics. We need leaders who seek office as a public service, not as a career, who are indifferent to parties and popularity.

Australia is one of the few advanced nations that employs compulsory voting. At seventeen, Aussies are bombarded with government mailings that warn of a fine if they fail to vote. Several of the leaders interviewed here found it literally laughable that Americans must register before voting; the nation most fervently exporting democracy has one of the most lackluster electoral systems in the developed world.

The American decline is not fully written; this is the most innovative and well-educated society the world has ever known. Nothing guarantees that fact will remain true, though, and reforms are crucial to our continued prosperity. An era of scarcity—which, after centuries of resource wealth, is entirely certain—demands a government that moves decisively. And that is exactly what we lack.

ACKNOWLEDGMENTS

This was a magnificent adventure, unlikely and uncharted, as great ones often seem to be. There was a session with a foremost statesman in the bowels of a Madrid hotel, laborers carting racks of chairs and screeching tables between rooms behind us. There was a conversation with a Nobel laureate in an empty ballroom beneath the Georgetown Four Seasons, a novice trumpeter practicing down the hall. There was a voice recorder left in the seat-back pocket of 33B on Scandinavian Air flight 903, heroically recovered by a flight attendant in Stockholm two days later, and a bank teller who wiped away numerous overdrafts in exchange for a copy of the book. I grew up in a town without a stoplight, where I would come home, on occasion, to dairy cows grazing in my yard. But there were moments this year when the world felt like it was at my fingertips, like nothing could go wrong and no one would refuse my calls. And there were months when this felt hopelessly out of reach. I was sure, more often than not, that these interviews would end up in a shoebox, relegated to a closet corner. This was an incredible adventure, and I thank all of those who gave it life.

First and foremost, a great debt is owed to Cody Shearer, without whom this book would have never lifted from napkin notes. His enthusiasm and drive were the lifeblood of this project from start to finish, and I am immeasurably grateful.

Derek and Marva Shearer also treated me as a son, welcoming me into their lives; I thank them for the inspiration and the laughs. I must thank Paul Flum and Giuseppe Messuti, without whom I could have never embarked on this adventure, and Larry Flynt, whose support and friendship I'm continuously thankful for.

Steve Clemons and his New America Foundation gave me the legitimacy to chase this dream and a quiet corner to hammer away at its roughest edges. Thank you to Danielle Maxwell and Simone Frank for the endless stream of coffee and tea, and the reams of paper that this book slowly emerged from.

My agent, Larry Weissman, believed in this project and its young author. At Palgrave, Emily Carleton and Laura Lancaster were infinitely patient with me. I apologize and thank them both. Alan Bradshaw, Michelle Fitzgerald, Siobhan Paganelli, Suzanne Fowler, and Abigail Coften made up a terrific team, and I thank them all.

Thank you to José María Aznar and John Major, Nobel laureate Martti Ahttsaari and Alejandro Toledo, all of whom sat down with me before I knew what I was doing. I apologize for having taken your time and thank you for your insights.

Nasim Ashraf, Ahron Bregman, Pavel Palezchenko, Ho Tong Yen, Don Russell, and Bob Walker were each links in chains of improbability; I thank them all. Martin Walker, Marc Cooper, Martin Carnoy, Giandominico Picco, Nicholas Schmidle, Craig Unger, Sy Hersh, David Hoffman, Martin Indyk, William Shawcross, Steve Coll, James Fallows, Robert Parry, Jeffrey Lewis, Gareth Evans, Robert Lehreman, Amjad Atallah, Joergen Oerstroem Moeller, Paul Wilson, Fabian Lieschke, Frank Levinson, Steve Wasserman, Chris Norton, Jonathan Granoff, Thomas Hoberman, Daniel Freifeld, Silvia Pescador, Sabina Tancevova, Sam Sherraden, and many others shared ideas and helped shape this project. I'm indebted to them all, and, undoubtedly, to many others I have forgotten here.

To the friends and cousin that got me drunk and made me dinner when they saw that I was at wits' ends and absolutely broke, I thank you, and will gladly return the favor if ever there is a chance. Thank you to my advisor, Barak Mendelsohn, for forcing me to think with some structure, and for taking time to read my chapters amid piles of his own. Alyx Beckwith also read several early chapters and helped me to think about how it all might coalesce, as did my grandmother, Mary Innis-Buchanan. Lauren Stewart, I hope, will always be my first set of eyes. Thank you to Joel Censer for helping me wrestle with words at the deadline. Thanks also to Arden and Roberta Sams, Bob Wilsusen and Karen Magovern, Wade Jackson, Zach Noren, Kaity O'Keefe, Charlie Rubin, Ben Mansbach, Nir Rosen, Liz Wu, Maggie Severns, Mckee Floyd, Courtney Bowditch, Thomas Medaglia, Jen Spector, Neal Danis, Annie Mendez, Brian Venturo, Adam Goldstein and Ben Polak, Matt and Michelle Sams, and Lee and Gabe. And to the Stern Center of Vermont for teaching a dyslexic to read.

I must thank my parents, Ann and George, and sisters, Laura and Sara, who have always given me the courage to dash off into the world, as well as a place to crash when ambition outstretched reason. They have encouraged me, supported me, and, ultimately, left me alone—all at just the right moments.

One evening in September 2009, when I was all but certain this project would fail, a swan, the cob of a beautiful Czech family, swam up to me along the bank of the Vltava River, and stared at me for the better part of ten minutes. As a passing couple stopped, noticing the two of us looking at each other warily, he shook his head and swam off toward the other bank and after his family.

Perhaps he was looking for a bit of bread, perhaps he was offering the same to me.

Thank you, Dana.

PHOTOGRAPHS

Photo of Fernando Henrique Cardoso, ca. 1985, page 5, courtesy of Acervo Pres. F.H. Cardoso, Instituto Fernando Henrique Cardoso—IFHC.

Photo of Ricardo Lagos on the program De Cara El Pais in 1988, page 23, courtesy of Fundacion Democracia y Desarrollo.

Photo of Gro Bruntland, page 43, courtesy of Labour Movement Archives and Library.

Photo of Václav Havel on April 27, 1978, page 61, courtesy of Libri Prohibiti.

Photo of Mikhail Gorbachev in 1986, page 77, courtesy of akg-images / RIA Nowosti.

Photo of F. W. de Klerk at a press conference in Pretoria in1989, page 93, courtesy of African Pictures / akg-images.

Photo of Pervez Musharraf, undated portrait ca. 1999, page 115, courtesy of Reuters.

Photo of Ehud Barak as a Lt. General from 1991, page 137, courtesy of Reuters.

Photo of Bill Clinton campaigning for Congress in 1974, page 157, courtesy of the William J. Clinton Presidential Library.

Photo of Jimmy Carter in the Georgia governor's office, ca. 1971, page 171, courtesy of the Jimmy Carter Presidential Library.

Photo of Helmut Schmidt as chancellor in 1974, page 187, courtesy of akg-images.

Photo of Goh Chok Tong as minister for defence and second minister for health in 1984, page 201, courtesy of the National Archives of Singapore.

Photo of Paul Keating at the National Press Club as treasurer in 1984, page 221, courtesy of the National Archives of Australia: A1680, 27/8/84/54.

NOTES

INTRODUCTION

1. *Edwards, $400 cuts:* John Solomon, "Splitting Hairs," *Washington Post,* July 5, 2007, C01.
2. *"jeremiad complex":* James Fallows, "How America Can Rise Again," *The Atlantic,* January/February 2010. http://www.theatlantic.com/magazine/archive/2010/01/how-america-can-rise-again/7839/; also, Sacvan Bercovitch, *American Jeremiad* (Madison: University of Wisconsin Press, 1980), 62.
3. *Flynn, "seen them fall apart":* Fallows, "How America."
4. *"we face scarcity":* Jorgen Ostrom Moller, "The Return of Malthus," *American Interest,* July/August 2008, 27.

CHAPTER 1: FERNANDO HENRIQUE CARDOSO

1. *"you will need to leave Brazil":* Fernando Henrique Cardoso, *The Accidental President of Brazil* (New York: Public Affairs, 2007), 95.
2. *Delivering machine guns:* Cardoso, *The Accidental President,* 106.
3. *"41 percent of Brits believe climate change even exists":* Peter Riddell and Ben Webster, "Climate Change Is Not Our Fault, Say Most Voters," *Times* (London), Nov. 14, 2009, 1.
4. *"36 percent of Americans believe that it's human driven":* "Fewer Americans See Solid Evidence of Global Warming," Pew Research Center, Oct. 22, 2009. http://people-press.org/report/556/global-warming.
5. *"Brazil is the land of the future":* Cardoso, *The Accidental President,* 6.
6. *"see the page of history turn":* Cardoso, *The Accidental President,* 121.

CHAPTER 2: RICARDO FROILÁN LAGOS ESCOBAR

1. *"make the economy scream:"* Robert Dallek, *Nixon and Kissinger: Partners in Power* (New York: HarperCollins, 2007), 234; *"everything short of a Dominican Republic–type action:"* Ruth Blakely, *State Terrorism and Neoliberalism: The North in the South* (Taylor & Francis US, 2009), 95.
2. *Pinochet attacked by Marxists:* Heraldo Muñoz, *The Dictator's Shadow* (New York: Basic Books, 2008), 166–69.
3. *Arrest of Lagos:* Muñoz, *Dictator's Shadow,* 175, 176.
4. De Cara El Pais *video:* http://www.youtube.com/watch?v=yMpN–1joVzY.
5. *"the finger of Chile":* Steven J. Stern, *Battling for Hearts and Minds: Memory Struggles in Pinochet's Chile* (Durham, NC: Duke University Press, 2006), 381.

6. *"did not grasp the impact"* and, below, *June 9 on television:* Muñoz, *Dictator's Shadow,* 193.

7. *Thatcher six-month study of reforms:* John Lee Anderson, "The Dictator," *New Yorker,* Oct. 18, 1998. http://www.newyorker.com/archive/1998/10/19/1998_10_19_044_TNY_LIBRY_000016635.

8. *Pinochet unemployment 30 percent:* "Chile: Out of the Frying Pan and Into the Fire," *Newsweek,* June 27, 1983, 56; *Lagos unemployment 8.1 percent:* "Can a Socialist Save Chile's Market?" *Euromoney,* Jan. 2006.

9. *2010 Quadrennial Defense Review,* 108, 109. http://www.defense.gov/qdr/images/QDR_as_of_12Feb10_1000.pdf.

10. *Weber, "The political publicist":* Max Weber, H. H. Gerth, Hans Heinrich Gerth, Charles Wright Mills, and Bryan S. Turner, *From Max Weber: Essays in Sociology* (London: Routledge Psychology Press, 1991), 96.

11. *Lincoln controlled by events:* David Von Drehle, "How Obama and McCain Would Lead," *Time,* Oct.30, 2008. http://www.time.com/time/politics/article/0,8599,1854818,00.html.

12. *Napoleon, "never was truly my own master":* Emmanuel-Auguste-Dieudonné Las Cases (comte de), *Mémorial de Sainte Hélène: Journal of the Private Life and Conversations of the Emperor Napoleon at Saint Helena,* vol. 4 (London: H. Colburn, 1823), 133 (digitized by University of Michigan, 2008).

CHAPTER 3: GRO HARLEM BRUNDTLAND

1. *"dusting gets done":* Fred Hauptfuhrer, "On Top of the World," *People,* April 20, 1987. http://www.people.com/people/archive/article/0,20096098,00.html.

2. *"Viking warrior incarnate":* Liv O'Hanlon, "Too Big for Her Roots: She Made Enemies in Cairo, but the World May Need Norway's Leader," *Independent,* Sept. 11, 1994, 17.

3. *80 percent of recession job loss suffered by men:* Catherine Rampell, "As Layoffs Surge, Women Pass Men in Job Force," *New York Times,* Feb. 5, 2009; J. B. Morely, "US Labour Market in 2008: Economy in Recession," Bureau of Labor and Statistics, March 2009, 4. www.bls.gov/opub/mlr/2009/03/art1full.pdf.

4. *Women 30 to 44 outpace male earnings:* Richard Fry and D'Vera Cohn, "Women, Men and the New Economics of Marriage," *Pew Research,* March 19, 2010. http://pewsocialtrends.org/pubs/750/new-economics-of-marriage#prc-jump.

5. *Set binding targets for 37 industrialized nations:* United Nations Framework Convention on Climate Change. http://unfccc.int/kyoto_protocol/items/2830.php.

6. *Leaving office:* Gro Harlem Brundtland, *Madame Prime Minister* (New York: Farrar, Straus & Giroux, 2002), 428.

7. *BBC poll:* James Robbins, "Free Market Fatally Flawed, Says Survey," *BBC,* Nov. 9, 2009. http://news.bbc.co.uk/2/hi/8347409.stm.

8. *Yeltsin goes for pizza:* Taylor Branch, *The Clinton Tapes: Wrestling History with the President* (New York: Simon & Schuster, 2009), 198.

9. *Nuclear football and Yeltsin:* David Hoffman, "Cold War Doctrines Refuse to Die," *Washington Post*, March 15, 1998, A1.

CHAPTER 4: VÁCLAV HAVEL

1. *Philosophy and sports car:* David Remnick, "Exit Havel," *New Yorker*, Feb. 17, 2003. http://www.newyorker.com/archive/2003/02/17/030217 fa_fact1?currentPage=all.
2. *emergency packet:* Remnick, "Exit Havel."
3. *Tramps and cops:* Václav Havel and Karel Hvížala, *Disturbing the Peace* (New York: Knopf, 2008), 108.
4. *Wringing stained sheets:* Jonathen Glancey, "Václav Havel Didn't Sleep Here," *Independent*, May 14, 1995. http://www.independent.co.uk/arts-entertainment/travel-vaclav-havel-didnt-sleep-here–1619562.html.
5. *No longer faced fear:* Havel and Hvížala: *Disturbing the Peace*, 144.
6. *"on the submarine":* Václav Havel, *To the Castle and Back* (New York: Vintage, 2007), 223.
7. *"mafia capitalism":* Havel, *To the Castle*, 21.
8. *Sisyphus:* Remnick, "Exit Havel"; and Václav Havel and Paul Robert Wilson, *Toward a Civil Society* (Prague: Lidové Noviny, 1994), 92.
9. *Main enemy, "contaminated moral environment":* Gregory Feifer, "The Velvet Surrender," *New Republic*, Sept. 23, 2010, 24.
10. *"entrepreneurs of identity":* Stephen Reicher and Nick Hopkins, *Self and Nation* (London: Sage, 2001), 49.
11. *Moscow exploited corruption, flag, and increased influence:* Feifer, "Velvet Surrender," 22–25.

CHAPTER 5: MIKHAIL SERGEYEVICH GORBACHEV

1. *"two Gorbachevs":* Robert G. Kaiser, *Why Gorbachev Happened* (New York: Simon & Schuster, 1991), 18.
2. *Yulia Karagondia reprimanded:* David Remnick, *Lenin's Tomb* (New York: Vintage Books, 1994), 157.
3. *Stalin starving own nation:* Timothy Snyder, "The Coming Age of Slaughter," *New Republic*, Oct. 28, 2010, 20–21.
4. *Nearly half Privolnoye starved:* Mikhail Sergeyevich Gorbachev, *Manifesto for Earth: Action Now for Peace, Global Justice, and a Sustainable Future* (London: Clairview Books, 2006), 10.
5. *All night to see Stalin's coffin:* Mikhail Sergeyevich Gorbachev and Zdeneck Mlynar, *Conversations with Gorbachev on Perestroika, the Prague Spring, and the Crossroads of Socialism,* trans. George Shriver (New York: Columbia University Press, 2002), 21.
6. *Gorbachev in Politburo at 47:* George J. Church, "Person of the Year 1987: Mikhail Sergeyevich Gorbachev." http://www.time.com/time/subscriber/personoftheyear/archive/stories/1987.html.
7. *"We can't on go living like this."* David E. Hoffman, *The Dead Hand* (New York: Doubleday, 2009), 189.
8. *Reagan, "if they keep dying on me:"* Ronald Reagan, *An American Life* (New York: Simon & Schuster, 1990), 611.

9. *Alberta farm milk production:* Hoffman, *The Dead Hand,* 183; from *Narodnoye Khozyaistvo SSSR,* v. 1983 g. p. 269.

10. *Tomato war:* Jonathan Steele, *Eternal Russia: Yeltsin, Gorbachev and the Mirage of Democracy* (Cambridge: Harvard University Press, 1994), 121.

11. *"Achilles heel of socialism":* Gorbachev and Mlynar, *Conversations with Gorbachev,* 160.

12. *Capitalism in 500 days:* David E. Hoffman, *Oligarchs: Wealth and Power in the New Russia* (New York: Public Affairs Books, 2003), 47.

13. *Response of vast middle to reforms:* Kaiser, *Why Gorbachev Happened,* 69.

14. *Gorbachev at G7:* Pavel Palazchenko, *My Years with Gorbachev* (University Park: Pennsylvania State University Press, 1997), 294–95.

15. *"Only Thatcher":* "Mikhail Gorbachev: Russia's Elder Statesman Still at Home with Power, *Independent,* June 7, 2010. http://www.independent.co.uk/news/people/profiles/mikhail-gorbachev-russias-elder-statesman-still-at-home-with-power-1993279.html.

16. *"Yeltsin . . . will not give in":* Anatoly S. Chernyaev, *My Six Years with Gorbachev,* trans. Robert English and Elizabeth Tucker (University Park: Pennsylvania State University Press, 2000), 376.

17. *Yeltsin on tank:* Hoffman, *The Dead Hand,* 374.

18. *"nothing more difficult":* Niccolò Machiavelli, *The Prince,* translated by W. K. Marriott, http://books.google.com.

19. *Prosperous, strong, dependent:* Palazchenko, *My Years with Gorbachev,* 292–93.

20. *Mack political violence study:* Andrew Mack, "Human Security Report 2005," Simon Fraser University. http://www.hsrgroup.org/human-security-reports/2005/overview.aspx.

CHAPTER 6: FREDERIK WILLEM DE KLERK

1. "Coloureds" is a South African term for mixed race individuals; it was one of four official racial categories used by the apartheid structure, but is still used today. It does not carry a negative connotation, nor is it perceived as a derogatory term.

2. *On February 2, 1990, "quantum leap," "done it all":* Alistair Sparks, "The Secret Revolution," *New Yorker,* April 11, 1994, 74.

3. *De Klerk as minister of education:* Dickson A. Mungazi, *The Last Defenders of the Laager: Ian D. Smith and F. W. de Klerk* (Westport: Greenwood Publishing, 1998), 140; Biodun Jeyifo, "An Interview with Nadine Gordimer: Harare," *Callaloo* (16: 4), Feb. 1992 (Baltimore: Johns Hopkins University Press), 923.

4. *Erica Adams's account:* David B. Ottaway, "The Romance That Rocked South Africa," *Washington Post,* Feb. 4, 1991, B1.

5. *"racial grouping is the only truth":* Alistair Haddon Sparks, *Tomorrow Is Another Country: Inside the Story of South Africa's Road to Change* (Chicago: University of Chicago Press, 1996), 93.

6. *"standing in the council chamber of God" sermon:* Sparks, *Tomorrow Is Another Country,* 99.

7. *Mandela at petrol station:* Sparks, *Tomorrow Is Another Country,* 39.
8. *Most unequal cities in the world:* "Urban Divide: Unequal Cities," March, 2010. The United Nations: www.unhabitat.org/documents/ SOWC10/R8.pdf.
9. *HIV infection rates:* "HIV in South Africa 'Levels Off,'" *BBC,* June 9, 2009, http://news.bbc.co.uk/2/hi/africa/8091489.stm; "South Africa National HIV Prevalence, Incidence, Behaviour, and Communication Survey, 2008," Human Sciences Research Council, www.hsrc.ac.za/ Document–3611.phtml.
10. *"loser-takes-all":* Patti Waldmeir, *Anatomy of a Miracle: The End of Apartheid and the Birth of a New South Africa* (New Brunswick: Rutgers University Press, 1998), 178.
11. *"bitterness in his heart":* Author's interview, February 3, 2009.

CHAPTER 7: PERVEZ MUSHARRAF

1. *Death of Bhutto:* Andrew Buncombe and Omar Waraich, "Inquiry into Bhutto's Death Fails to Satisfy Supporters," *Independent,* Feb. 9, 2009, 32.
2. *Pakistan's pursuit of nuclear weapons, sanctions:* Zahid Hussein, *Frontline Pakistan* (New York: Columbia University Press, 2008), 162–70.
3. *Pakistan's nuclear security, US response team:* Seymour M. Hersh, "Defending the Arsenal," *New Yorker,* Nov. 16, 2009. http://www.new yorker.com/reporting/2009/11/16/091116fa_fact_hersh?current Page=all.
4. *"blanket overflight and landing rights":* Immediately after 9/11 Musharraf accepted all US demands, before walking back the permissions days later. Seth G. Jones, *In the Graveyard of Empires: America's War in Afghanistan* (New York: W. W. Norton & Company, 2010), 89.
5. *30,000 orphans:* "Steps Towards Peace: Putting Kashmiris First," International Crisis Group, June 3, 2010, 5; Steve Coll, "Kashmir: The Time Has Come," *New York Review of Books,* Sept. 30, 2010, 82.
6. *Free Kashmir:* Coll, "Kashmir: The Time Has Come," 83.
7. *Audacious peace initiative:* Steve Coll, "The Back Channel: India and Pakistan's Secret Kashmir Talks," *New Yorker,* March 2009, 39–51.
8. *Solution was "inevitable":* "Kashmir Solution Inevitable: Musharraf," *ANI,* Feb. 8, 2008. http://www.thaindian.com/newsportal/south-asia/ kashmir-solution-inevitable-musharraf_10016798.html.
9. *"far less patient now":* Author's interview, June 29, 2009.
10. *"end up like Kashmir":* Author's interview, May 15, 2010.

CHAPTER 8: EHUD BARAK

1. *"I can't do it":* Martin Indyk, *Innocent Abroad: An Intimate Account of American Peace Diplomacy in the Middle East* (New York: Simon & Schuster, 2009), 251. When I asked Barak about this incident, he denied Ambassador Indyk's account.
2. *Pianist and a knack for picking locks:* Connie Bruck, "The Commando," *New Yorker,* April 17, 2000, 83.

3. *Campaign advertisement:* Stanley B. Greenberg, *Dispatches from the War Room* (New York: St. Martin's Press, 2009), 275.

4. *News of Yonatan Netanyahu's death:* Deborah Sontag, "Two Who Share a Past Are Rivals for Israel's Future," *New York Times,* April 20, 1999. http://query.nytimes.com/gst/fullpage.html?res=9C03E6DC163 AF933A15757C0A96F958260&pagewanted=all.

5. *"a high-quality mechanical watch":* Sontag, "Two Who Share a Past."

6. *Fatah's role in the coup:* David Rose, "The Gaza Bombshell," *Vanity Fair,* April 2008. http://www.vanityfair.com/politics/features/2008/04/ gaza200804.

7. The Barak offer has been the subject of a great deal of controversy and has been recounted by a number of summit participants. Barak certainly made mistakes, and the rushed schedule of the talks unnerved Arafat. Barak's decision to try to forge peace with the Syrians first was interpreted as an attempt to isolate the Palestinians by removing a key supporter, and it likely was. Further, Barak discarded a number of the steps outlined in Rabin's Oslo accords; he had never supported the agreement, and broke publicly with Rabin when the accords were signed. He was fearful it provided for too much Palestinian autonomy too quickly and would endanger Israel. But the abandonment of gradual steps in favor of a grand bargain further frayed Arafat's nerves rather than allaying his anxiety. See Robert Malley and Hussein Agha, "Camp David: The Tragedy of Errors," *New York Review of Books,* Aug. 9, 2001. http://www.nybooks.com/articles/archives/2001/aug/09/ camp-david-the-tragedy-of-errors/?pagination=false; Indyk, *Innocent Abroad,* 325–40.

8. *"inner cabinet":* Bruck, "The Commando," 82.

9. *"one of the terror organizations":* Greenberg, *Dispatches from the War Room,* 281.

10. *"an apartheid state":* "Ehud Barak Breaks the Apartheid Barrier," *Economist,* Feb. 15, 2010. http://www.economist.com/node/21004833.

CHAPTER 9: WILLIAM JEFFERSON CLINTON

1. When trying to win his support for his wife, Bill Clinton is alleged to have told Ted Kennedy, "A few years ago, this guy would have been getting us coffee." In the heat of the campaign, the comment was taken as racism, rather than a reference to inexperience.

   Before the South Carolina primary—which the Clintons, before unexpectedly losing Iowa, thought they could win because of Bill's popularity among the black populace—a reporter asked, "What does it say about Barack Obama that it takes two of you to beat him?" Clinton chuckled, commented that the question was bait, then offered: "Jesse Jackson won South Carolina twice, in '84 and '88. And he ran a good campaign. And Senator Obama's run a good campaign here; he's run a good campaign everywhere. He's got a—He's a good candidate with a good organization." A number of news organizations cut Clinton's response after "'88," their intended inference being that South Carolina is an easy primary for black candidates. *Coffee:* John Heilemann and

Mark Halperin, *Game Change: Obama and the Clintons, McCain and Palin, and the Race of a Lifetime* (New York: HarperCollins, 2010), 218; *Jesse Jackson:* Andrew Malcolm, "In His Own Words: Bill Clinton on Barack Obama and Jesse Jackson," *Los Angeles Times,* Jan. 31, 2008. http://latimesblogs.latimes.com/washington/2008/01/lin-his-own-wor.html.

2. *"I think they were wrong":* "Clinton: I was wrong to listen to advice on credit derivatives," *ABC NEWS,* April 17, 2010. http://blogs.abc news.com/politicalpunch/2010/04/clinton-rubin-and-summers-gave-me-wrong-advice-on-derivatives-and-i-was-wrong-to-take-it.html.

3. *"cut his head open":* Stanley B. Greenberg, *Dispatches from the War Room* (New York: St. Martin's Press, 2009), 60.

4. *Shuttles back and forth to Durham:* John Gartner, *In Search of Bill Clinton: A Psychological Biography* (New York: Macmillan, 2009), 128.

5. *Chelsea Clinton, "none of the men . . . live past sixty":* Carol Felsenthal, *Clinton in Exile: A President Out of the White House* (New York: William Morrow, 2008), 300.

6. *Jim Johnson calm:* David Maraniss, *First in His Class: The Biography of Bill Clinton* (New York: Simon & Schuster, 1996), 116.

7. *Leopoulos, watch Clinton read:* Carolyn Staley, "The Music of Friendship," in *The Clintons of Arkansas: An Introduction by Those Who Know Them Best,* ed. Ernest Dumas (Fayetteville: University of Arkansas Press, 1993), 38.

8. *"don't give a rip about public opinion":* Diane Blair, "Of Darkness and Light," in *The Clintons of Arkansas,* ed. Dumas, 68.

CHAPTER 10: JAMES EARL CARTER, JR.

1. *"Passionless Presidency":* James Fallows, "The Passionless Presidency: The Trouble with Jimmy Carter's Administration," *Atlantic Monthly,* May 1979. http://www.theatlantic.com/past/docs/unbound/flashbks/pres/fallpass.htm.

2. *Fuel efficiency doubled:* Garry Wills, "The Strange Success of Jimmy Carter," *New York Review of Books,* Oct. 28, 2010, 23; Thomas L. Friedman, *Hot Flat, and Crowded: Why We Need a Green Revolution and How It Can Renew America* (New York: Farrar, Straus & Giroux, 2008), 18.

3. *"Crisis of Confidence" speech and 11-point bounce:* Kevin Mattson, *What the Heck Are You Up To, Mr. President?* (New York: Bloomsbury, 2009), 204. Full speech, 207.

4. *Racism in 1970 governor's race:* Burton Ira Kaufman and Scott Kaufman, *The Presidency of James Earl Carter* (Lawrence: University of Kansas Press, 2006), 9.

5. *"not easy for me to accept criticism":* Mattson, *What the Heck Are You Up To,* 136.

6. *Only 30 million heard:* Mattson, *What the Heck Are You Up To,* 21.

7. *"power to persuade":* Richard Neustadt, *Presidential Power and the Modern Presidents* (New York: Simon & Schuster, 1991), 29.

8. Carter "not big enough for the game": Jonathan Carr, *Helmut Schmidt: Helmsman of Germany* (London: Weidenfeld & Nicolson, 1985), 124.

9. *Schmidt's psychological attitude:* Jimmy Carter, *White House Diary* (New York: Farrar, Straus & Giroux, 2010), 172.

CHAPTER 11: HELMUT HEINRICH WALDEMAR SCHMIDT

1. *"learned his socialism":* Giles Radice, *The New Germans* (London: M. Joseph, 1995), 93.

2. *"Mr. Mayor, you're in my way here":* Jonathan Carr, *Helmut Schmidt: Helmsman of Germany* (London: Weidenfeld and Nicolson, 1985), 29.

3. *"the world is not too small":* "Freiheit ist das Feuer, ist der helle Schein, solange es noch lodert ist die Welt nicht zu klein," trans. Fabian Lieschke, *Carleton Germanic Papers,* vols. 17–19, 1990, digitized, April 8, 2008.

4. *Schmidt at the Cologne Synagogue:* Helmut Schmidt and Wolfram F. Hanrieder, *Helmut Schmidt: Perspectives on Politics* (Boulder: Westview Press, 1982), 196.

CHAPTER 12: GOH CHOK TONG

1. *"a welcome green lung":* "About Istana," last modified June 16, 2010, http://www.istana.gov.sg/AboutIstana/index.html.

2. *"birdcage economy":* Evan Osnos, "Boom Doctor," *New Yorker,* Oct.11, 2010, 46.

3. *Government wages at two-thirds public salaries:* Lee Kuan Yew, "Third World to First" (New York: HarperCollins, 2000), 169.

4. *government acted as a partner:* Stan Sesser, "A Nation of Contradictions," *New Yorker,* Jan. 13, 1992, 50.

5. *Sales of* Cosmopolitan *allowed:* Gary Rodan, "Singapore in 2004: Long-Awaited Leadership Transition," *University of California Press, Asian Survey,* 45:1 (Jan.-Feb. 2005), 142.

6. *never lost a case:* Clark Hoyt, "Censored in Singapore," *New York Times,* April 3, 2010. http://www.nytimes.com/2010/04/04/opinion/04pubed.html.

7. *Goh as "wooden":* Sonny Yap, Richard Lim, and Leong Weng Kam, *Men in White* (Singapore: Singapore Press Holdings, 2009), 435.

8. *China's 863 program:* Evan Osnos, "Green Giant," *New Yorker,* Dec. 21, 2009.

9. *Question whether a vibrant scientific culture is possible:* Editorial, "China's Challenges," *Nature,* July 2008. http://www.nature.com/nature/journal/v454/n7203/full/454367a.html; Osnos, "Green Giant."

10. *"For every Lee Kuan Yew":* Osnos, "Boom Doctor."

11. *Influence over cabinet but no control:* John Edwards, *Keating: the Inside Story* (New York: Viking, 1996), 445.

12. *T-shirt shack in Hawaii:* Todd Purdram, "Washington, We Have a Problem," *Vanity Fair,* Aug. 2010. http://www.vanityfair.com/online/daily/2010/08/can-washington-be-fixed.html.

CHAPTER 13: PAUL JOHN KEATING

1. *Keating coup:* John Edwards, *Keating: The Inside Story* (New York: Viking, 1996), 432.
2. *Debt boom, twice GDP:* Edwards, *Keating: The Inside Story,* 264.
3. *Neo-classical antiques:* Valerie Lawson, "The Other Man in Keating's Life," *Sydney Morning Herald,* March 23, 1991, 14.
4. *"amongst savages":* Mad About Music, Sept. 6, 2009, http://www.wqxr.org/programs/mam/2009/sep/06/transcript/.
5. *Keating on Churchill:* Edwards, *Keating: The Inside Story,* 427.
6. *"Keating on the attack":* Don Watson, *Recollections of a Bleeding Heart: A Portrait of Paul Keating PM* (New York: Knopf, 2002), 506.
7. *"pansies" and "Rosy":* P. Costigan, "Keating . . . Out of Slight," *Sunday Mail,* Feb. 23, 1986.
8. *"warm lettuce" and "brain-dead":* "Keating Shoots from the Lip," *Advertiser,* April 3, 1992.
9. *Dared them to follow:* Paul Kelly, *The End of Certainty* (St. Leonard's, New South Wales: Allen & Unwin, 1992), 166.
10. *Hawke's parting advice:* Kelly, *The End of Certainty,* 658, from *Australian Financial Review,* Jan. 7, 1992.
11. *Lang's advice and "shower of sparks":* Watson, *Recollections of a Bleeding Heart,* 11–12, 19.
12. *"history takes care of itself":* "The Asia We Have to Have," *Sydney Morning Herald,* March 10, 2000, 14.
13. *Bullies:* Roderick M. Kramer, "The Great Intimidators," *Harvard Business Review* 84:2 (2006), 94; Joseph S. Nye Jr., *The Powers to Lead* (New York: Oxford University Press, 2008), 81.
14. *"Keep a hinterland":* Author's interview, June 23, 2009.
15. *Obama and Cameron:* Richard Woods, "Barack Obama: He Came. He Saw. He, er, Left." *Sunday Times,* July 27, 2008. http://www.timesonline.co.uk/tol/news/politics/article4407467.ece.

INDEX